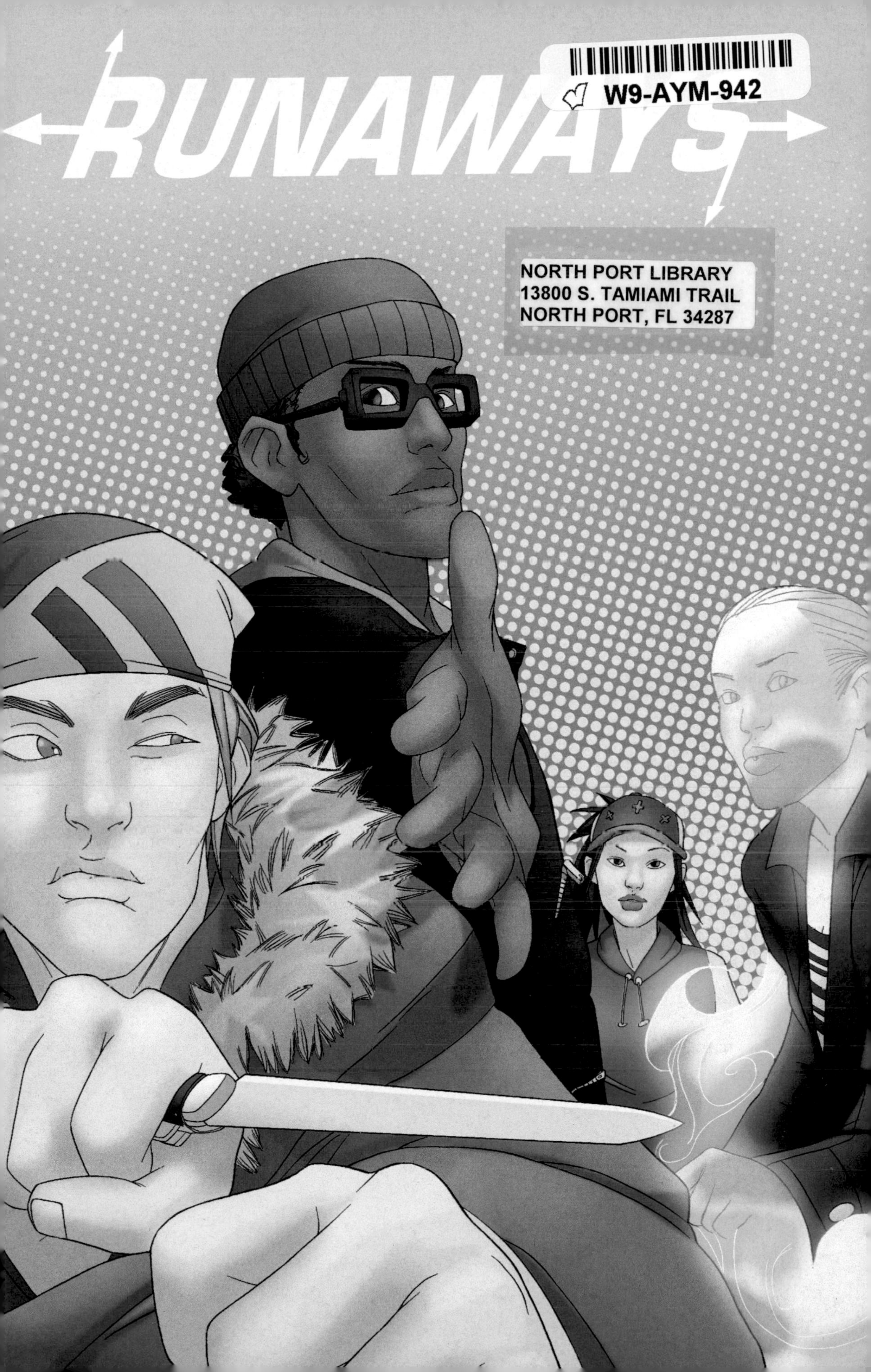

RUNAWAYS

RUNAWAYS

WRITER: **BRIAN K. VAUGHAN**

PENCILS: **ADRIAN ALPHONA** (#7-10) & **TAKESHI MIYAZAWA** (#11-12)

INKS: **CRAIG YEUNG** (#7-10) & **DAVID NEWBOLD** (#11-12)

COLORS: **BRIAN REBER** (#7, #11-12) & **CHRISTINA STRAIN** (#8-10)

LETTERS: **VC's RANDY GENTILE** (#7-9, #11-12) & **CHRIS ELIOPOULOS** (#10)

COVER ART: **ADRIAN ALPHONA** & **CRAIG YEUNG** (#7), **JO CHEN** (#8-10)
AND **JOSH MIDDLETON** (#11-12)

ASSISTANT EDITOR: **MACKENZIE CADENHEAD**

EDITOR: **C.B. CEBULSKI**

RUNAWAYS CREATED BY **BRIAN K. VAUGHAN** & **ADRIAN ALPHONA**

3 1969 02568 4159

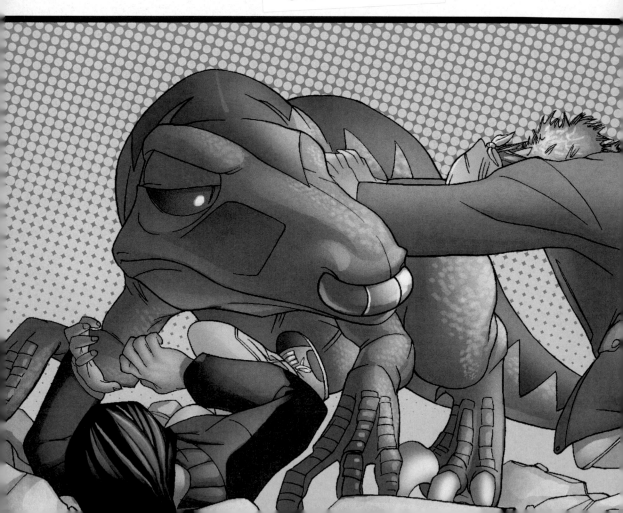

COLLECTION EDITOR: **JENNIFER GRÜNWALD**
ASSISTANT EDITOR: **CAITLIN O'CONNELL**
ASSOCIATE MANAGING EDITOR: **KATERI WOODY**
EDITOR, SPECIAL PROJECTS: **MARK D. BEAZLEY**
VP PRODUCTION & SPECIAL PROJECTS: **JEFF YOUNGQUIST**
SVP PRINT, SALES & MARKETING: **DAVID GABRIEL**

EDITOR IN CHIEF: **AXEL ALONSO**
CHIEF CREATIVE OFFICER: **JOE QUESADA**
PUBLISHER: **DAN BUCKLEY**
EXECUTIVE PRODUCER: **ALAN FINE**

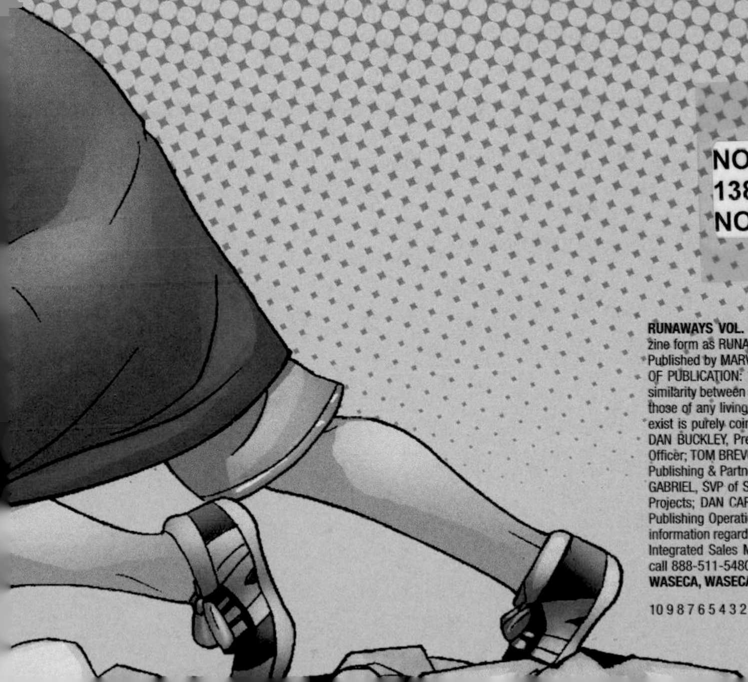

NORTH PORT LIBRARY
13800 S. TAMIAMI TRAIL
NORTH PORT, FL 34287

RUNAWAYS VOL. 2: TEENAGE WASTELAND. Contains material originally published in magazine form as RUNAWAYS #7-12. Second edition. First printing 2017. ISBN# 978-1-302-90500-2. Published by MARVEL WORLDWIDE, INC., a subsidiary of MARVEL ENTERTAINMENT, LLC. OFFICE OF PUBLICATION: 135 West 50th Street, New York, NY 10020. Copyright © 2017 MARVEL No similarity between any of the names, characters, persons, and/or institutions in this magazine with those of any living or dead person or institution is intended, and any such similarity which may exist is purely coincidental. **Printed in the U.S.A.** ALAN FINE, President, Marvel Entertainment; DAN BUCKLEY, President, TV, Publishing & Brand Management; JOE QUESADA, Chief Creative Officer; TOM BREVOORT, SVP of Publishing; DAVID BOGART, SVP of Business Affairs & Operations, Publishing & Partnership; C.B. CEBULSKI, VP of Brand Management & Development, Asia; DAVID GABRIEL, SVP of Sales & Marketing, Publishing; JEFF YOUNGQUIST, VP of Production & Special Projects; DAN CARR, Executive Director of Publishing Technology; ALEX MORALES, Director of Publishing Operations; SUSAN CRESPI, Production Manager; STAN LEE, Chairman Emeritus. For information regarding advertising in Marvel Comics or on Marvel.com, please contact Vit DeBellis, Integrated Sales Manager, at vdebellis@marvel.com. For Marvel subscription inquiries, please call 888-511-5480. **Manufactured between 12/23/2016 and 1/30/2017 by QUAD/GRAPHICS WASECA, WASECA, MN, USA.**

10 9 8 7 6 5 4 3 2 1

PREVIOUSLY:

TEENAGER ALEX WILDER AND FIVE OTHER ONLY CHILDREN
ALWAYS THOUGHT THEIR PARENTS WERE BORING LOS ANGELES SOCIALITES,
UNTIL THE KIDS WITNESS THE ADULTS MURDER A YOUNG GIRL IN SOME KIND OF
DARK SACRIFICIAL RITUAL. THE TEENS SOON LEARN THAT THEIR PARENTS ARE
PART OF A SECRET ORGANIZATION CALLED THE PRIDE, A COLLECTION OF CRIME
BOSSES, TIME-TRAVELING DESPOTS, ALIEN OVERLORDS, MAD SCIENTISTS, EVIL
MUTANTS AND DARK WIZARDS.

AFTER STEALING WEAPONS AND RESOURCES FROM THESE VILLAINOUS
ADULTS (INCLUDING A MYSTICAL STAFF, FUTURISTIC GAUNTLETS AND A
GENETICALLY ENGINEERED VELOCIRAPTOR NAMED OLD LACE), THE KIDS
RUN AWAY FROM HOME AND VOW TO BRING THEIR PARENTS TO JUSTICE. BUT
WHEN THE MEMBERS OF THE PRIDE FRAME THEIR CHILDREN FOR THE MURDER
THEY COMMITTED, THE FUGITIVE RUNAWAYS ARE FORCED TO RETREAT TO A
SUBTERRANEAN HIDEOUT NICKNAMED "THE HOSTEL." USING THE DIVERSE
POWERS AND SKILLS THEY INHERITED, THE RUNAWAYS NOW HOPE TO ATONE FOR
THEIR PARENTS' CRIMES BY HELPING THOSE IN NEED.

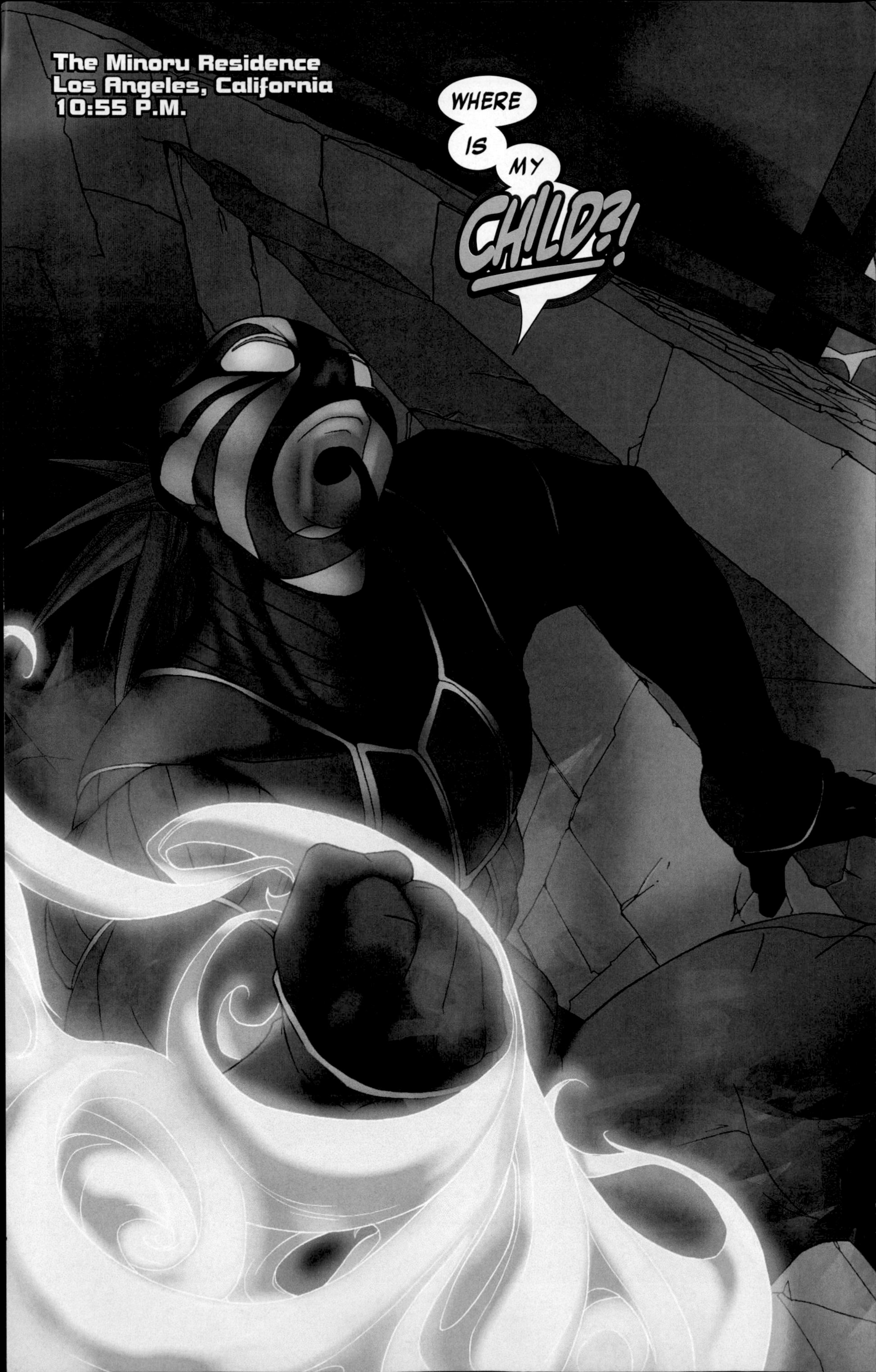
The Minoru Residence
Los Angeles, California
10:55 P.M.
WHERE IS MY CHILD?!

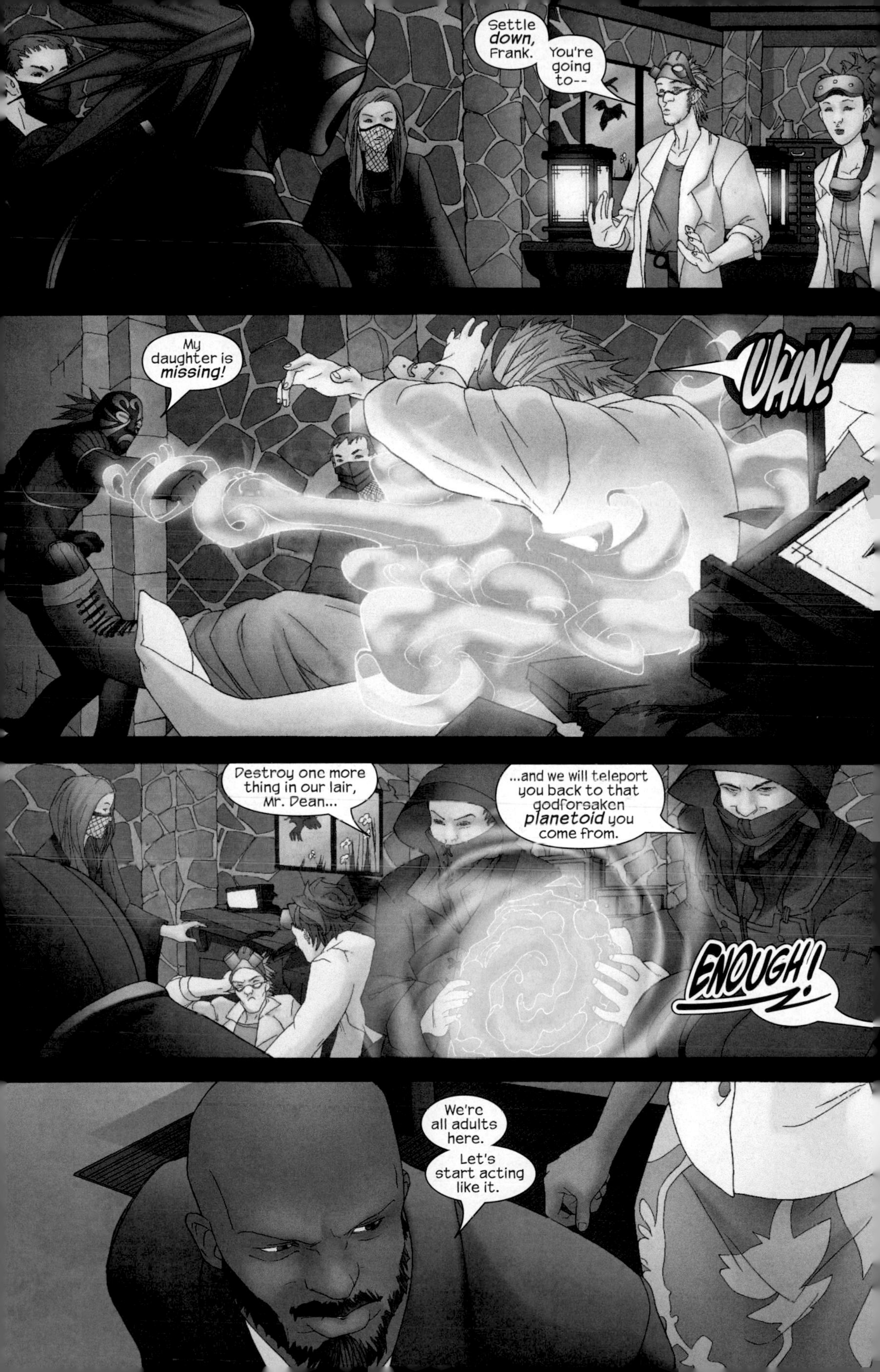
Settle down, Frank.
You're going to--
My daughter is missing!
UHN!
Destroy one more thing in our lair, Mr. Dean...
...and we will teleport you back to that godforsaken planetoid you come from.
ENOUGH!
We're all adults here.
Let's start acting like it.

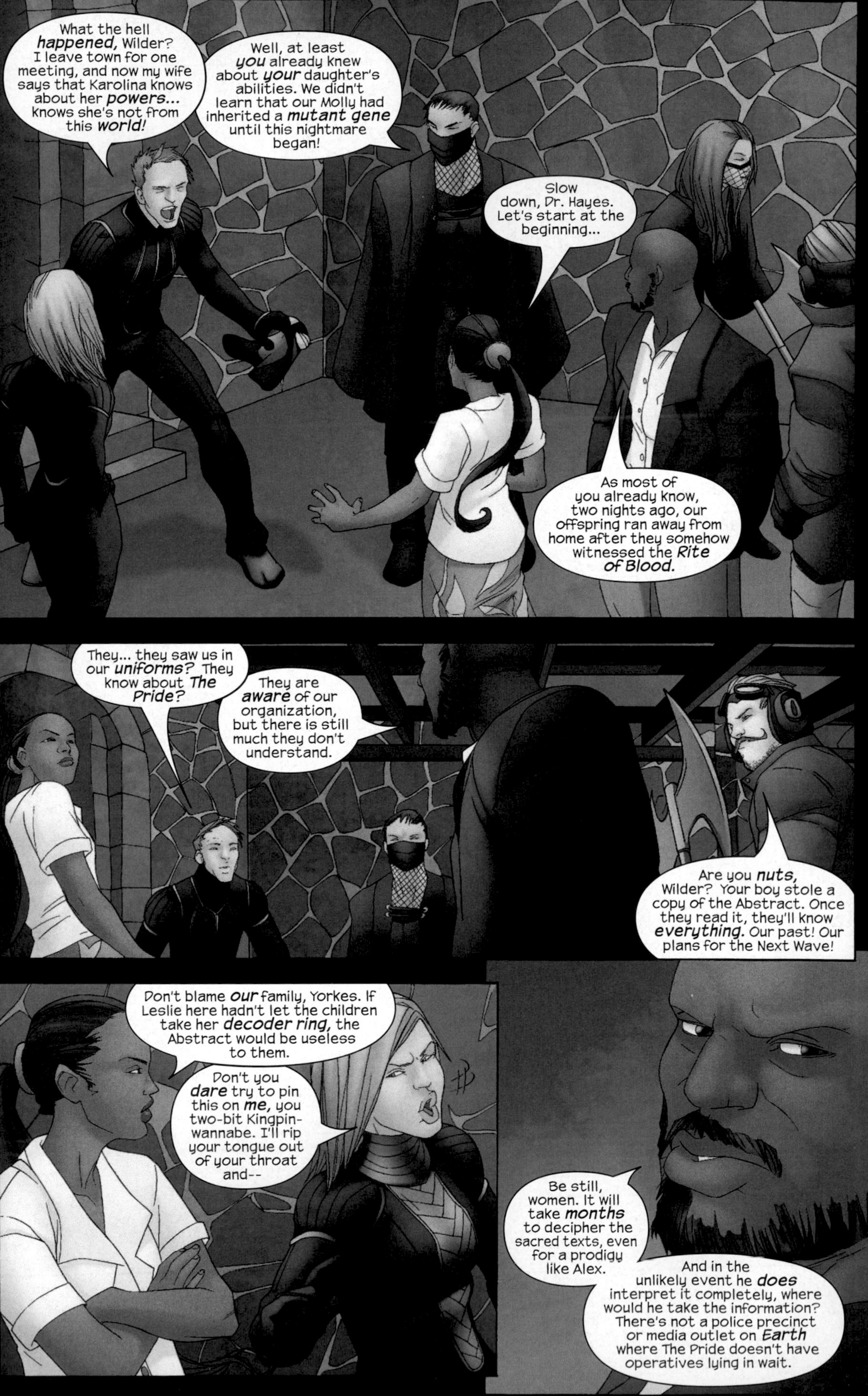

What the hell happened, Wilder? I leave town for one meeting, and now my wife says that Karolina knows about her powers... knows she's not from this world!
Well, at least you already knew about your daughter's abilities. We didn't learn that our Molly had inherited a mutant gene until this nightmare began!
Slow down, Dr. Hayes. Let's start at the beginning...
As most of you already know, two nights ago, our offspring ran away from home after they somehow witnessed the Rite of Blood.
They... they saw us in our uniforms? They know about The Pride?
They are aware of our organization, but there is still much they don't understand.
Are you nuts, Wilder? Your boy stole a copy of the Abstract. Once they read it, they'll know everything. Our past! Our plans for the Next Wave!
Don't blame our family, Yorkes. If Leslie here hadn't let the children take her decoder ring, the Abstract would be useless to them.
Don't you dare try to pin this on me, you two-bit Kingpin-wannabe. I'll rip your tongue out of your throat and--
Be still, women. It will take months to decipher the sacred texts, even for a prodigy like Alex.
And in the unlikely event he does interpret it completely, where would he take the information? There's not a police precinct or media outlet on Earth where The Pride doesn't have operatives lying in wait.

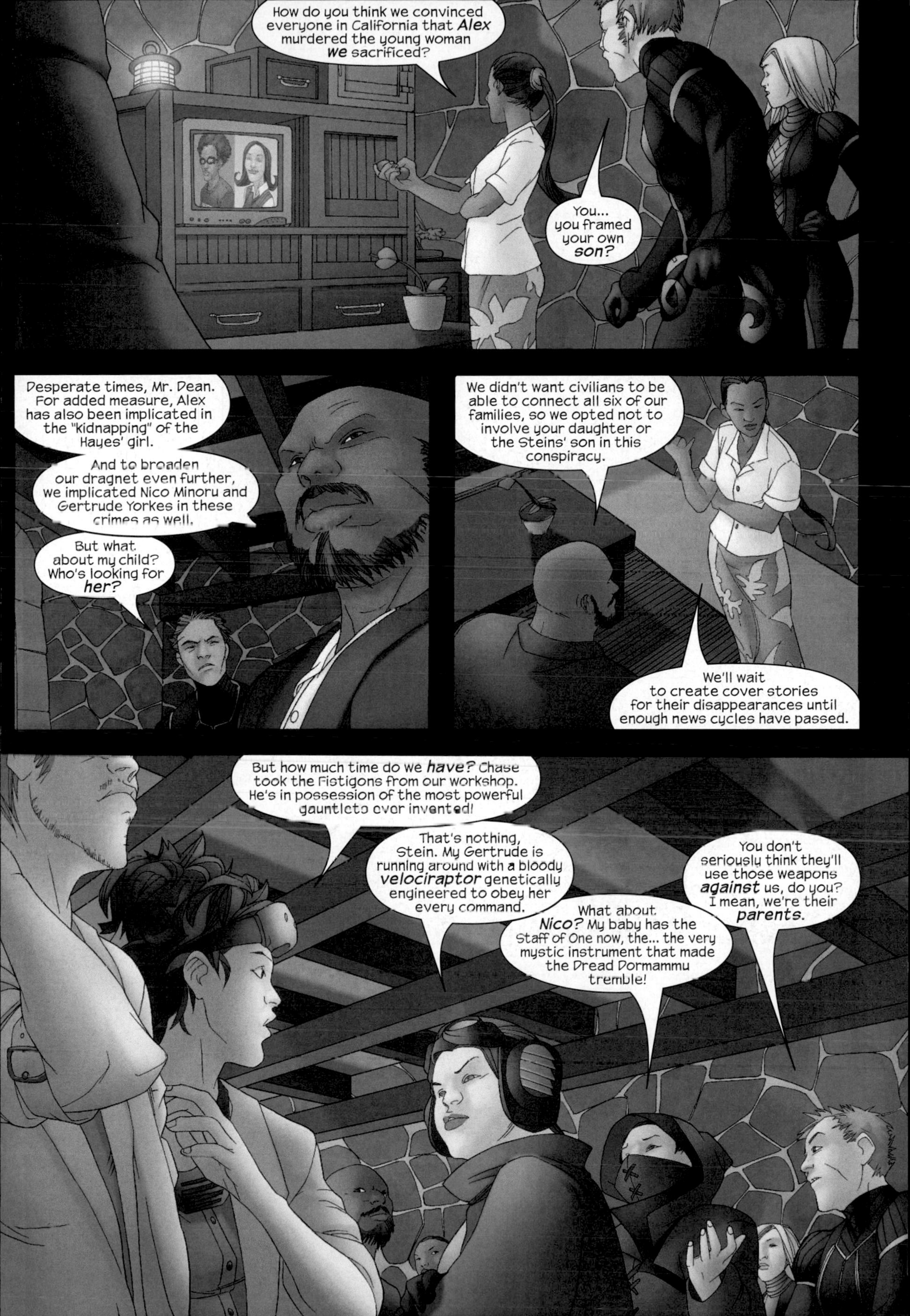
How do you think we convinced everyone in California that *Alex* murdered the young woman *we* sacrificed?
You... you framed your own *son?*
Desperate times, Mr. Dean. For added measure, Alex has also been implicated in the "kidnapping" of the Hayes' girl.
And to broaden our dragnet even further, we implicated Nico Minoru and Gertrude Yorkes in these crimes as well.
But what about my child? Who's looking for *her?*
We didn't want civilians to be able to connect all six of our families, so we opted not to involve your daughter or the Steins' son in this conspiracy.
We'll wait to create cover stories for their disappearances until enough news cycles have passed.
But how much time do we *have?* Chase took the Fistigons from our workshop. He's in possession of the most powerful gauntlets ever invented!
That's nothing, Stein. My Gertrude is running around with a bloody *velociraptor* genetically engineered to obey her every command.
What about *Nico?* My baby has the Staff of One now, the... the very mystic instrument that made the Dread Dormammu tremble!
You don't seriously think they'll use those weapons *against* us, do you? I mean, we're their *parents*.

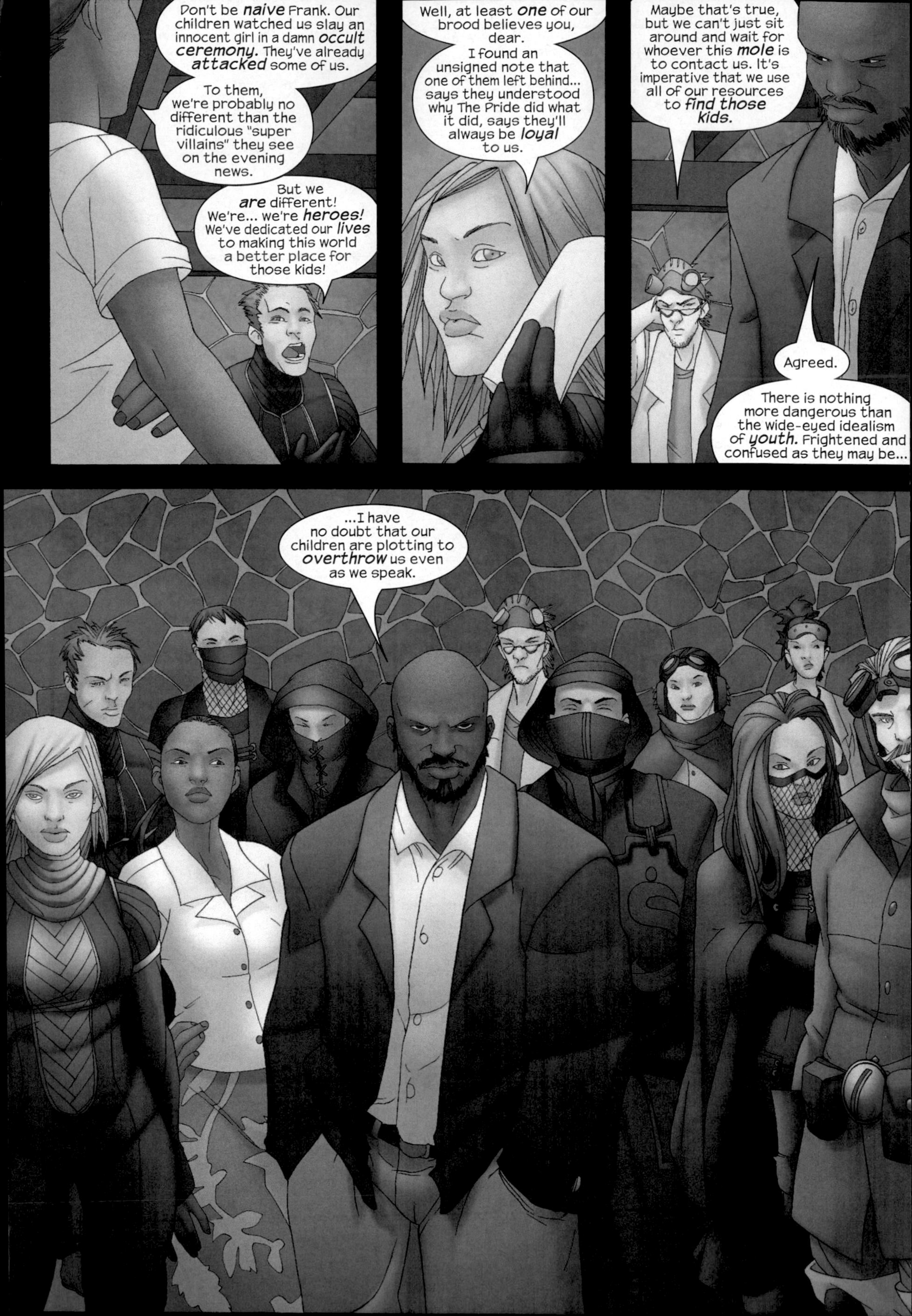
Don't be naive Frank. Our children watched us slay an innocent girl in a damn occult ceremony. They've already attacked some of us.
To them, we're probably no different than the ridiculous "super villains" they see on the evening news.
But we are different! We're... we're heroes! We've dedicated our lives to making this world a better place for those kids!
Well, at least one of our brood believes you, dear.
I found an unsigned note that one of them left behind... says they understood why The Pride did what it did, says they'll always be loyal to us.
Maybe that's true, but we can't just sit around and wait for whoever this mole is to contact us. It's imperative that we use all of our resources to find those kids.
Agreed.
There is nothing more dangerous than the wide-eyed idealism of youth. Frightened and confused as they may be...
...I have no doubt that our children are plotting to overthrow us even as we speak.

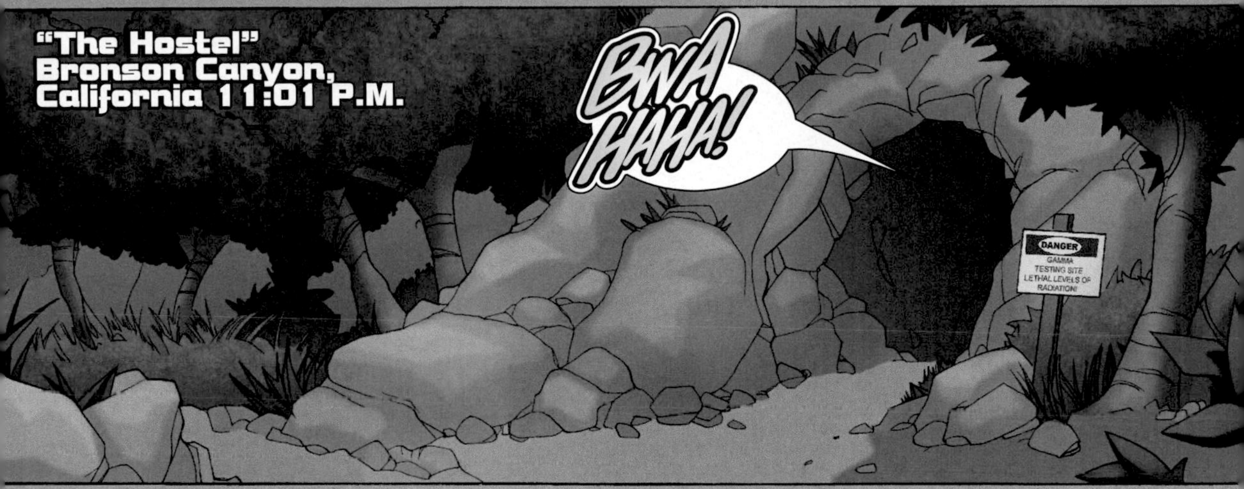
"The Hostel"
Bronson Canyon, California 11:01 P.M.
BWA HAHA!
DANGER
GAMMA TESTING SITE LETHAL LEVELS OF RADIATION!

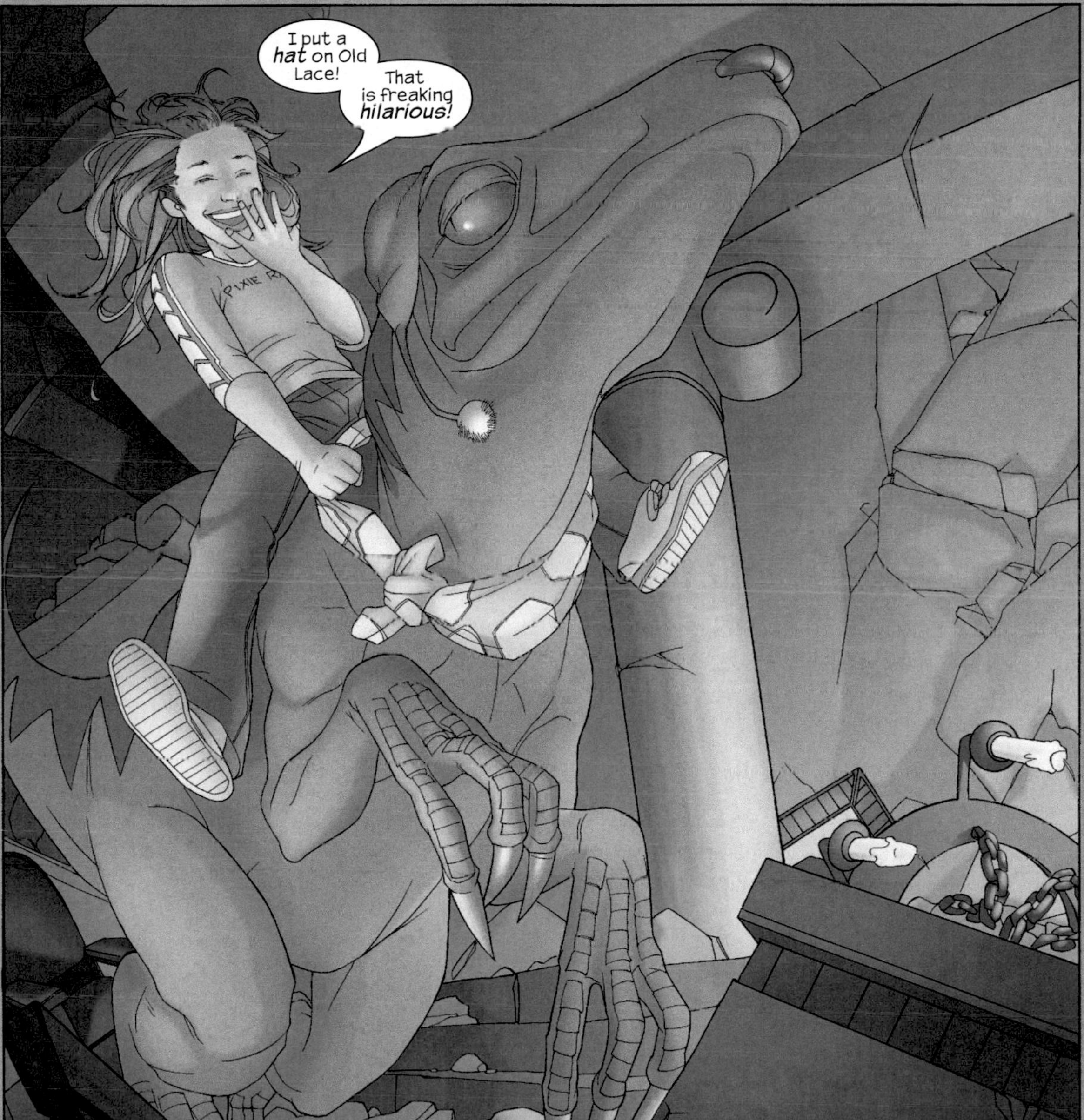
I put a *hat* on Old Lace!
That is freaking *hilarious!*

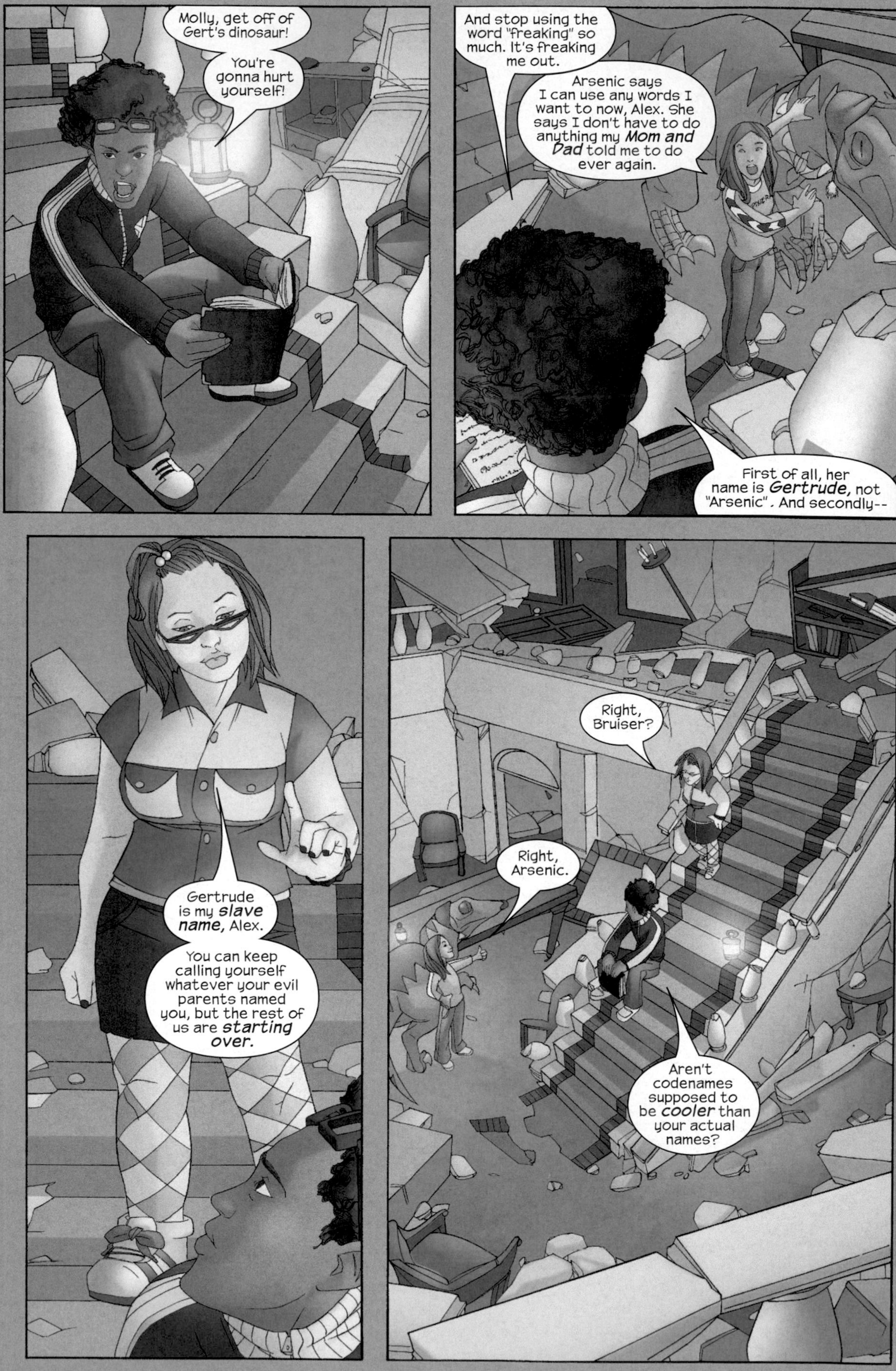

Molly, get off of Gert's dinosaur!
You're gonna hurt yourself!
And stop using the word "freaking" so much. It's freaking me out.
Arsenic says I can use any words I want to now, Alex. She says I don't have to do anything my Mom and Dad told me to do ever again.
First of all, her name is Gertrude, not "Arsenic". And secondly--
Gertrude is my slave name, Alex.
You can keep calling yourself whatever your evil parents named you, but the rest of us are starting over.
Right, Bruiser?
Right, Arsenic.
Aren't codenames supposed to be cooler than your actual names?

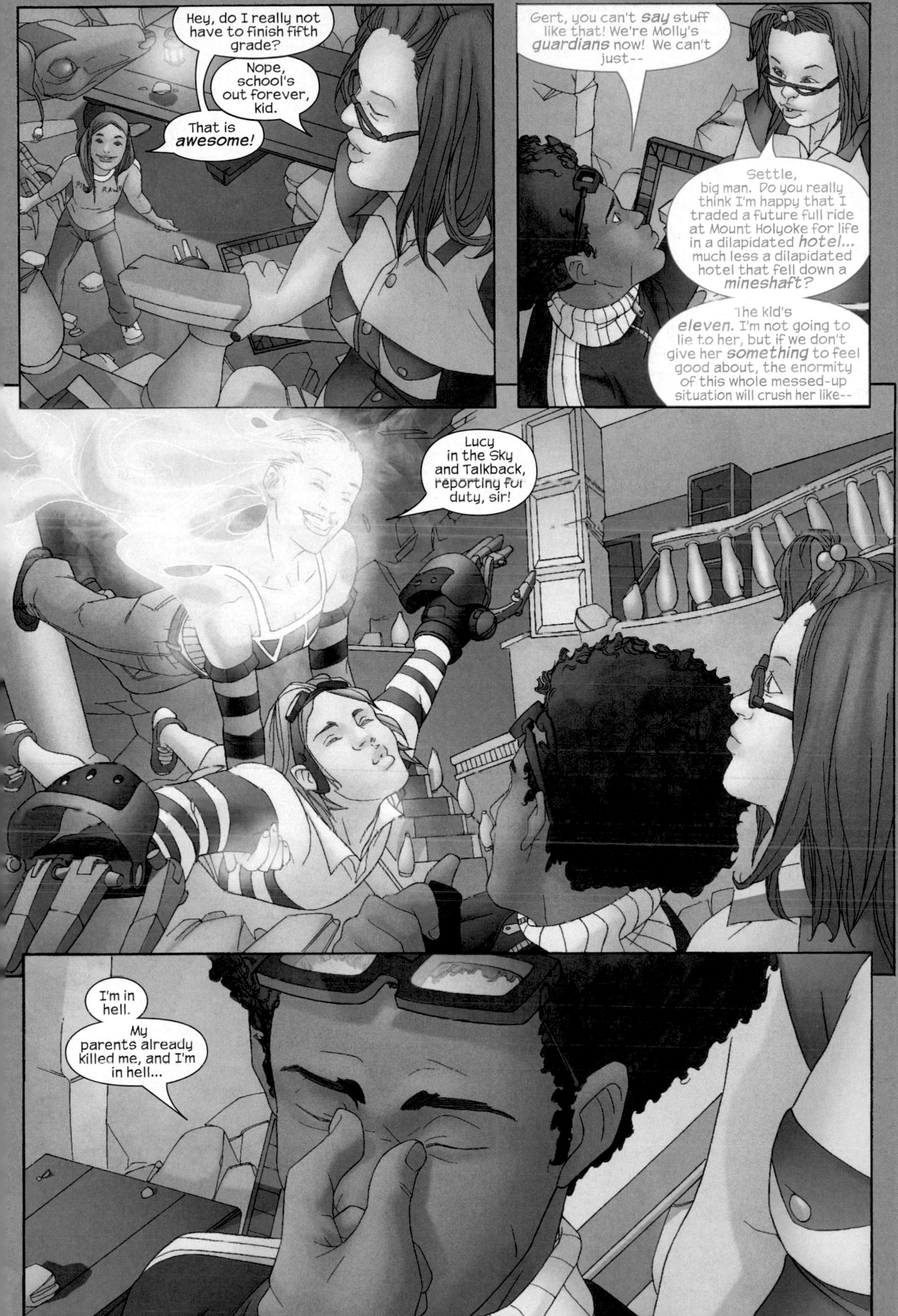
Hey, do I really not have to finish fifth grade?
Nope, school's out forever, kid.
That is *awesome!*
Gert, you can't *say* stuff like that! We're Molly's *guardians* now! We can't just--
Settle, big man. Do you really think I'm happy that I traded a future full ride at Mount Holyoke for life in a dilapidated *hotel...* much less a dilapidated hotel that fell down a *mineshaft?*
The kid's *eleven.* I'm not going to lie to her, but if we don't give her *something* to feel good about, the enormity of this whole messed-up situation will crush her like--
Lucy in the Sky and Talkback, reporting for duty, sir!
I'm in hell.
My parents already killed me, and I'm in hell...

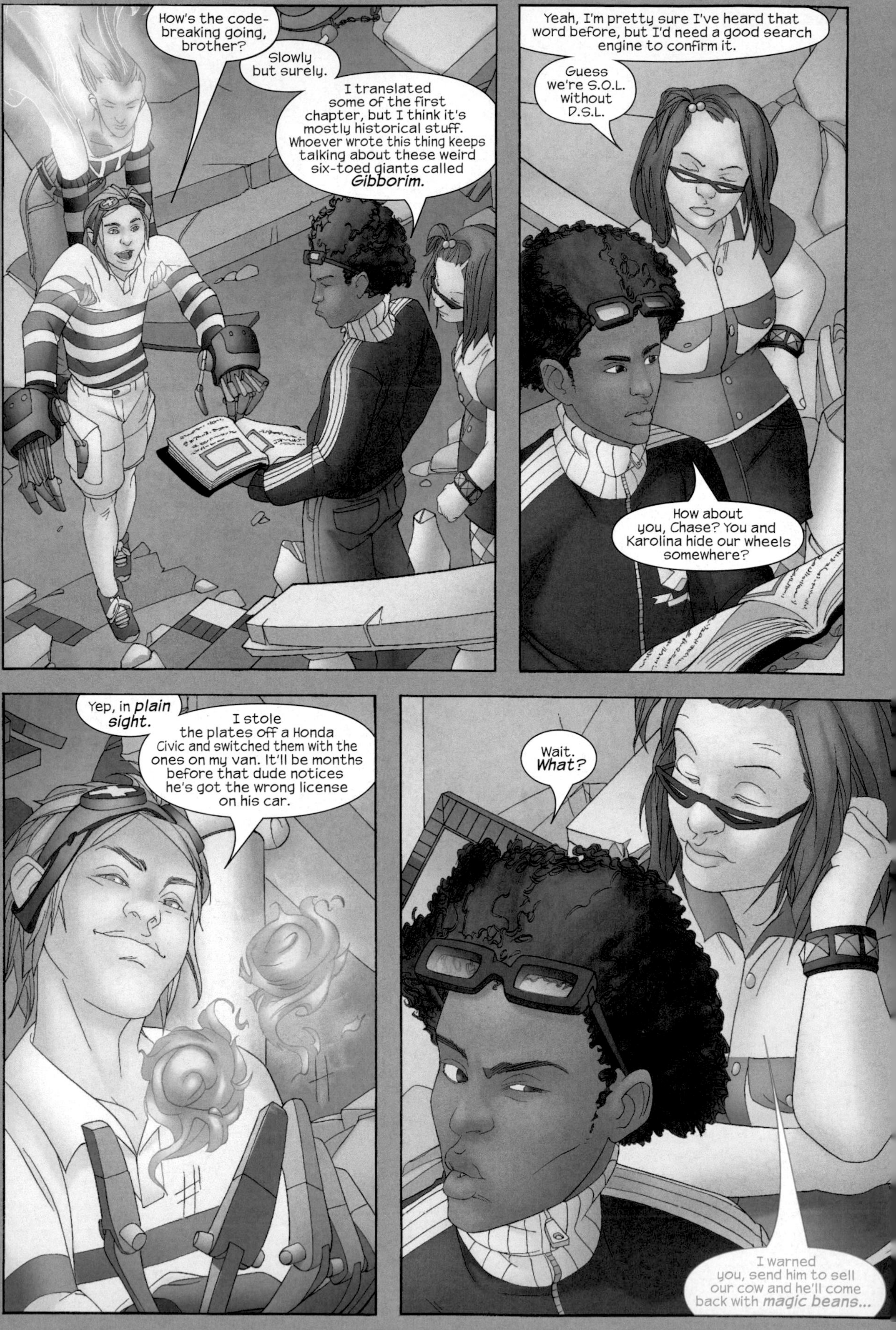
How's the code-breaking going, brother?
Slowly but surely.
I translated some of the first chapter, but I think it's mostly historical stuff. Whoever wrote this thing keeps talking about these weird six-toed giants called *Gibborim.*
Yeah, I'm pretty sure I've heard that word before, but I'd need a good search engine to confirm it.
Guess we're S.O.L. without D.S.L.
How about you, Chase? You and Karolina hide our wheels somewhere?
Yep, in *plain sight.*
I stole the plates off a Honda Civic and switched them with the ones on my van. It'll be months before that dude notices he's got the wrong license on his car.
Wait. *What?*
I warned you, send him to sell our cow and he'll come back with *magic beans...*

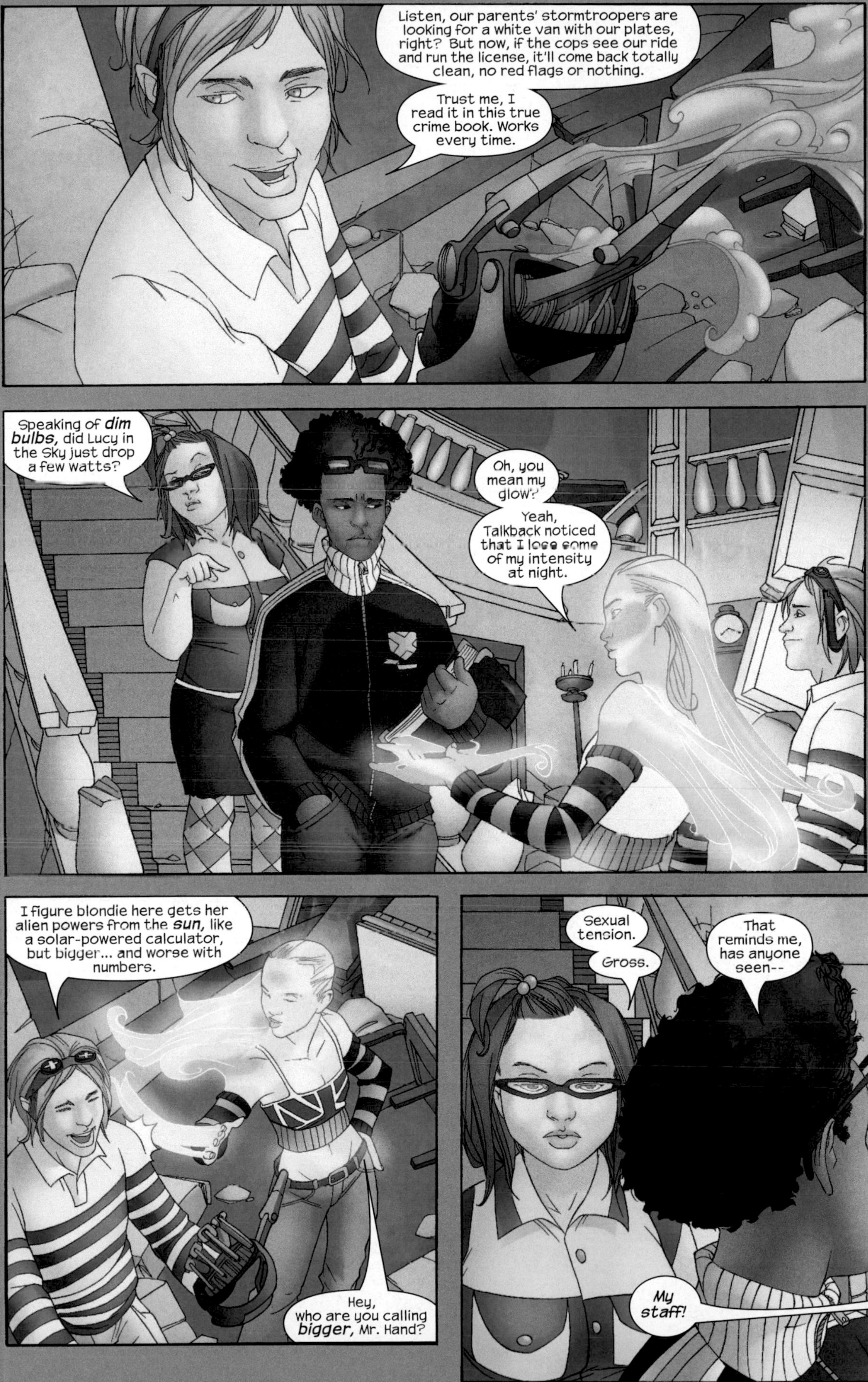
Listen, our parents' stormtroopers are looking for a white van with our plates, right? But now, if the cops see our ride and run the license, it'll come back totally clean, no red flags or nothing.
Trust me, I read it in this true crime book. Works every time.
Speaking of **dim bulbs,** did Lucy in the Sky just drop a few watts?
Oh, you mean my glow?
Yeah, Talkback noticed that I lose some of my intensity at night.
I figure blondie here gets her alien powers from the **sun,** like a solar-powered calculator, but bigger... and worse with numbers.
Hey, who are you calling **bigger,** Mr. Hand?
Sexual tension.
Gross.
That reminds me, has anyone seen--
My staff!

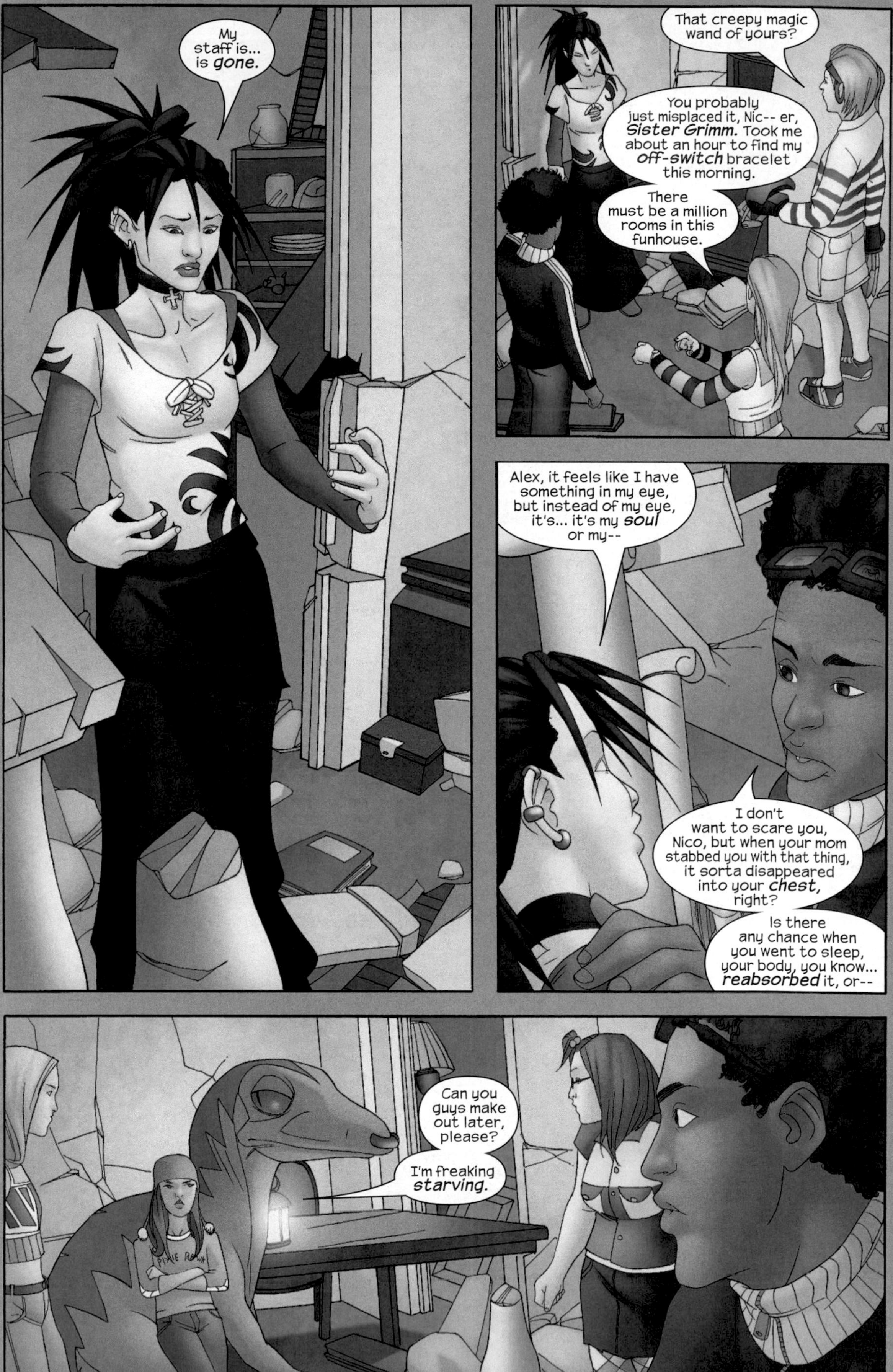
My staff is... is gone.
That creepy magic wand of yours?
You probably just misplaced it, Nic-- er, Sister Grimm. Took me about an hour to find my off-switch bracelet this morning.
There must be a million rooms in this funhouse.
Alex, it feels like I have something in my eye, but instead of my eye, it's... it's my soul or my--
I don't want to scare you, Nico, but when your mom stabbed you with that thing, it sorta disappeared into your chest, right?
Is there any chance when you went to sleep, your body, you know... reabsorbed it, or--
Can you guys make out later, please?
I'm freaking starving.

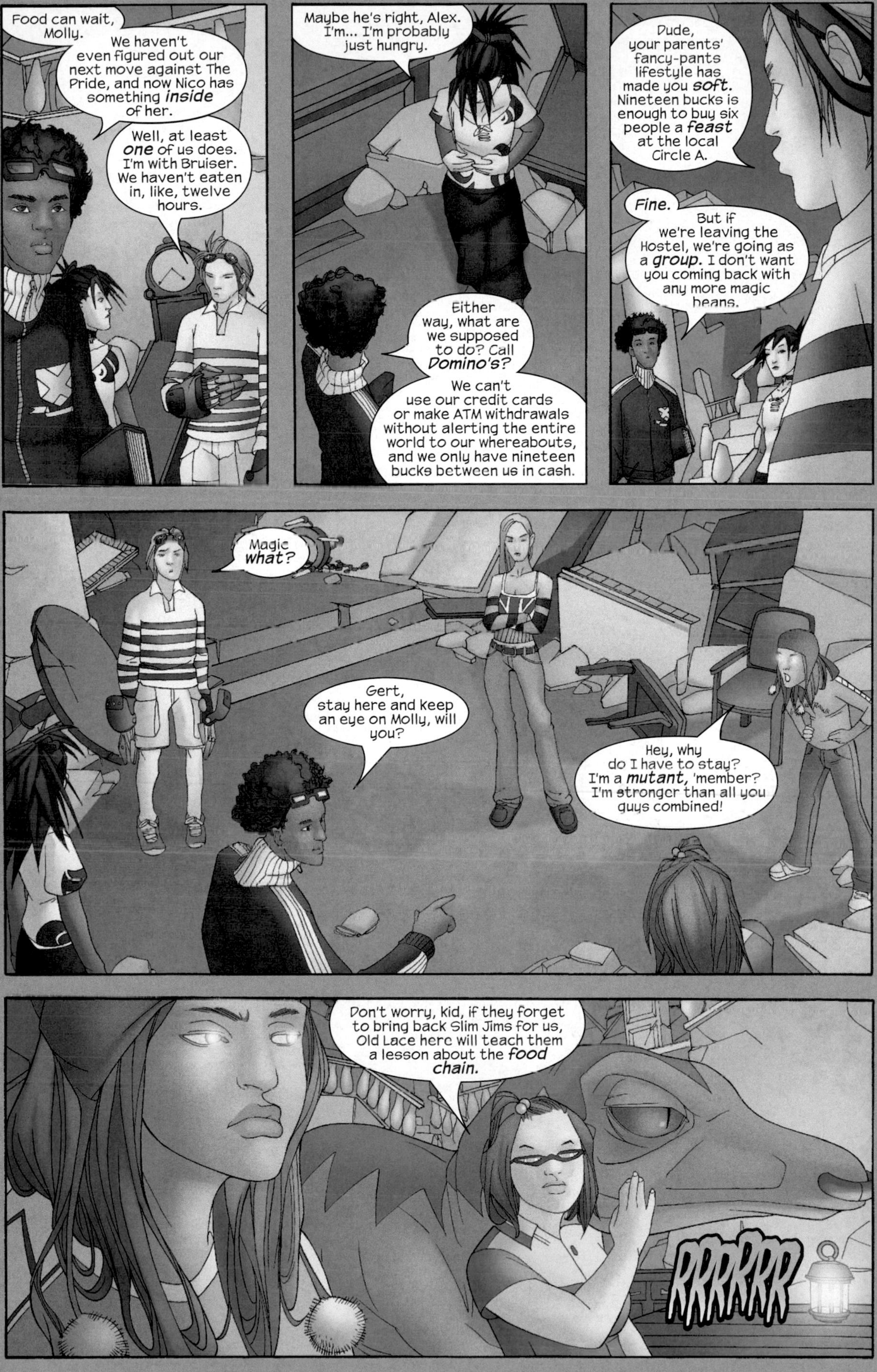
Food can wait, Molly.
We haven't even figured out our next move against The Pride, and now Nico has something *inside* of her.
Well, at least *one* of us does. I'm with Bruiser. We haven't eaten in, like, twelve hours.
Maybe he's right, Alex. I'm... I'm probably just hungry.
Either way, what are we supposed to do? Call *Domino's*?
We can't use our credit cards or make ATM withdrawals without alerting the entire world to our whereabouts, and we only have nineteen bucks between us in cash.
Dude, your parents' fancy-pants lifestyle has made you *soft.* Nineteen bucks is enough to buy six people a *feast* at the local Circle A.
Fine.
But if we're leaving the Hostel, we're going as a *group.* I don't want you coming back with any more magic beans.
Magic *what?*
Gert, stay here and keep an eye on Molly, will you?
Hey, why do I have to stay? I'm a *mutant,* 'member? I'm stronger than all you guys combined!
Don't worry, kid, if they forget to bring back Slim Jims for us, Old Lace here will teach them a lesson about the *food chain.*
RRRRRR

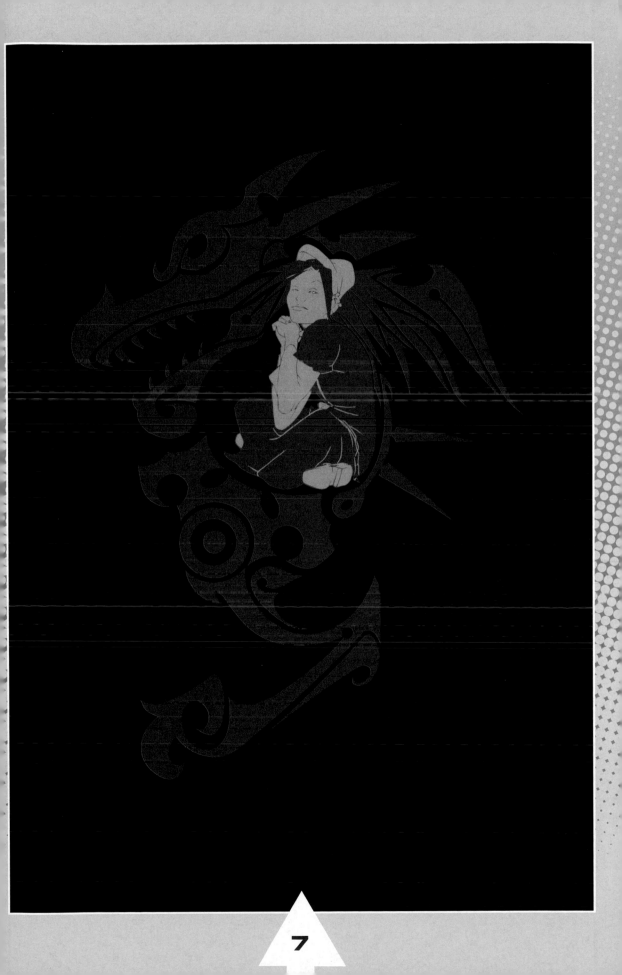

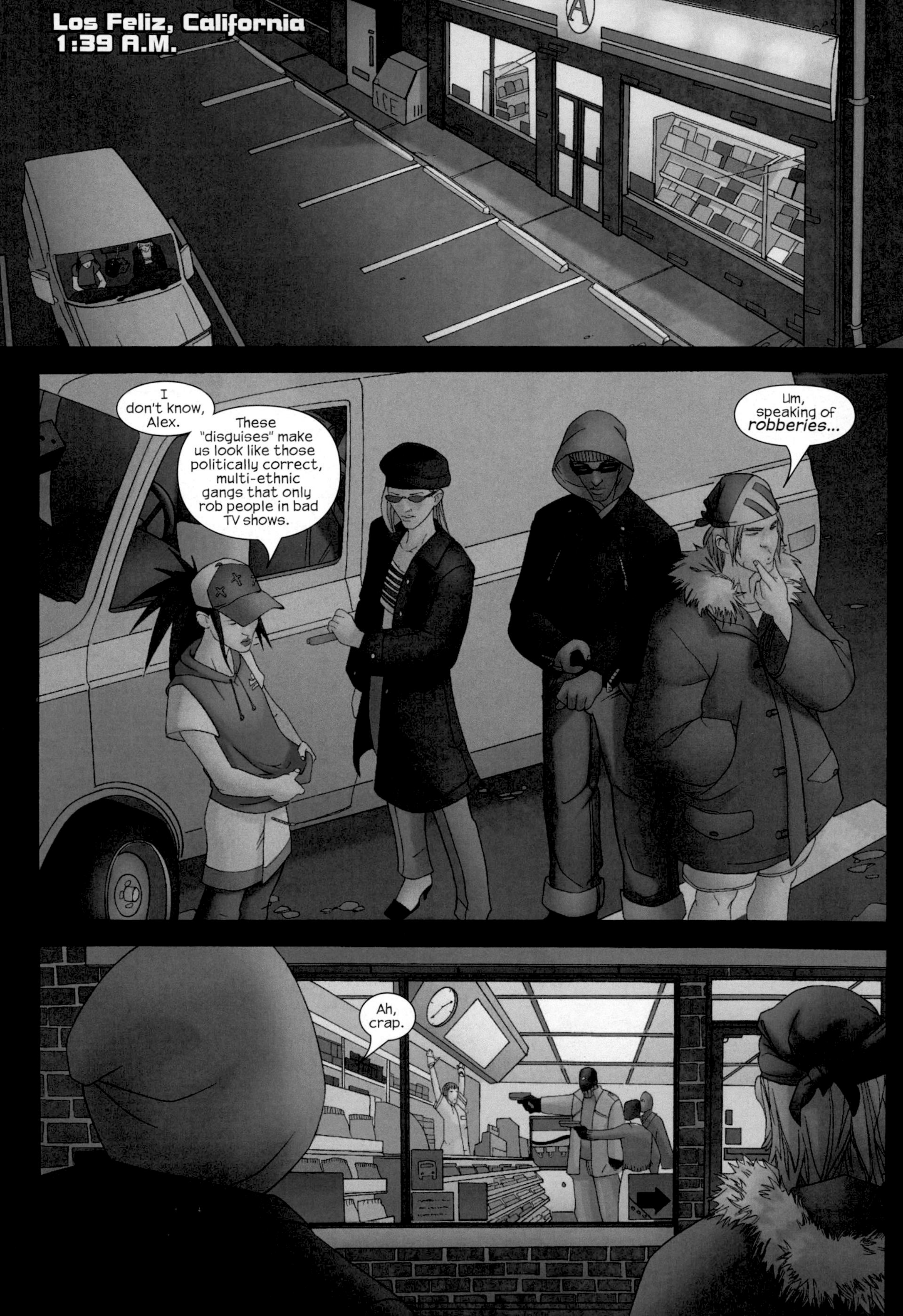

Los Feliz, California
1:39 A.M.
I don't know, Alex.
These "disguises" make us look like those politically correct, multi-ethnic gangs that only rob people in bad TV shows.
Um, speaking of *robberies...*
Ah, crap.

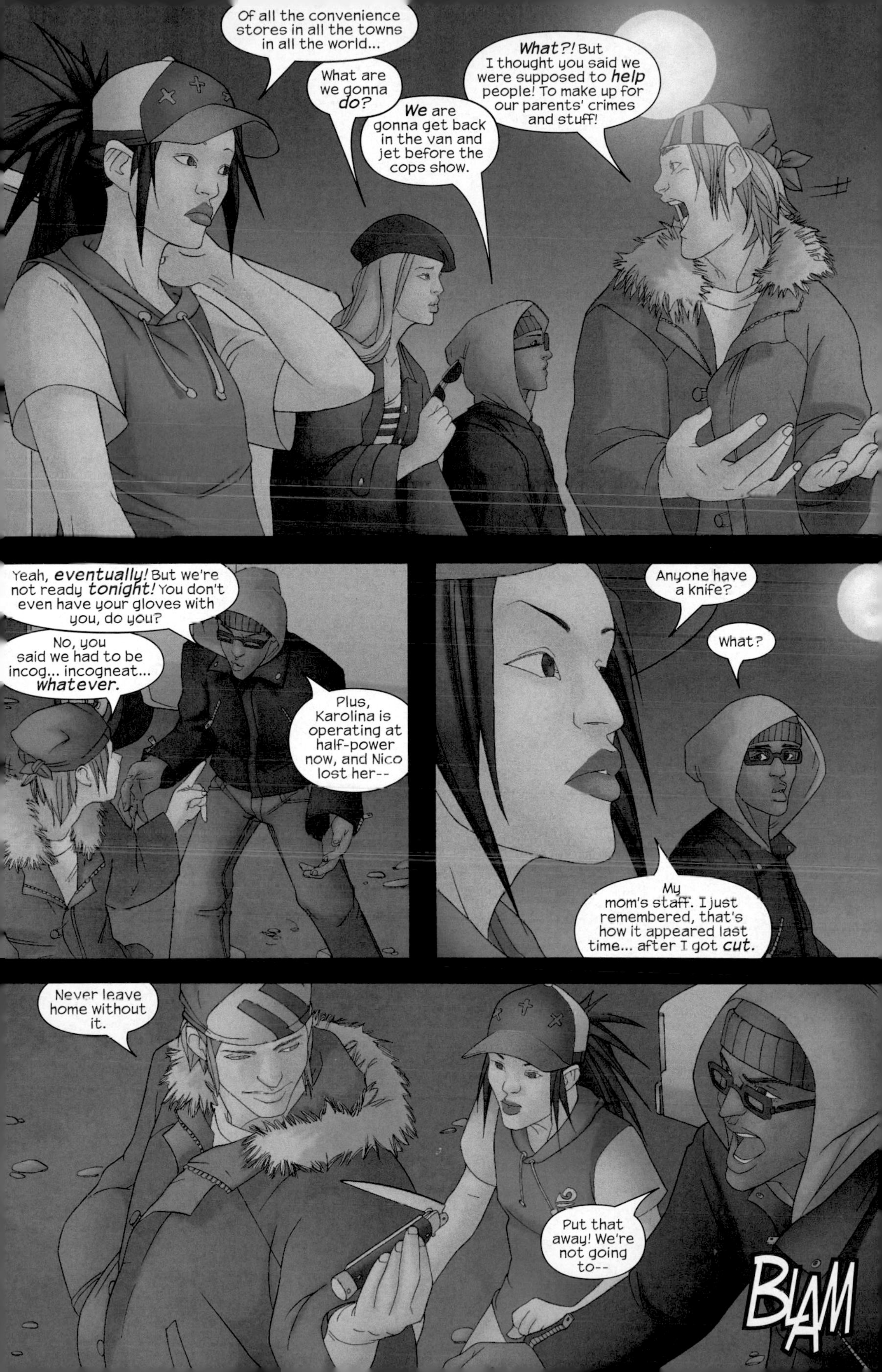

Of all the convenience stores in all the towns in all the world...
What are we gonna do?
We are gonna get back in the van and jet before the cops show.
What?! But I thought you said we were supposed to help people! To make up for our parents' crimes and stuff!
Yeah, eventually! But we're not ready tonight! You don't even have your gloves with you, do you?
No, you said we had to be incog... incogneat... whatever.
Plus, Karolina is operating at half-power now, and Nico lost her--
Anyone have a knife?
What?
My mom's staff. I just remembered, that's how it appeared last time... after I got cut.
Never leave home without it.
Put that away! We're not going to--
BLAM

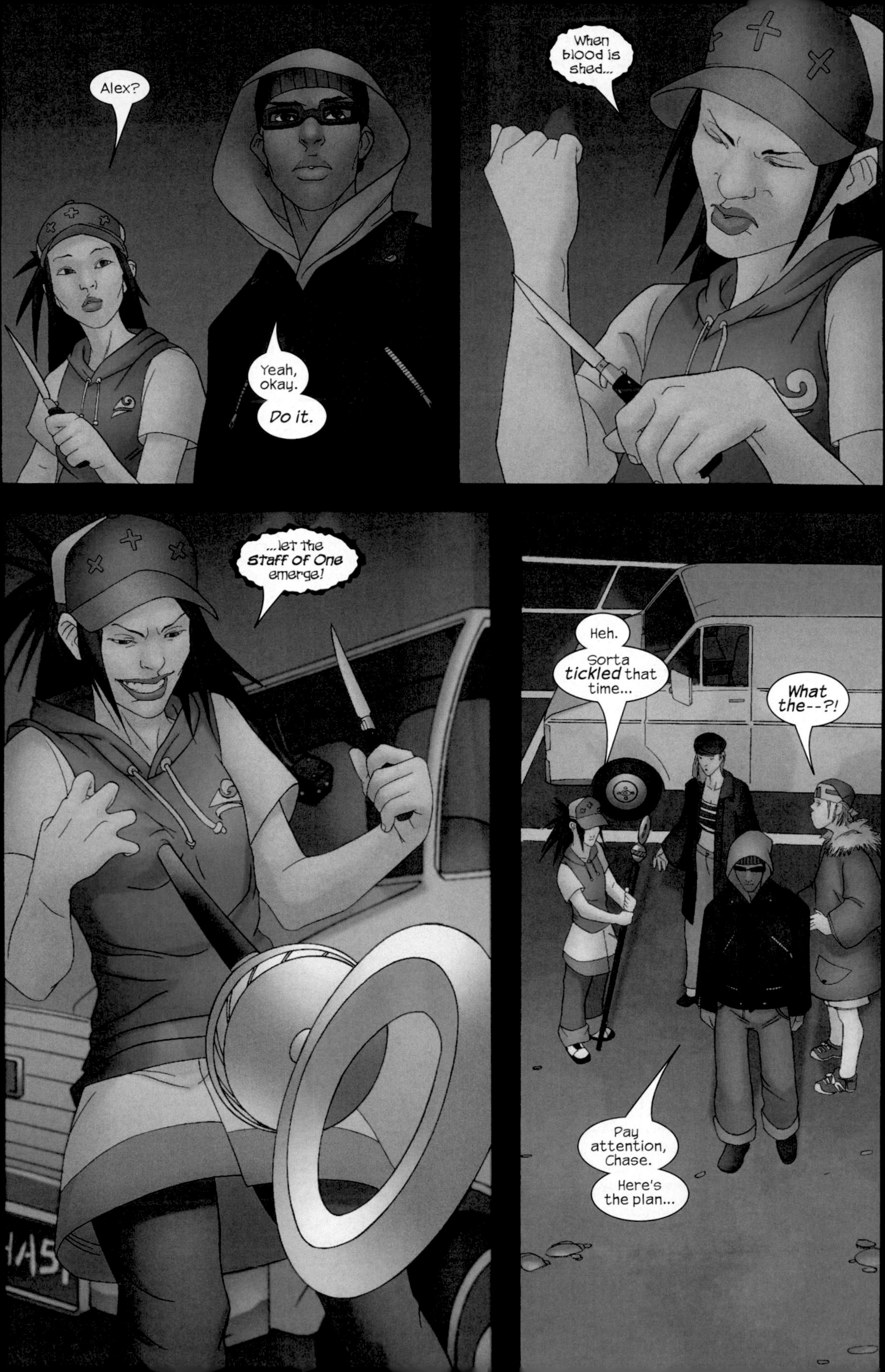
Alex?
Yeah, okay.
Do it.
When blood is shed...
...let the Staff of One emerge!
Heh.
Sorta tickled that time...
What the--?!
Pay attention, Chase.
Here's the plan...

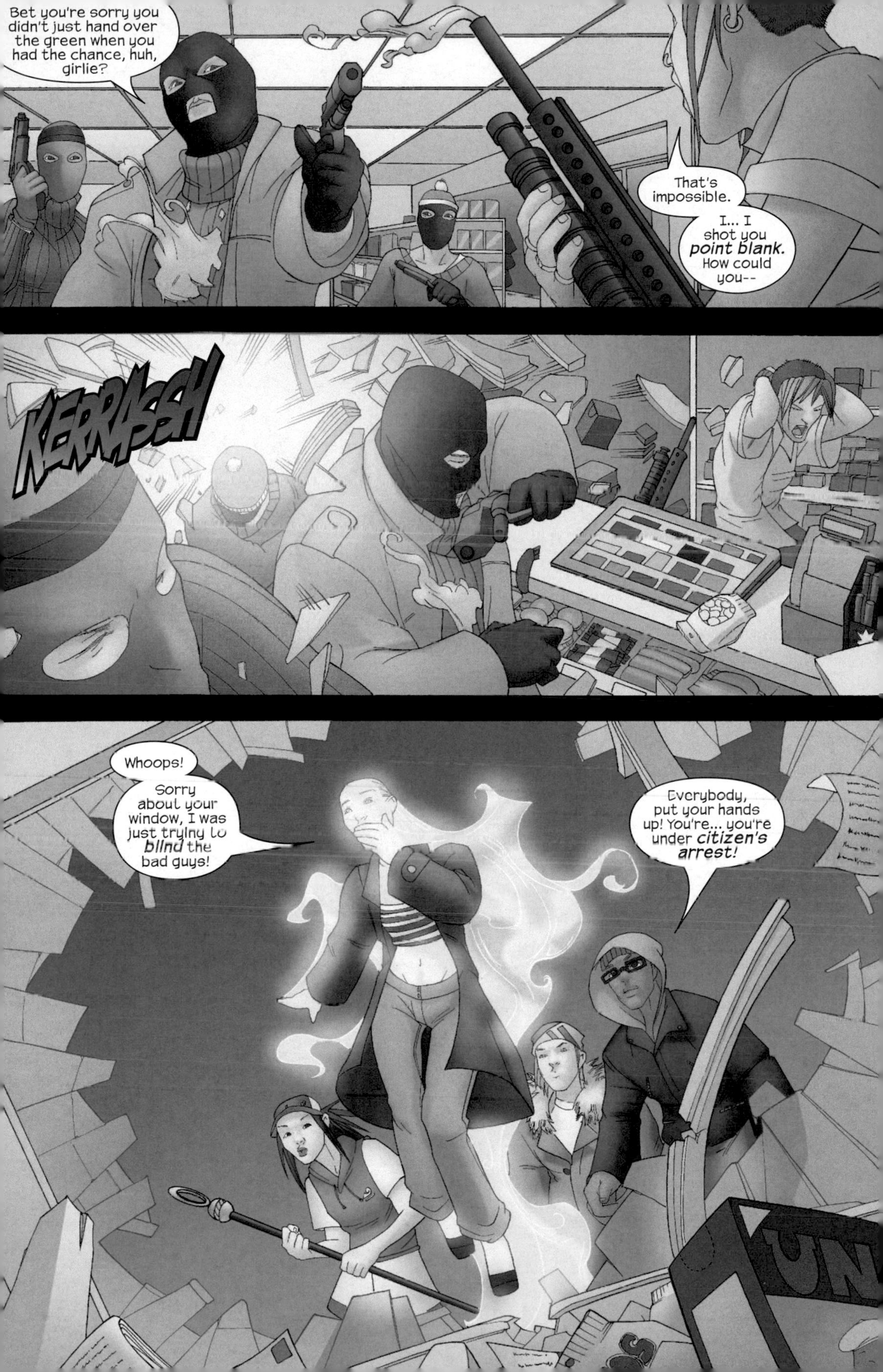
Bet you're sorry you didn't just hand over the green when you had the chance, huh, girlie?
That's impossible.
I... I shot you *point blank.* How could you--
KERRASSH
Whoops!
Sorry about your window, I was just trying to *blind* the bad guys!
Everybody, put your hands up! You're... you're under *citizen's arrest!*

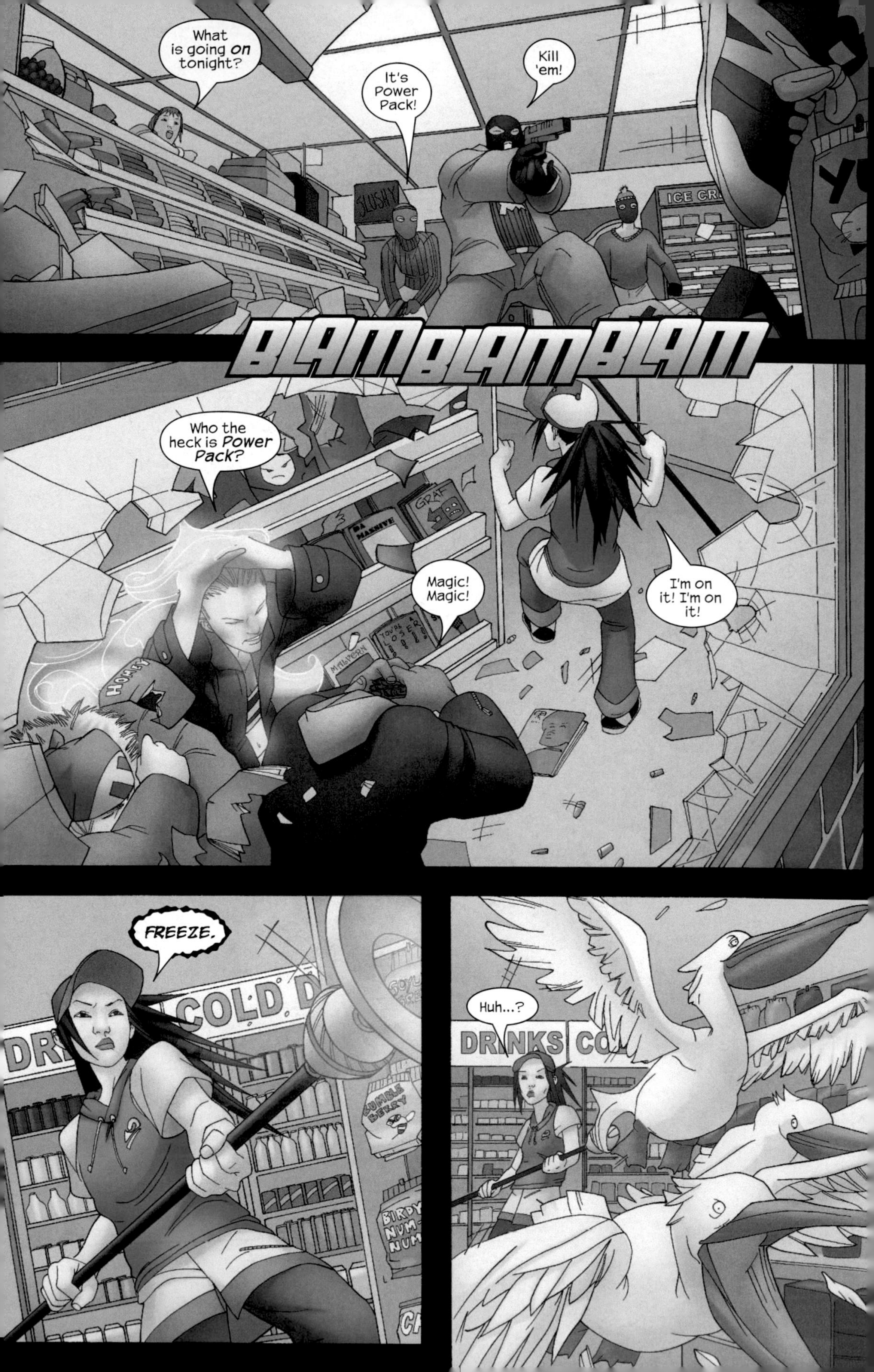
What is going *on* tonight?
It's Power Pack!
Kill 'em!
ICE CR
SLUSHY
BLAMBLAMBLAM
Who the heck is *Power Pack?*
Magic! Magic!
I'm on it! I'm on it!
FREEZE.
COLD D
Huh...?
DRINKS CO

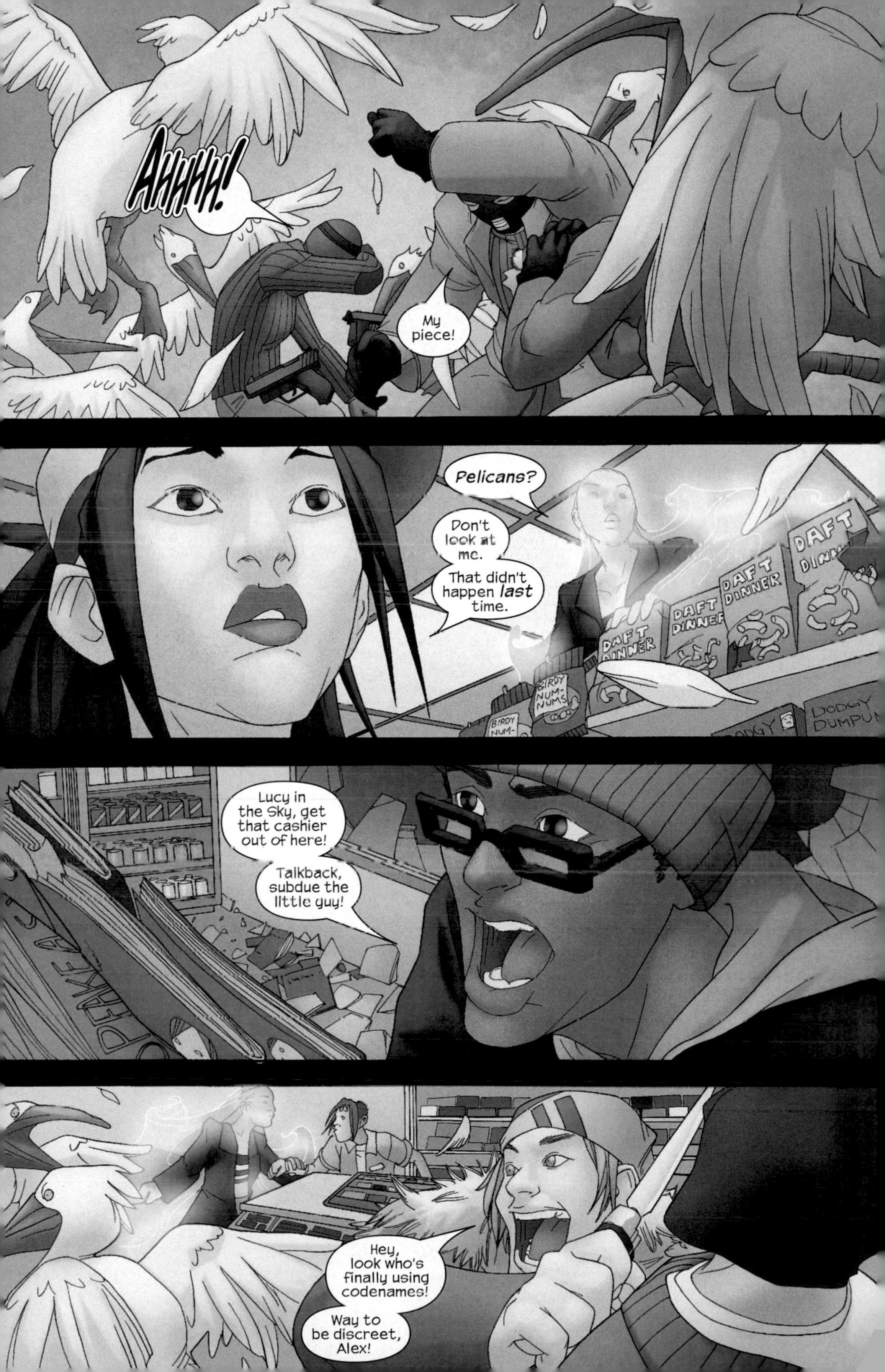
AHHHH!
My piece!
Pelicans?
Don't look at me.
That didn't happen *last* time.
DAFT DINNER
BIRDY NUM-NUMS
DODGY DUMPUN
Lucy in the Sky, get that cashier out of here!
Talkback, subdue the little guy!
Hey, look who's finally using codenames!
Way to be discreet, Alex!

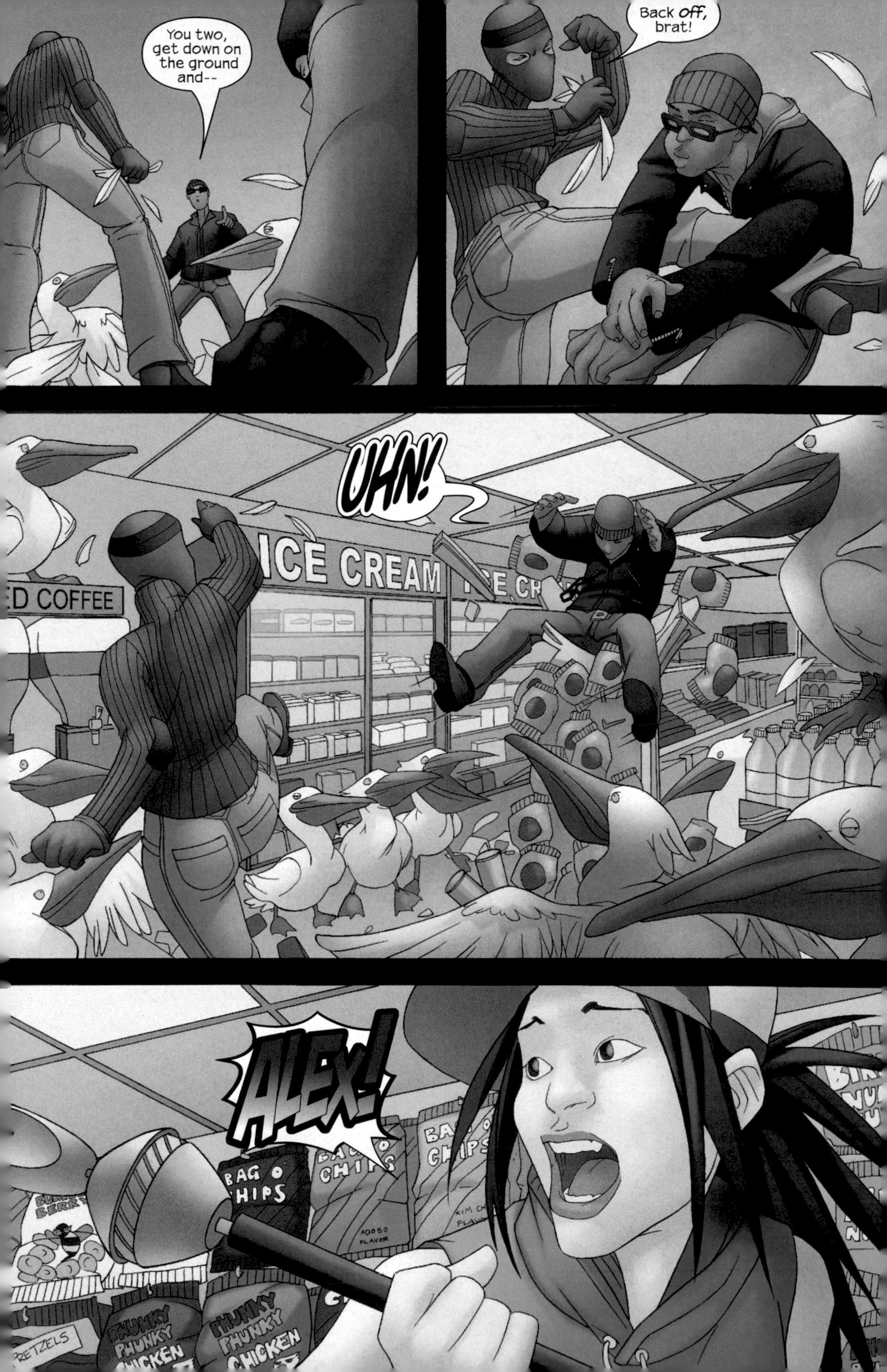
You two, get down on the ground and--
Back off, brat!
UHN!
ICE CREAM
ED COFFEE
ALEX!
BAG O' CHIPS
BAG O' CHIPS
BAG O' CHIPS
ADOBO FLAVOR
PHUNKY PHUNKY CHICKEN
PHUNKY PHUNKY CHICKEN
RETZELS

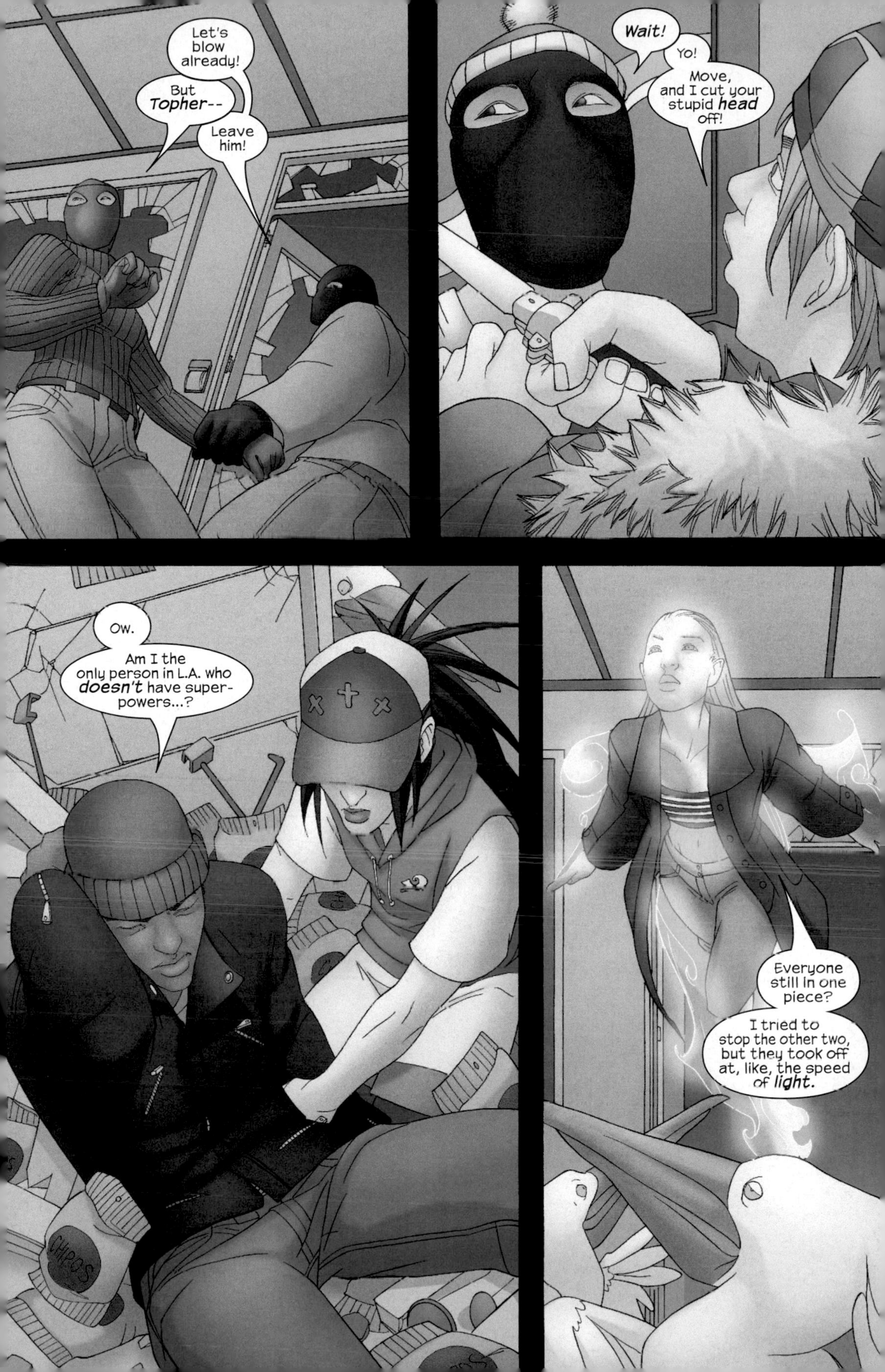

Let's blow already!
But Topher--
Leave him!
Wait!
Yo!
Move, and I cut your stupid head off!
Ow.
Am I the only person in L.A. who doesn't have super-powers...?
Everyone still in one piece?
I tried to stop the other two, but they took off at, like, the speed of light.
CHIPS

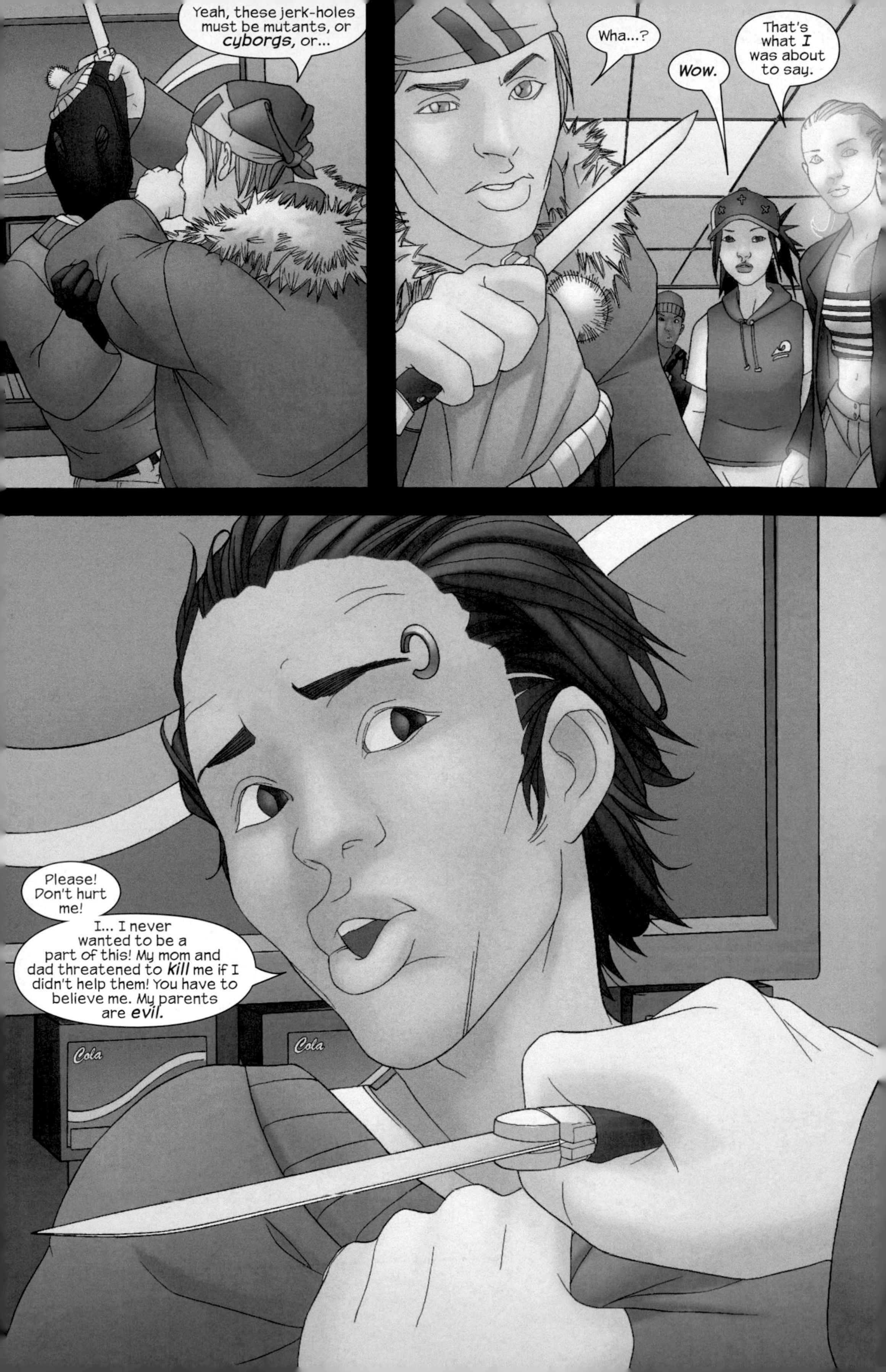
Yeah, these jerk-holes must be mutants, or *cyborgs*, or...
Wha...?
Wow.
That's what *I* was about to say.
Cola
Cola
Please! Don't hurt me!
I... I never wanted to be a part of this! My mom and dad threatened to *kill* me if I didn't help them! You have to believe me. My parents are *evil*.

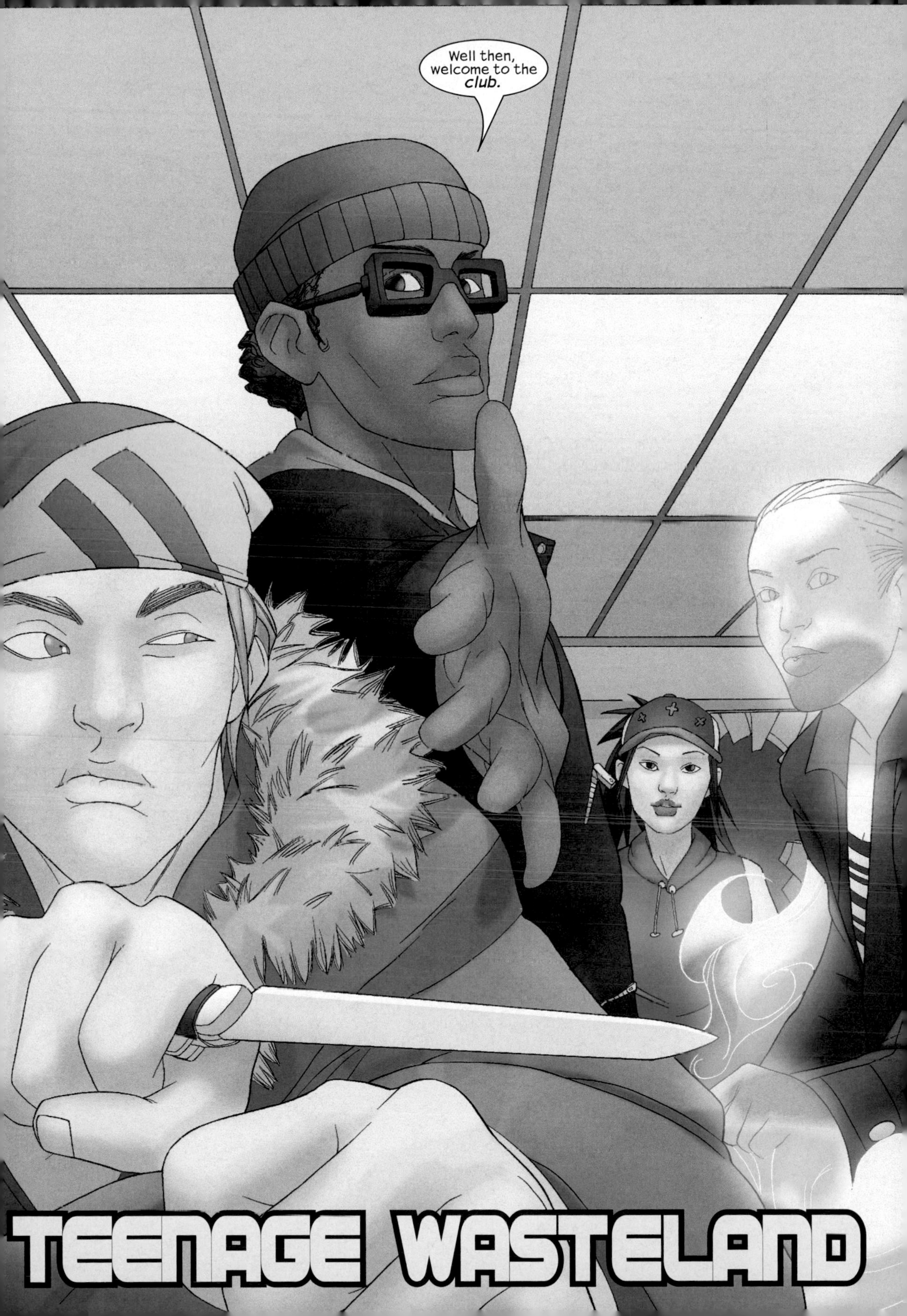
Well then, welcome to the *club.*
TEENAGE WASTELAND

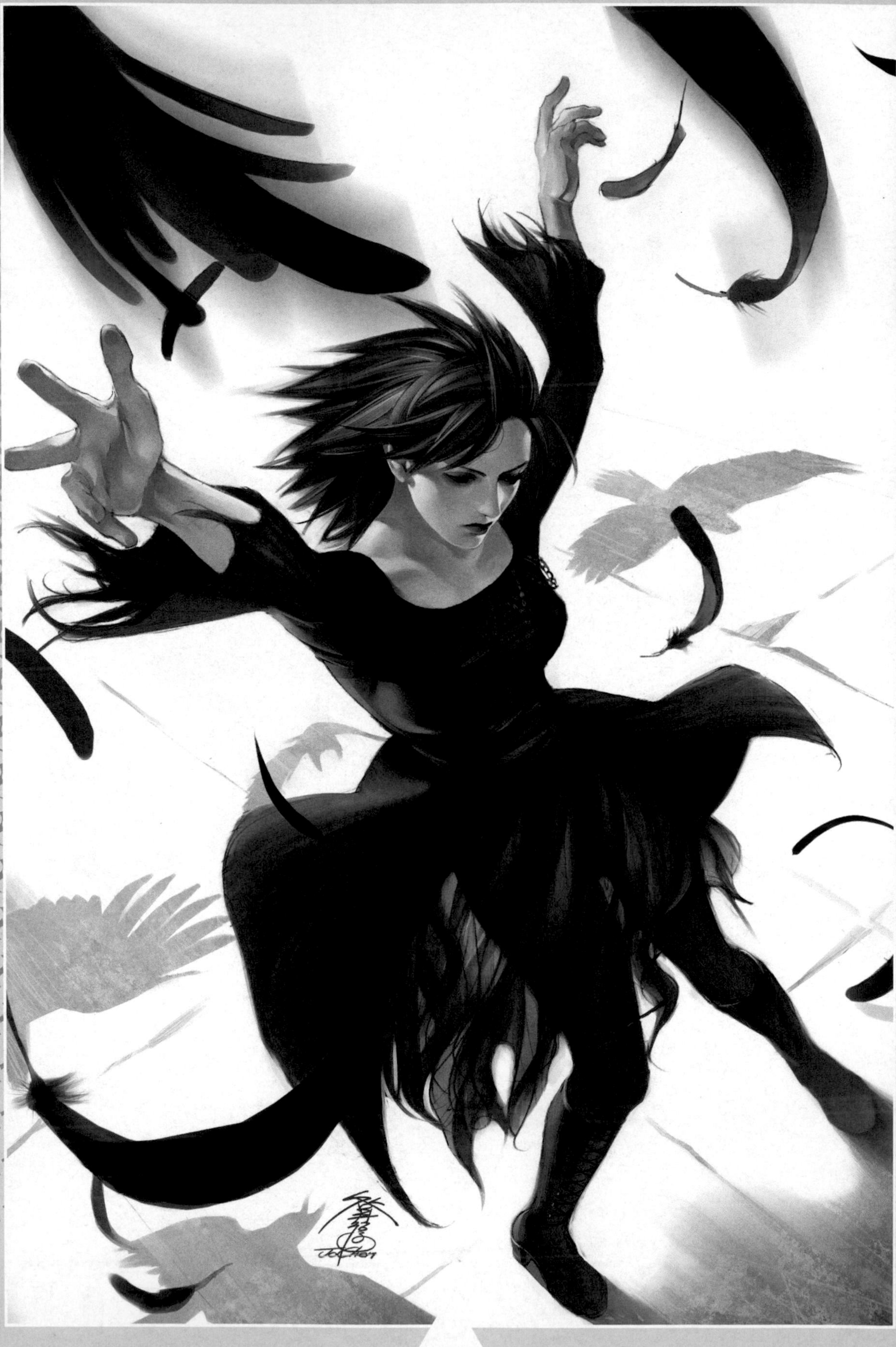

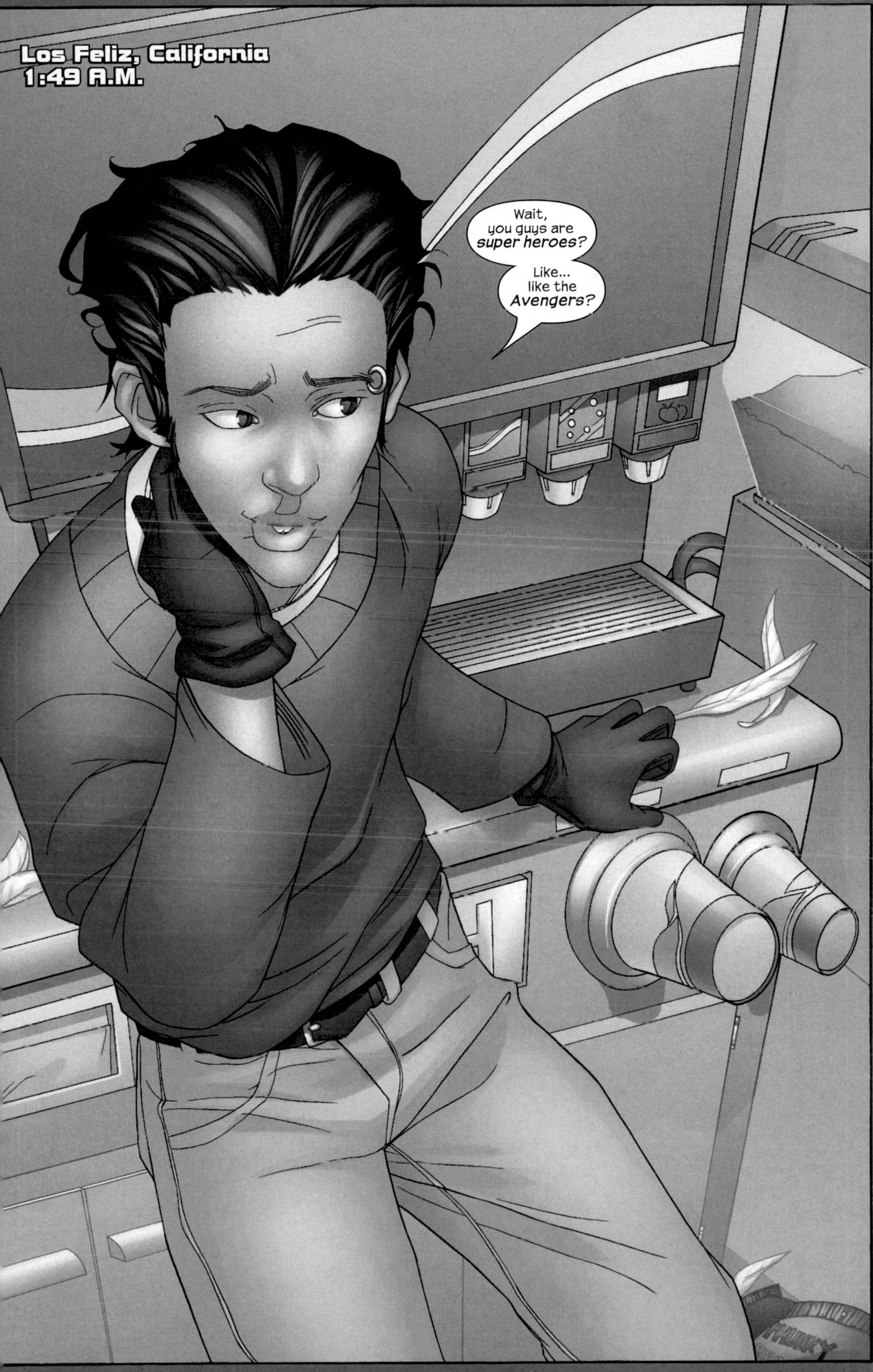
Los Feliz, California
1:49 A.M.
Wait, you guys are super heroes?
Like... like the Avengers?

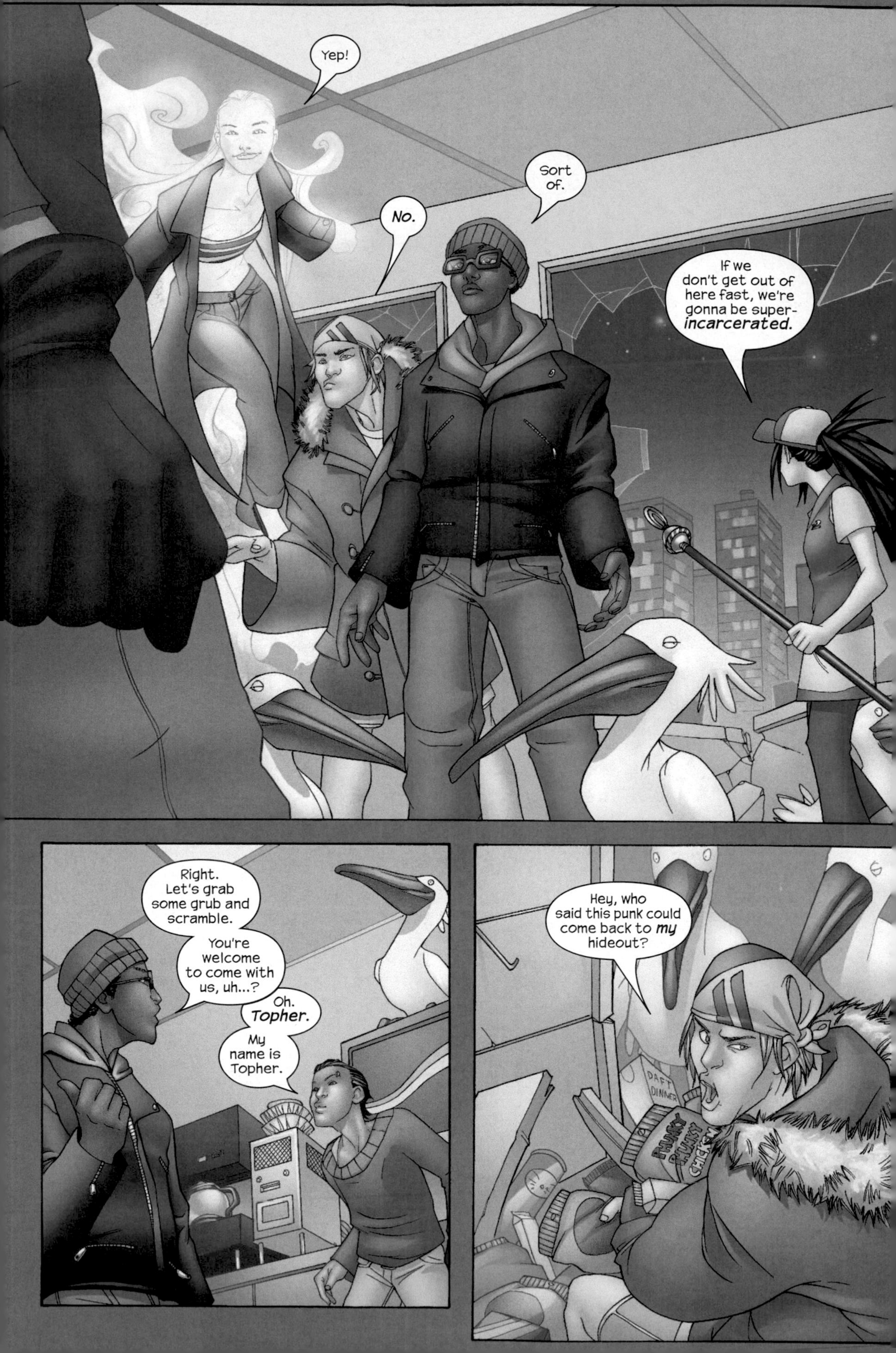
Yep!
No.
Sort of.
If we don't get out of here fast, we're gonna be super-*incarcerated.*
Right. Let's grab some grub and scramble.
You're welcome to come with us, uh...?
Oh. *Topher.*
My name is Topher.
Hey, who said this punk could come back to *my* hideout?

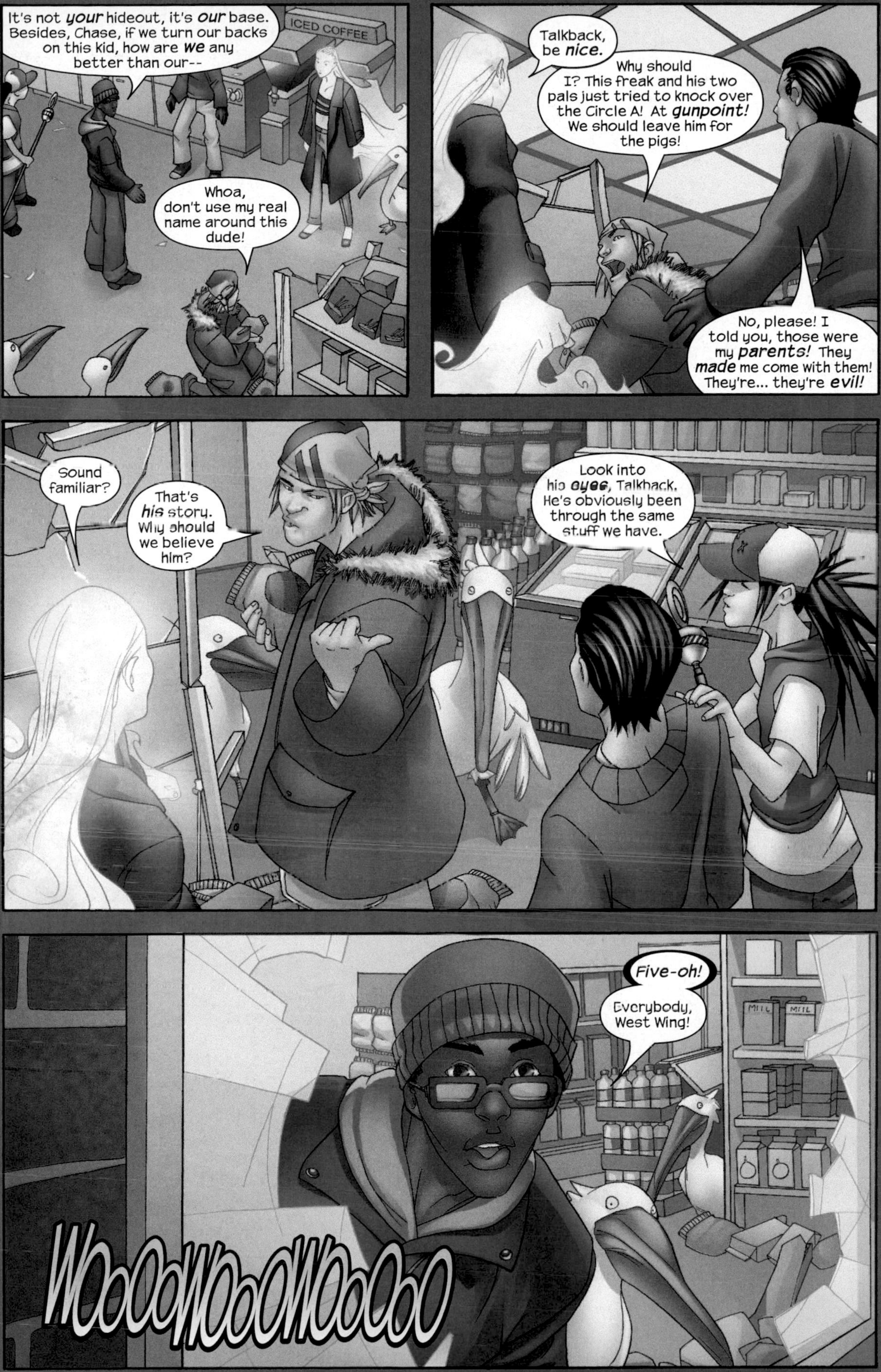
It's not your hideout, it's our base. Besides, Chase, if we turn our backs on this kid, how are we any better than our--
ICED COFFEE
Whoa, don't use my real name around this dude!
Talkback, be nice.
Why should I? This freak and his two pals just tried to knock over the Circle A! At gunpoint! We should leave him for the pigs!
No, please! I told you, those were my parents! They made me come with them! They're... they're evil!
Sound familiar?
That's his story. Why should we believe him?
Look into his eyes, Talkback. He's obviously been through the same stuff we have.
Five-oh!
Everybody, West Wing!
WOoOoWOoOWOoOoO

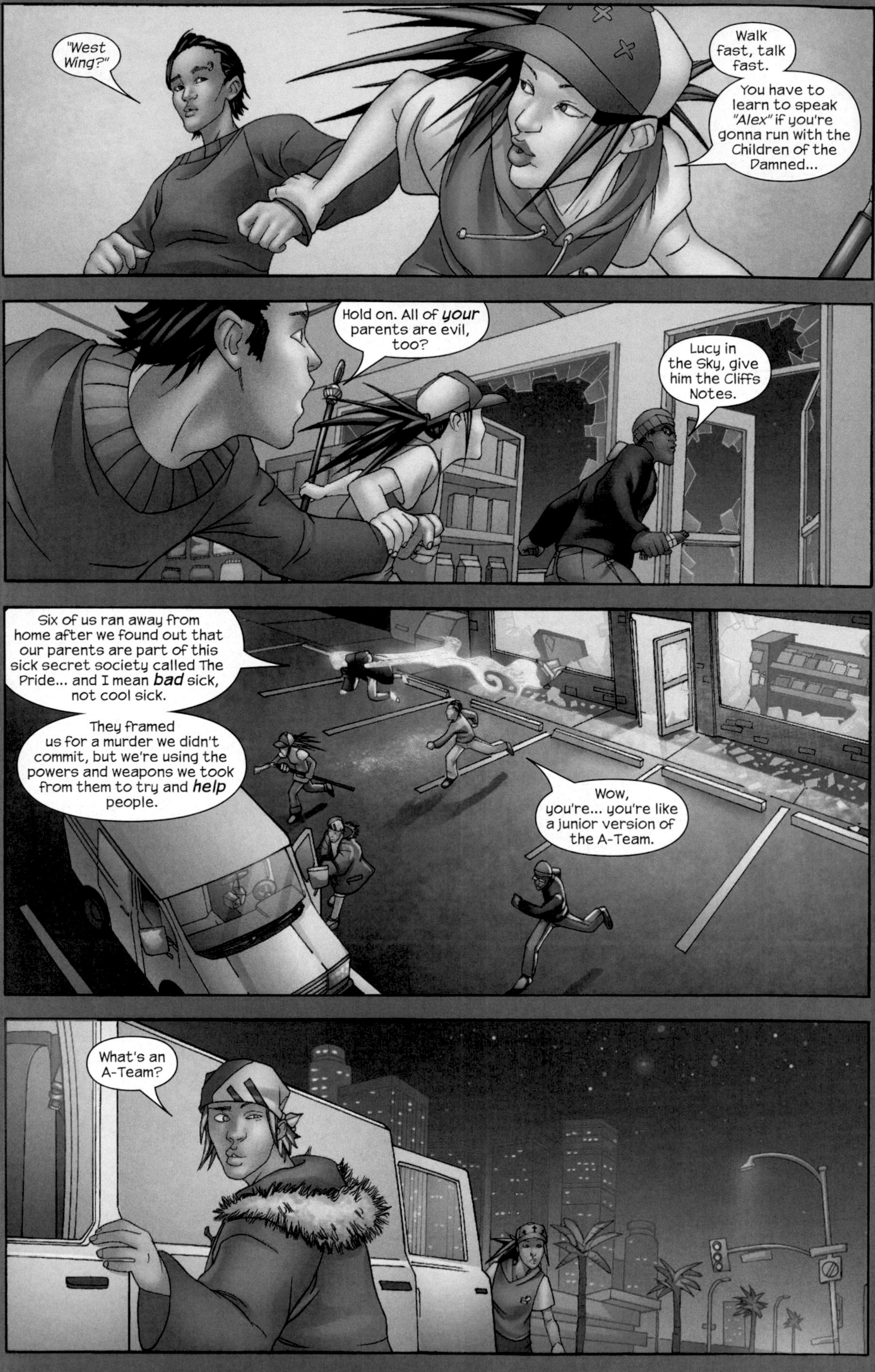
"West Wing?"
Walk fast, talk fast.
You have to learn to speak "Alex" if you're gonna run with the Children of the Damned...
Hold on. All of **your** parents are evil, too?
Lucy in the Sky, give him the Cliffs Notes.
Six of us ran away from home after we found out that our parents are part of this sick secret society called The Pride... and I mean **bad** sick, not cool sick.
They framed us for a murder we didn't commit, but we're using the powers and weapons we took from them to try and **help** people.
Wow, you're... you're like a junior version of the A-Team.
What's an A-Team?

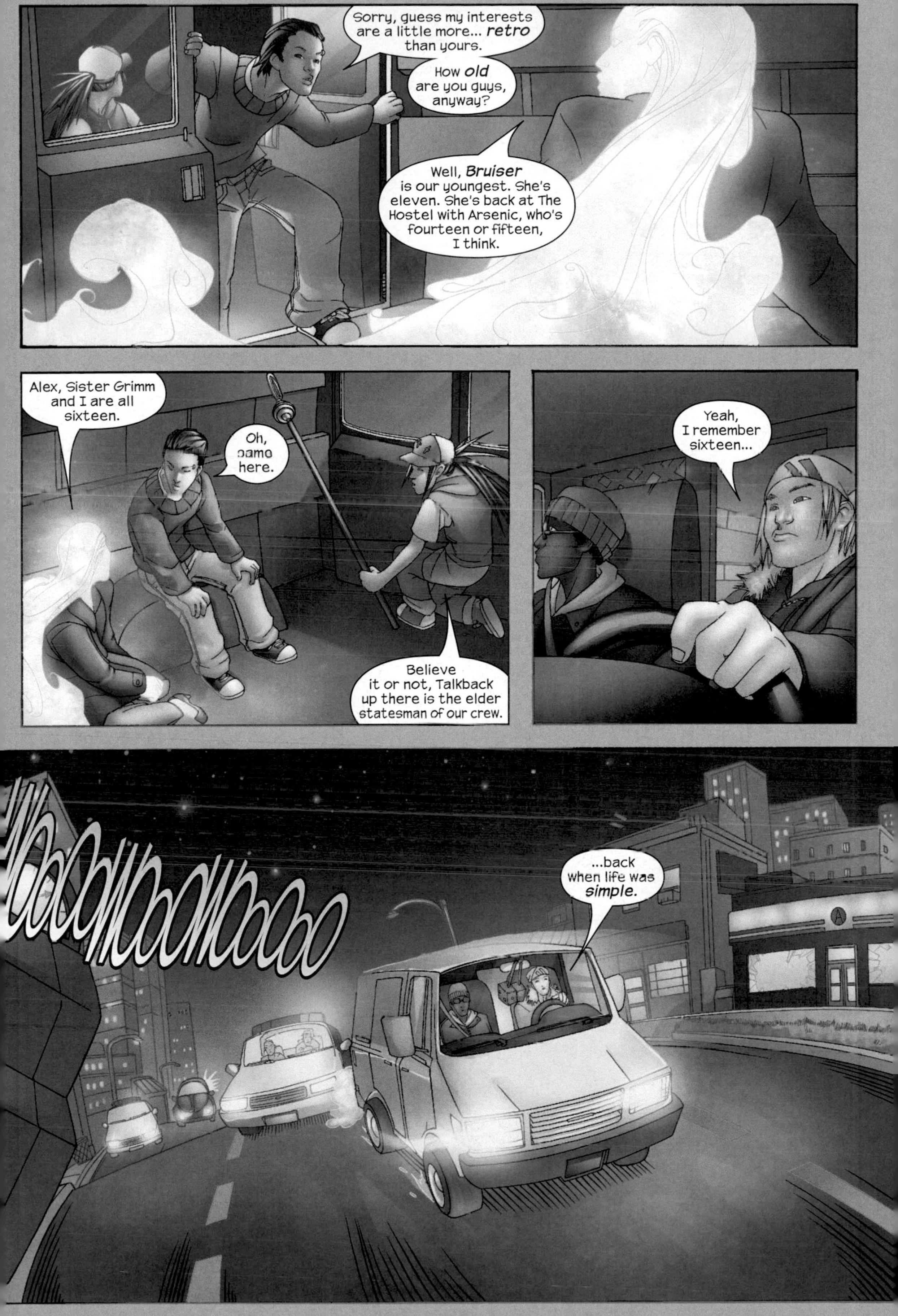
Sorry, guess my interests are a little more... retro than yours.
How old are you guys, anyway?
Well, Bruiser is our youngest. She's eleven. She's back at The Hostel with Arsenic, who's fourteen or fifteen, I think.
Alex, Sister Grimm and I are all sixteen.
Oh, same here.
Believe it or not, Talkback up there is the elder statesman of our crew.
Yeah, I remember sixteen...
WOOOWOOOWOOOOO
...back when life was simple.

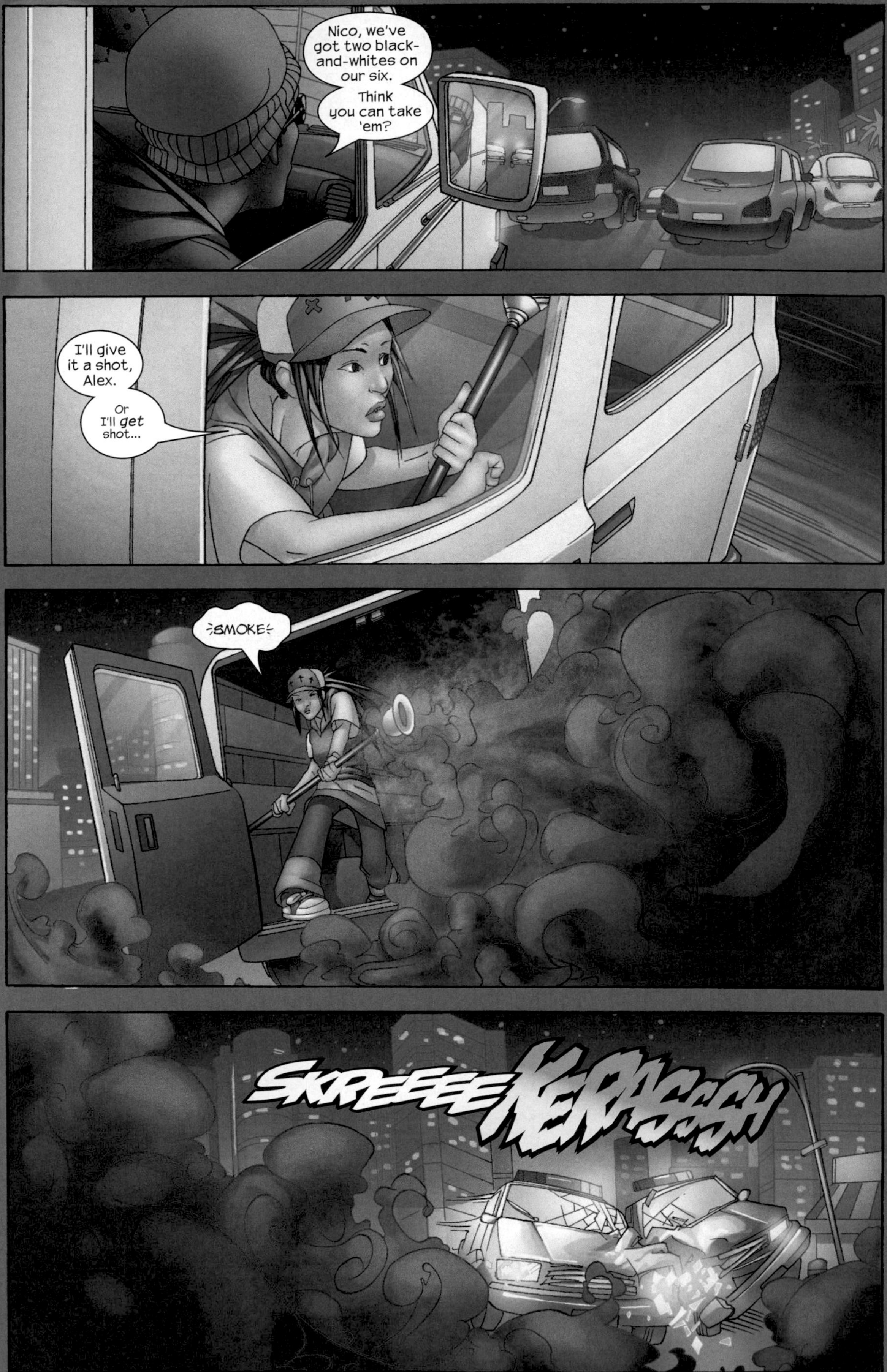
Nico, we've got two black-and-whites on our six.
Think you can take 'em?
I'll give it a shot, Alex.
Or I'll get shot...
SMOKE
SKREEEEE KERASSSH

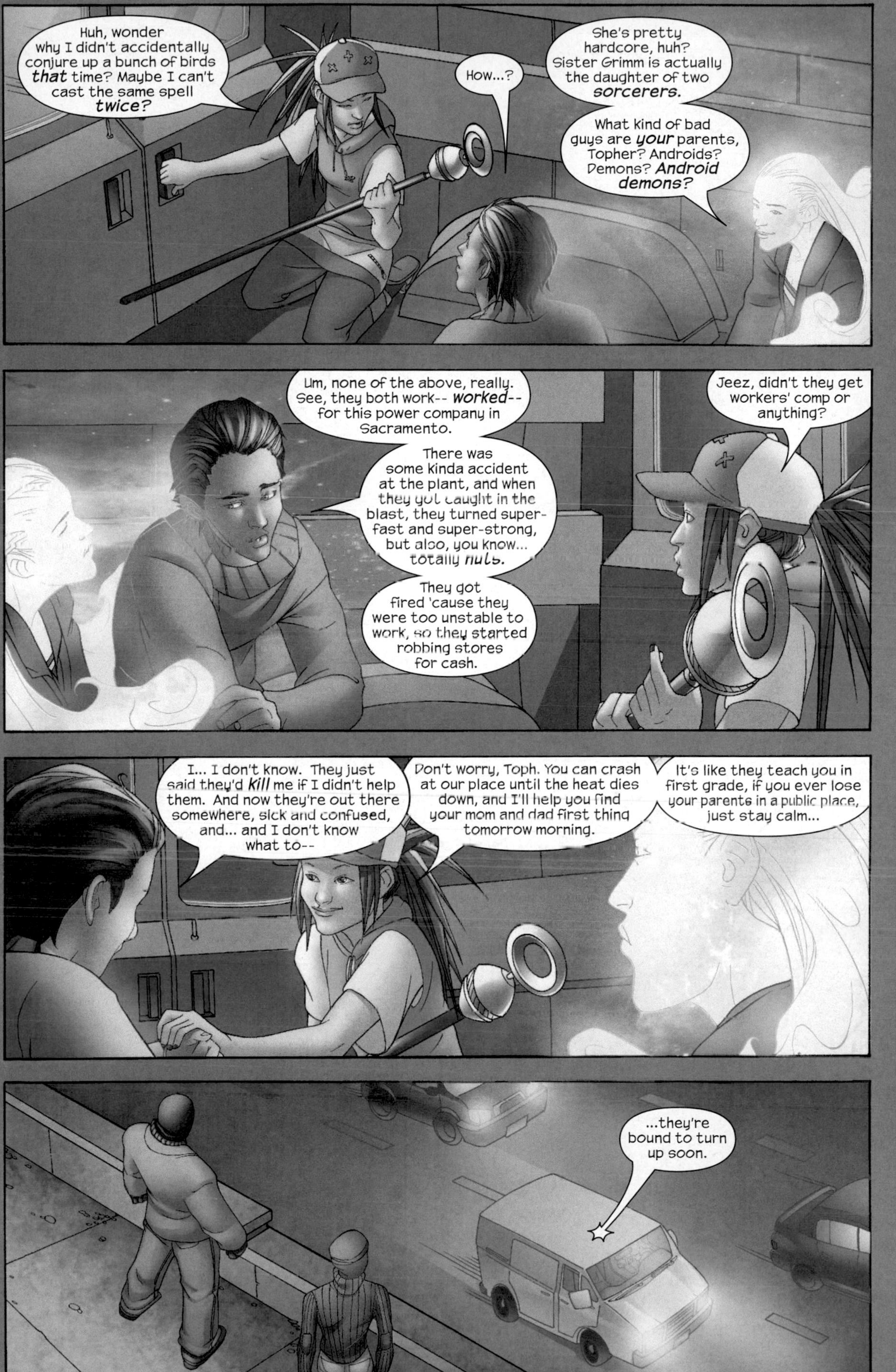
Huh, wonder why I didn't accidentally conjure up a bunch of birds that time? Maybe I can't cast the same spell twice?
How...?
She's pretty hardcore, huh? Sister Grimm is actually the daughter of two sorcerers.
What kind of bad guys are your parents, Topher? Androids? Demons? Android demons?
Um, none of the above, really. See, they both work-- worked-- for this power company in Sacramento.
There was some kinda accident at the plant, and when they got caught in the blast, they turned super-fast and super-strong, but also, you know... totally nuts.
They got fired 'cause they were too unstable to work, so they started robbing stores for cash.
Jeez, didn't they get workers' comp or anything?
I... I don't know. They just said they'd kill me if I didn't help them. And now they're out there somewhere, sick and confused, and... and I don't know what to--
Don't worry, Toph. You can crash at our place until the heat dies down, and I'll help you find your mom and dad first thing tomorrow morning.
It's like they teach you in first grade, if you ever lose your parents in a public place, just stay calm...
...they're bound to turn up soon.

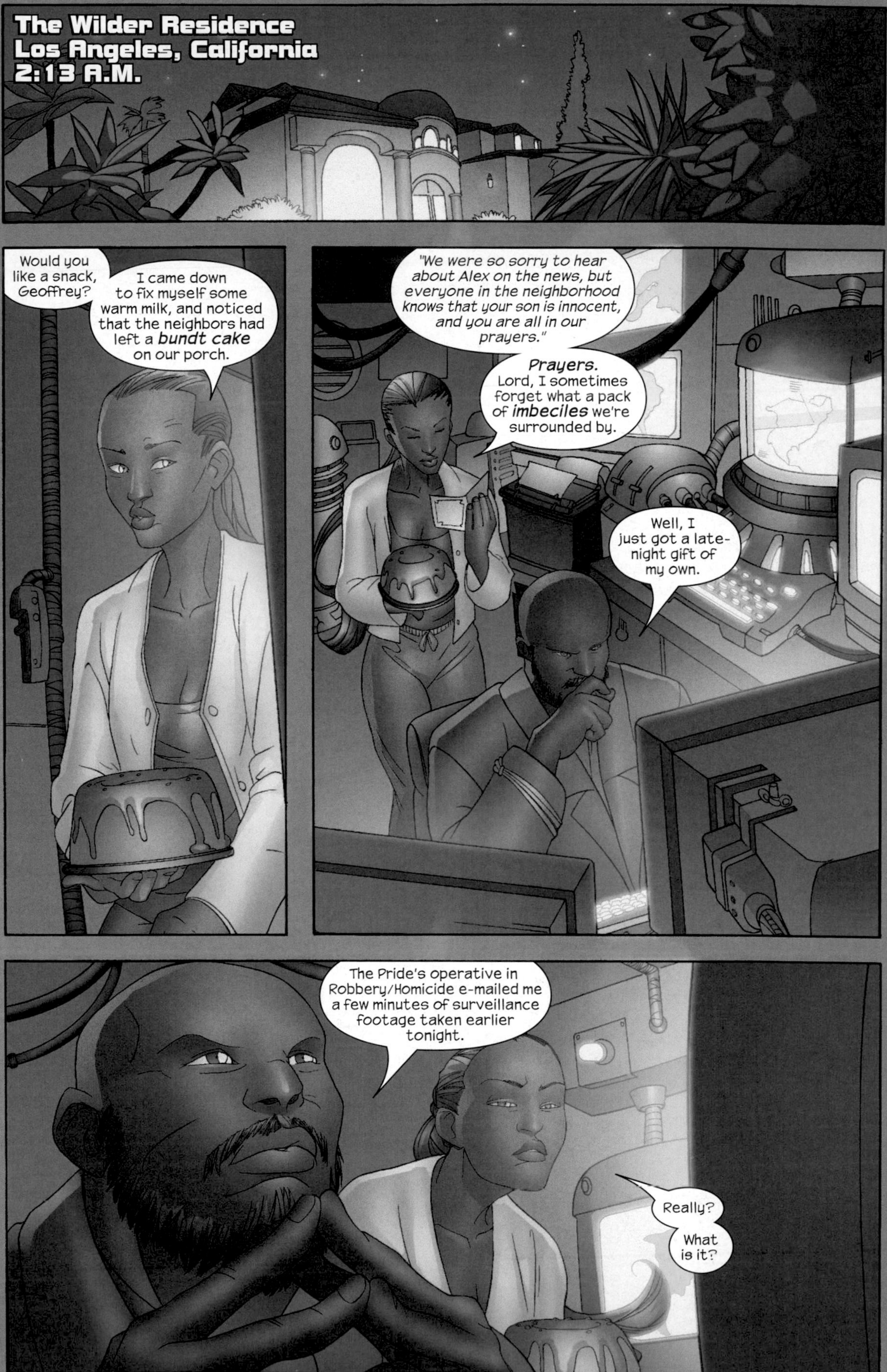

The Wilder Residence
Los Angeles, California
2:13 A.M.
Would you like a snack, Geoffrey?
I came down to fix myself some warm milk, and noticed that the neighbors had left a *bundt cake* on our porch.
"We were so sorry to hear about Alex on the news, but everyone in the neighborhood knows that your son is innocent, and you are all in our prayers."
Prayers. Lord, I sometimes forget what a pack of *imbeciles* we're surrounded by.
Well, I just got a late-night gift of my own.
The Pride's operative in Robbery/Homicide e-mailed me a few minutes of surveillance footage taken earlier tonight.
Really?
What is it?

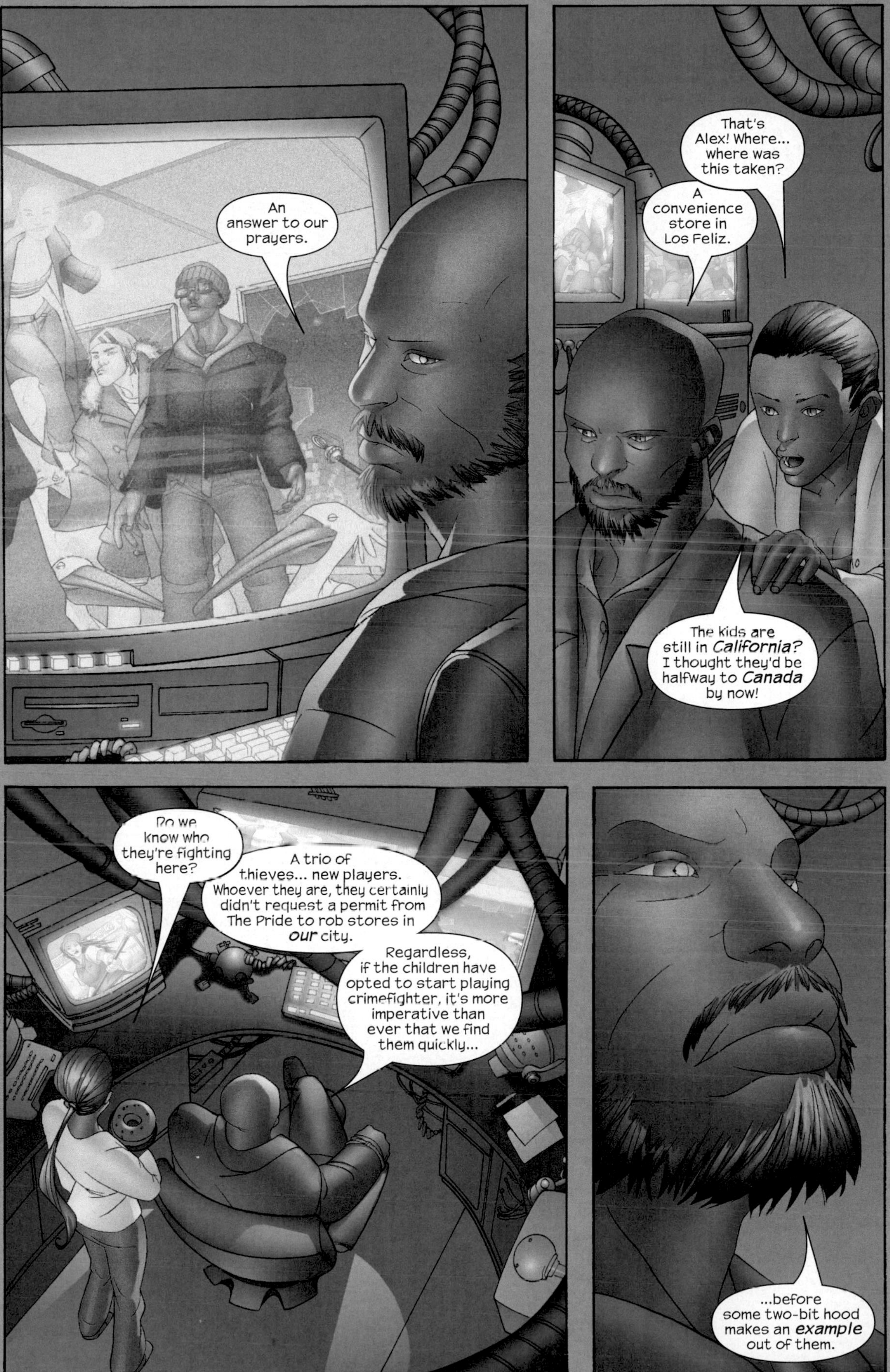
An answer to our prayers.
That's Alex! Where... where was this taken?
A convenience store in Los Feliz.
The kids are still in California? I thought they'd be halfway to Canada by now!
Do we know who they're fighting here?
A trio of thieves... new players. Whoever they are, they certainly didn't request a permit from The Pride to rob stores in our city.
Regardless, if the children have opted to start playing crimefighter, it's more imperative than ever that we find them quickly...
...before some two-bit hood makes an example out of them.

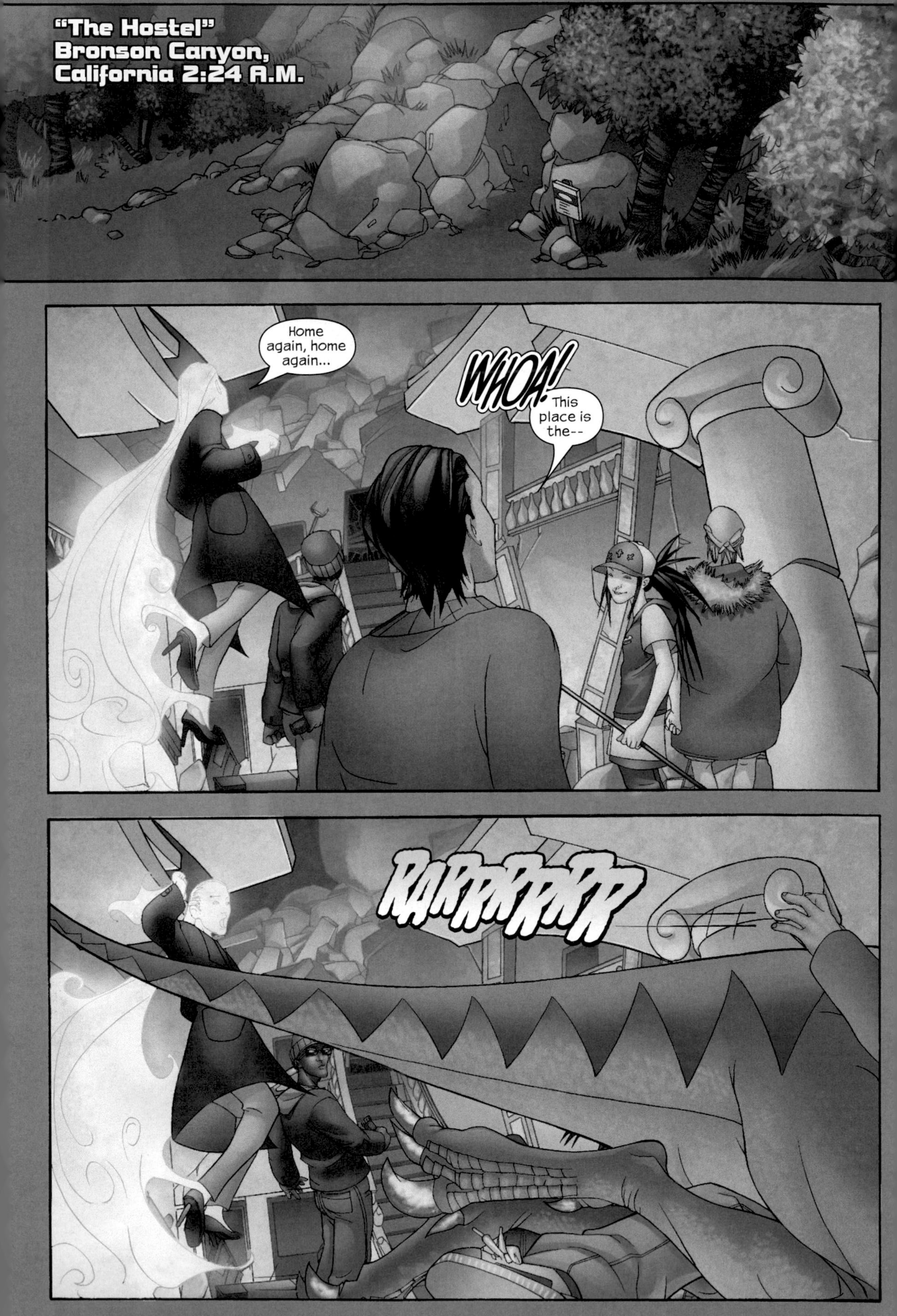
"The Hostel"
Bronson Canyon, California 2:24 A.M.
Home again, home again...
WHOA!
This place is the--
RARRRRRRR

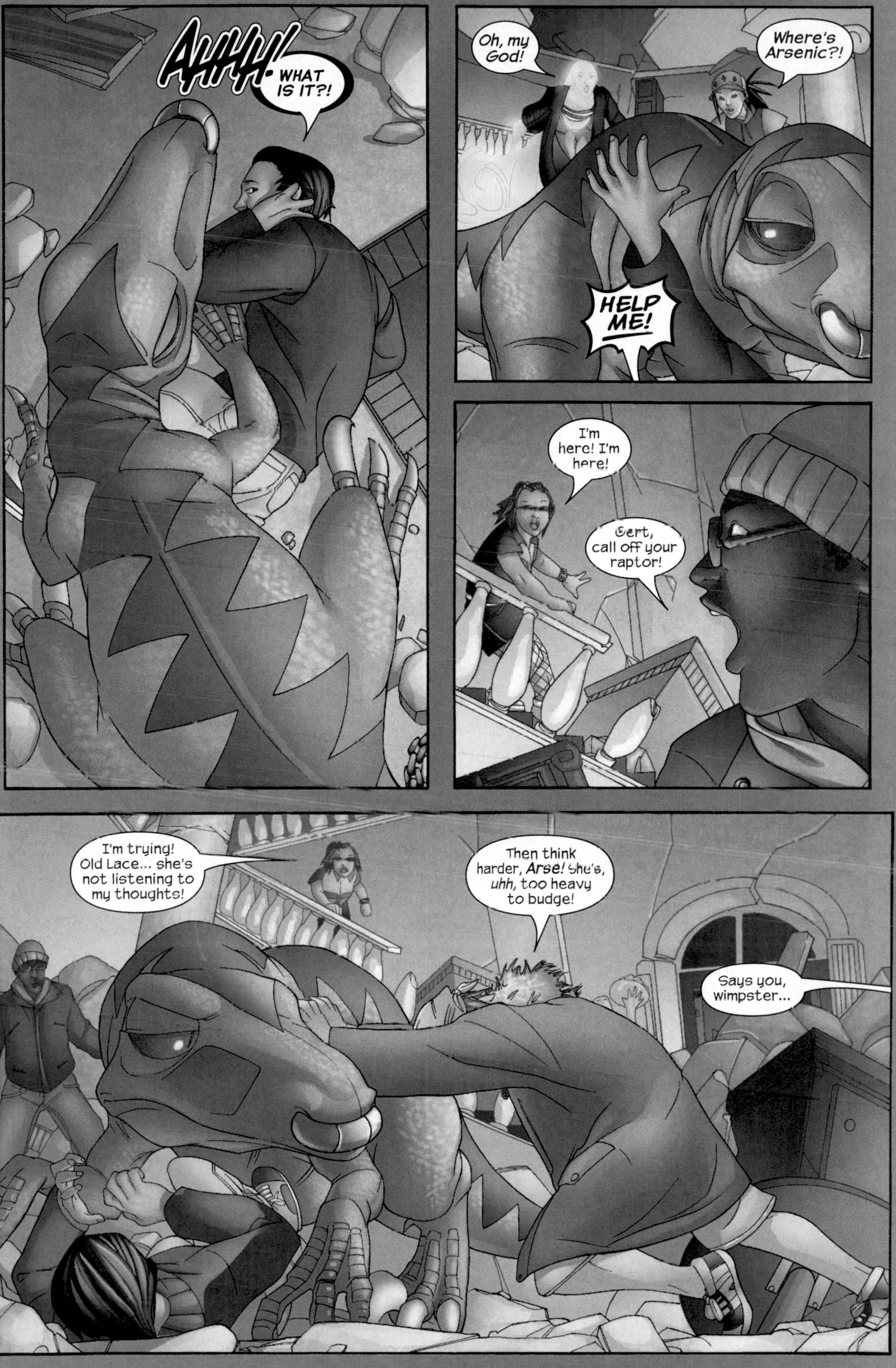
AHHH!
WHAT IS IT?!
Oh, my God!
Where's Arsenic?!
HELP ME!
I'm here! I'm here!
Gert, call off your raptor!
I'm trying! Old Lace... she's not listening to my thoughts!
Then think harder, Arse! She's, uhh, too heavy to budge!
Says you, wimpster...

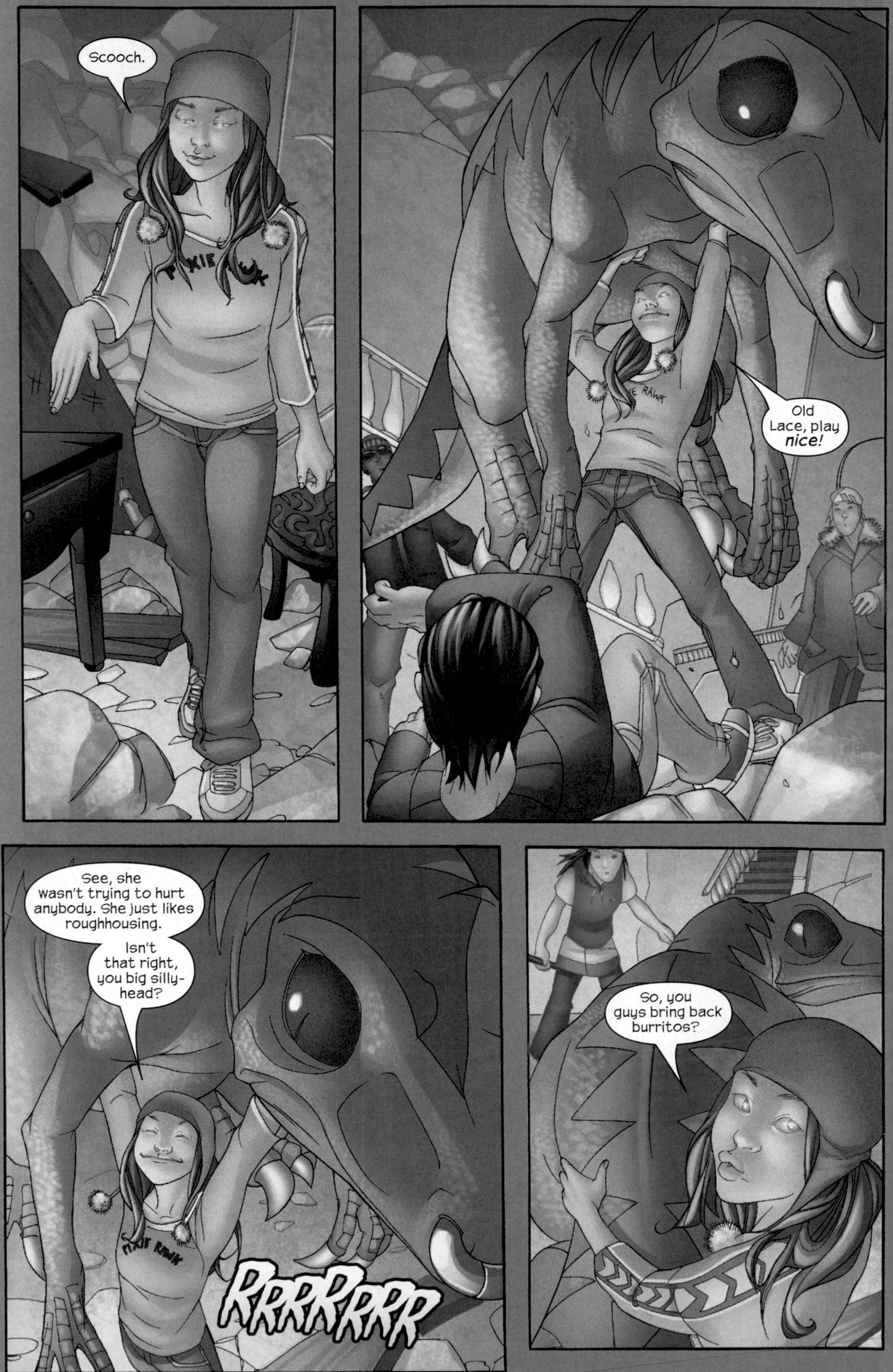
Scooch.
Old Lace, play *nice!*
See, she wasn't trying to hurt anybody. She just likes roughhousing.
Isn't that right, you big silly-head?
RRRRRRRR
So, you guys bring back burritos?

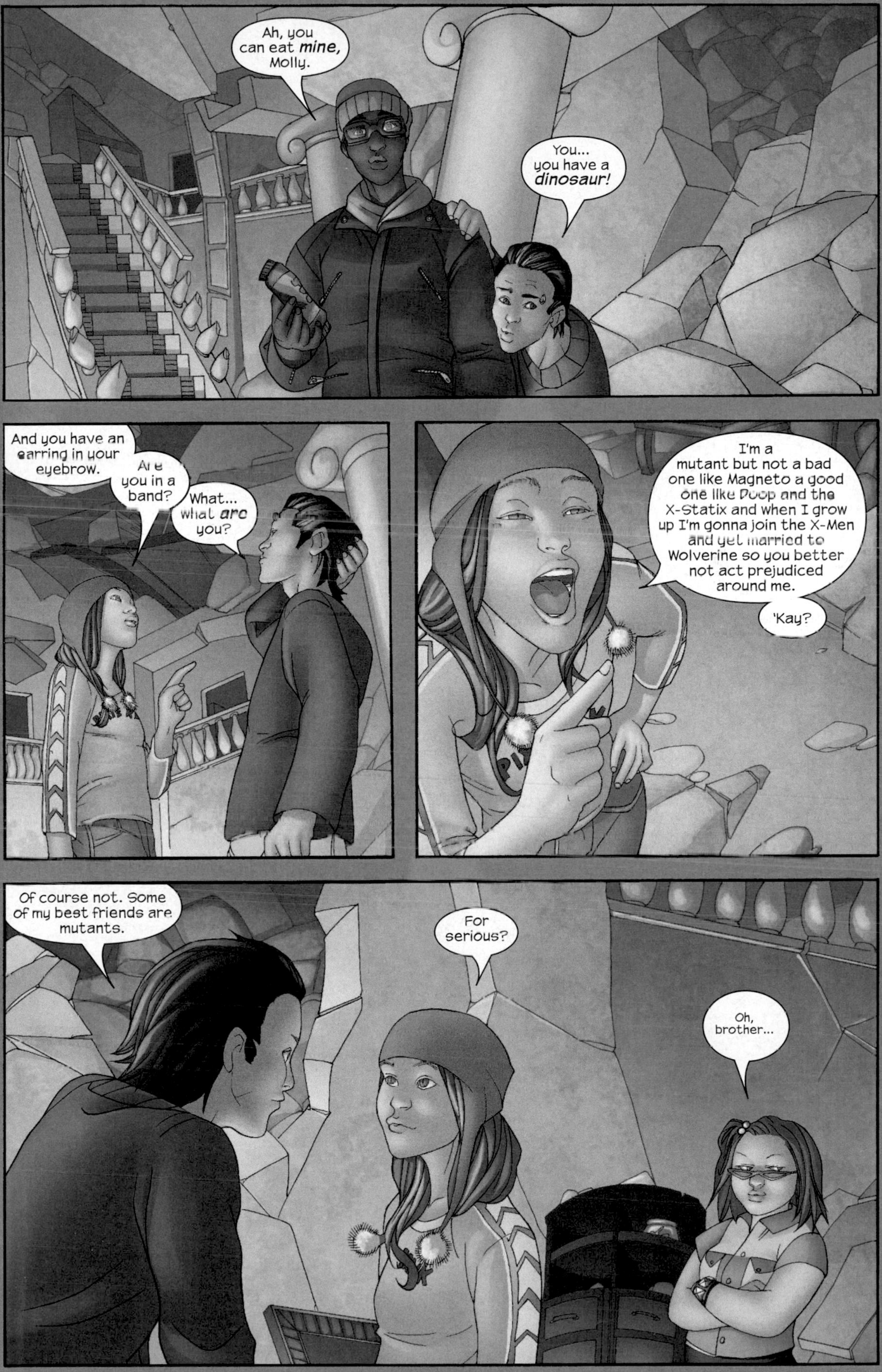
Ah, you can eat *mine,* Molly.
You... you have a *dinosaur!*
And you have an earring in your eyebrow.
Are you in a band?
What... what *are* you?
I'm a mutant but not a bad one like Magneto a good one like Doop and the X-Statix and when I grow up I'm gonna join the X-Men and get married to Wolverine so you better not act prejudiced around me.
'Kay?
Of course not. Some of my best friends are mutants.
For serious?
Oh, brother...

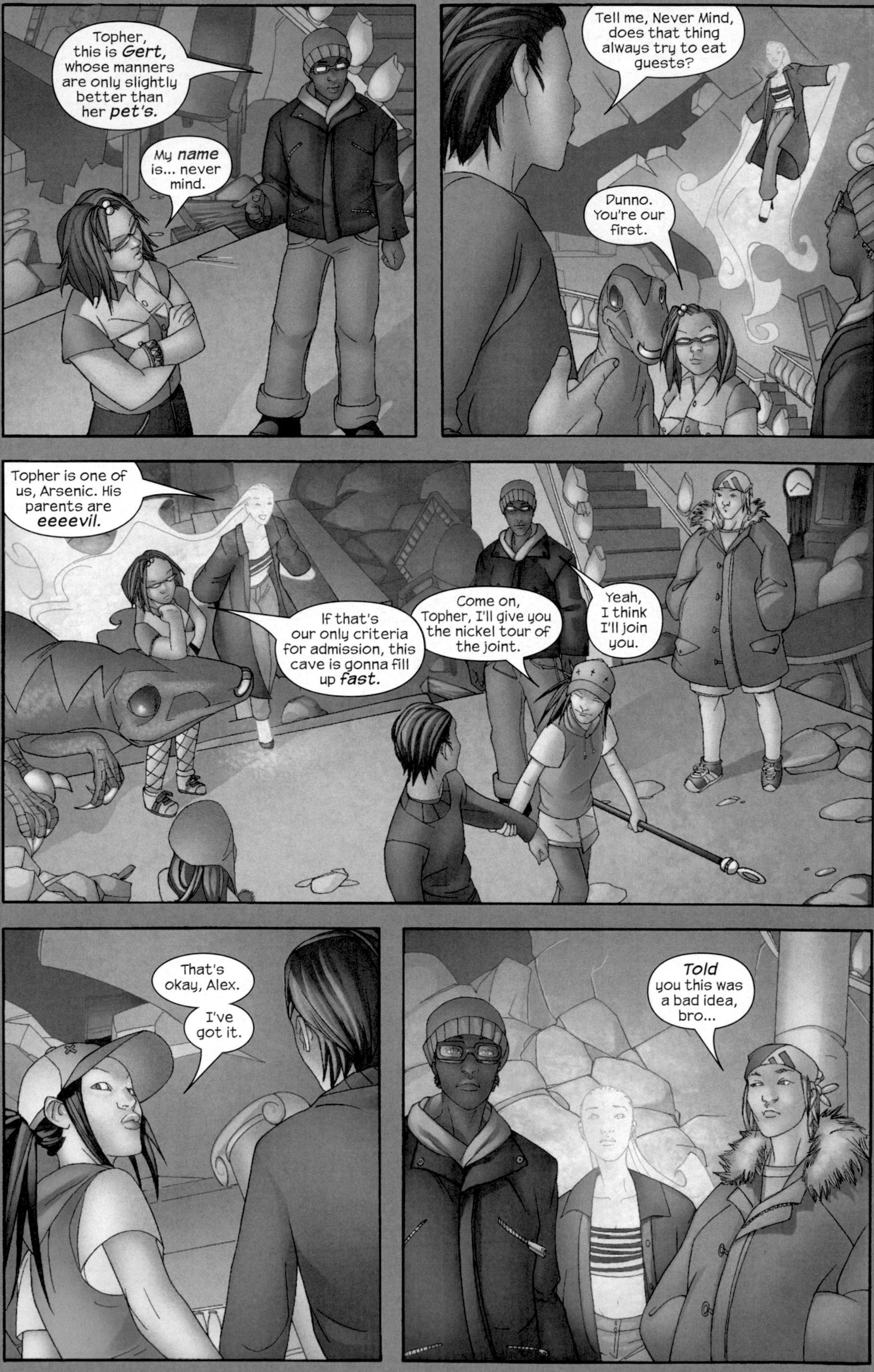
Topher, this is *Gert,* whose manners are only slightly better than her *pet's.*
My *name* is... never mind.
Tell me, Never Mind, does that thing always try to eat guests?
Dunno. You're our first.
Topher is one of us, Arsenic. His parents are *eeeevil.*
If that's our only criteria for admission, this cave is gonna fill up *fast.*
Come on, Topher, I'll give you the nickel tour of the joint.
Yeah, I think I'll join you.
That's okay, Alex.
I've got it.
Told you this was a bad idea, bro...

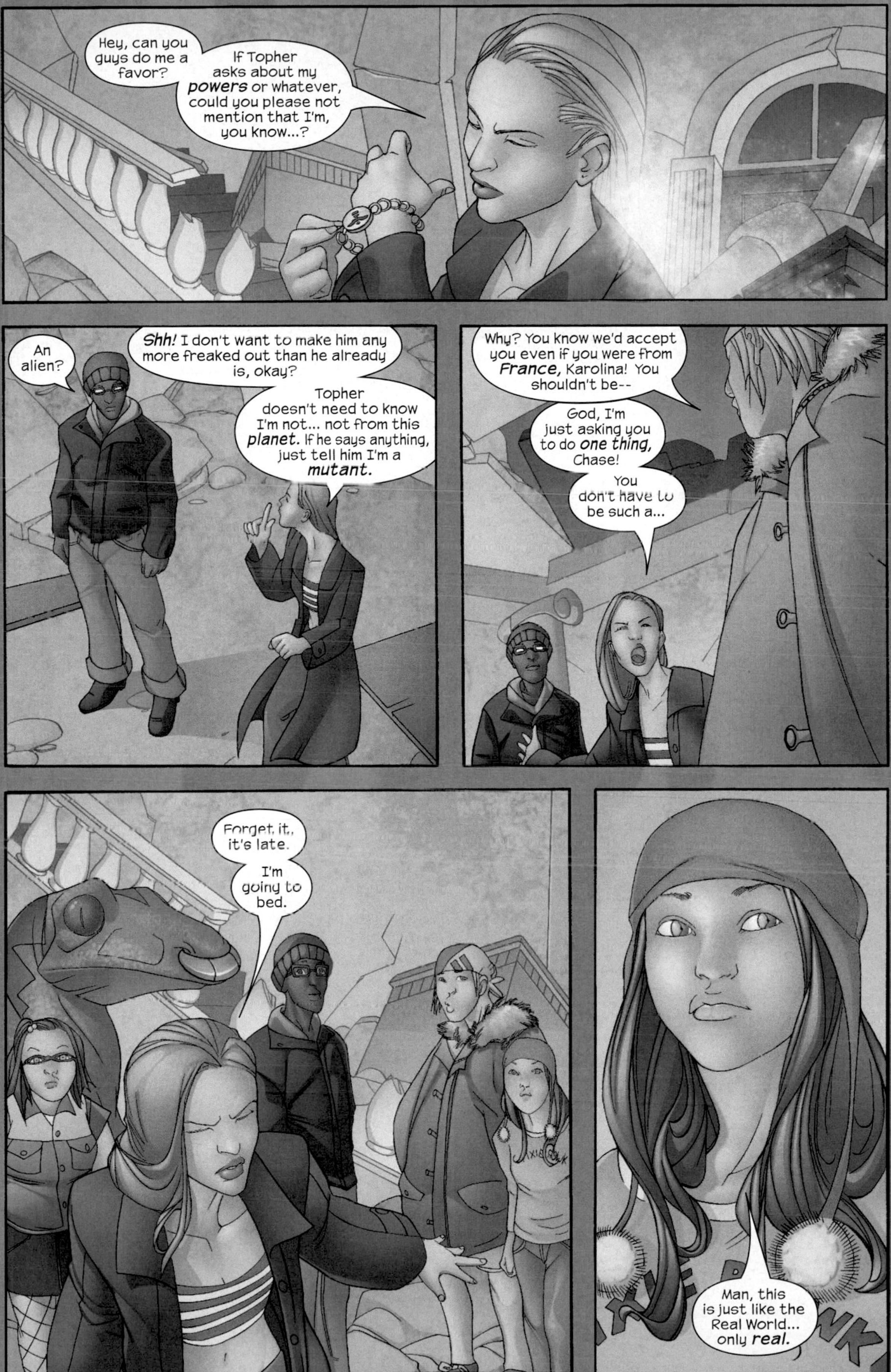
Hey, can you guys do me a favor?
If Topher asks about my powers or whatever, could you please not mention that I'm, you know...?
An alien?
Shh! I don't want to make him any more freaked out than he already is, okay?
Topher doesn't need to know I'm not... not from this planet. If he says anything, just tell him I'm a mutant.
Why? You know we'd accept you even if you were from France, Karolina! You shouldn't be--
God, I'm just asking you to do one thing, Chase!
You don't have to be such a...
Forget it, it's late.
I'm going to bed.
Man, this is just like the Real World... only real.

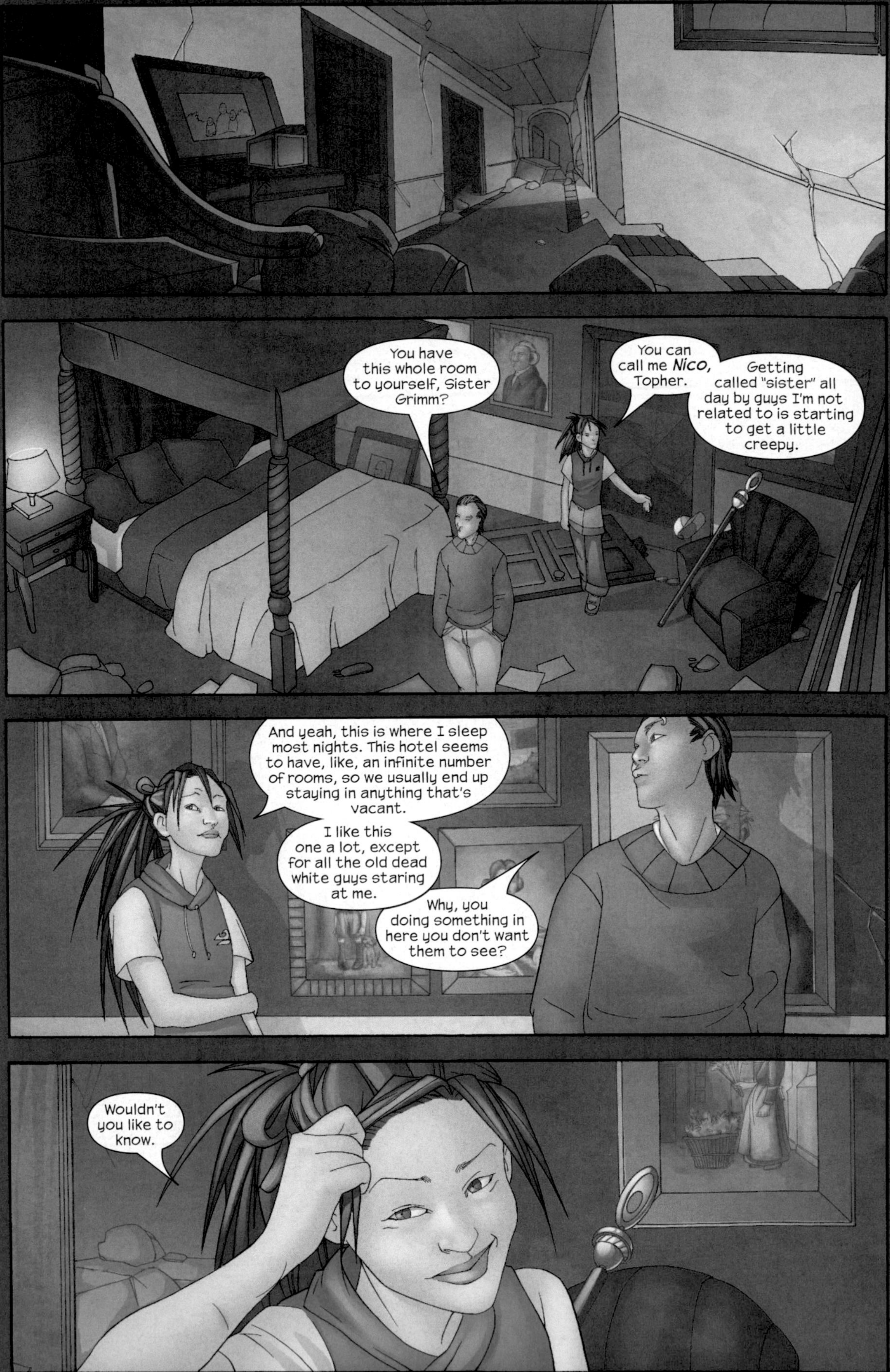
You have this whole room to yourself, Sister Grimm?
You can call me Nico, Topher.
Getting called "sister" all day by guys I'm not related to is starting to get a little creepy.
And yeah, this is where I sleep most nights. This hotel seems to have, like, an infinite number of rooms, so we usually end up staying in anything that's vacant.
I like this one a lot, except for all the old dead white guys staring at me.
Why, you doing something in here you don't want them to see?
Wouldn't you like to know.

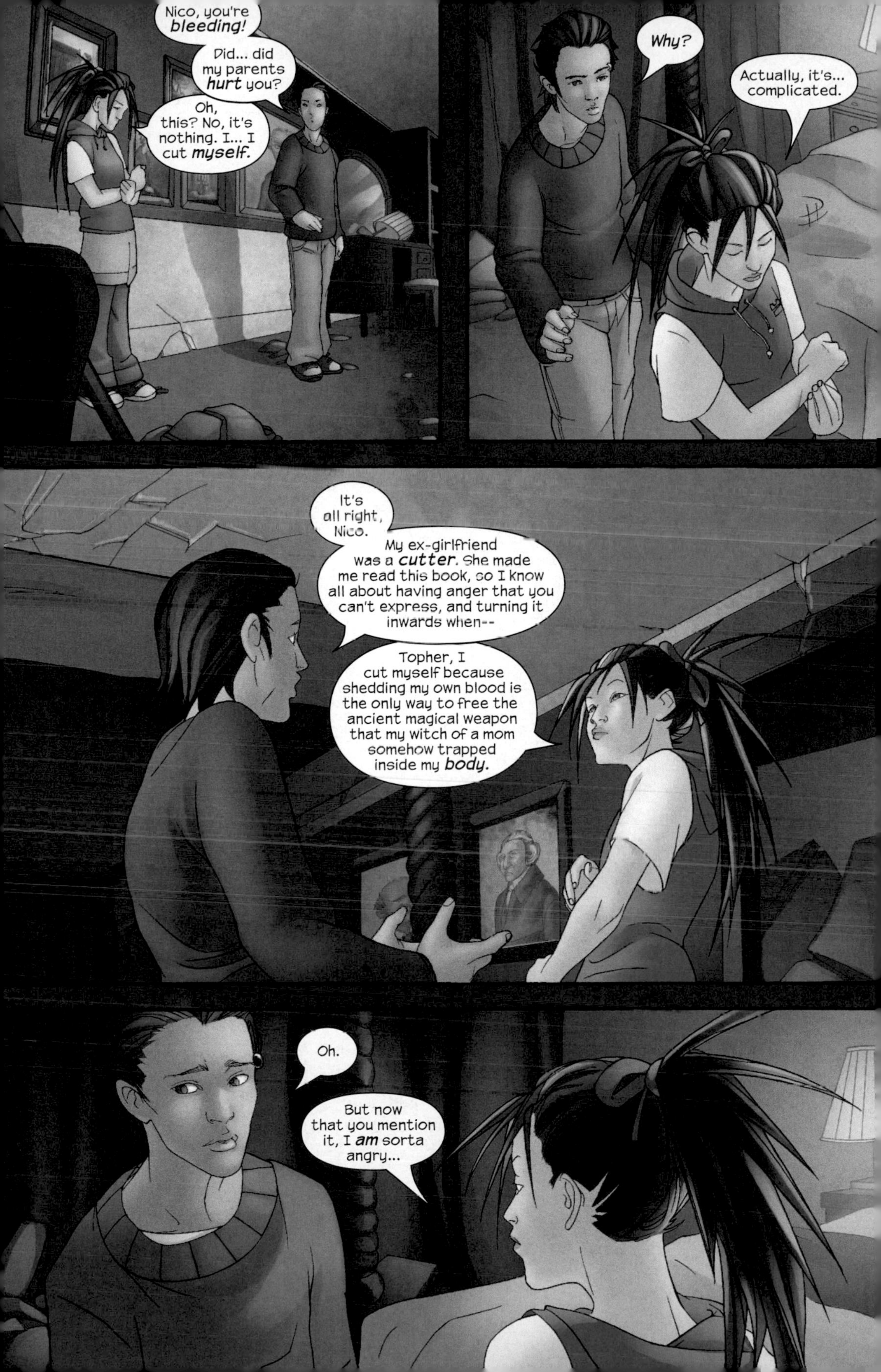
Nico, you're bleeding!
Did... did my parents hurt you?
Oh, this? No, it's nothing. I... I cut myself.
Why?
Actually, it's... complicated.
It's all right, Nico.
My ex-girlfriend was a cutter. She made me read this book, so I know all about having anger that you can't express, and turning it inwards when--
Topher, I cut myself because shedding my own blood is the only way to free the ancient magical weapon that my witch of a mom somehow trapped inside my body.
Oh.
But now that you mention it, I am sorta angry...

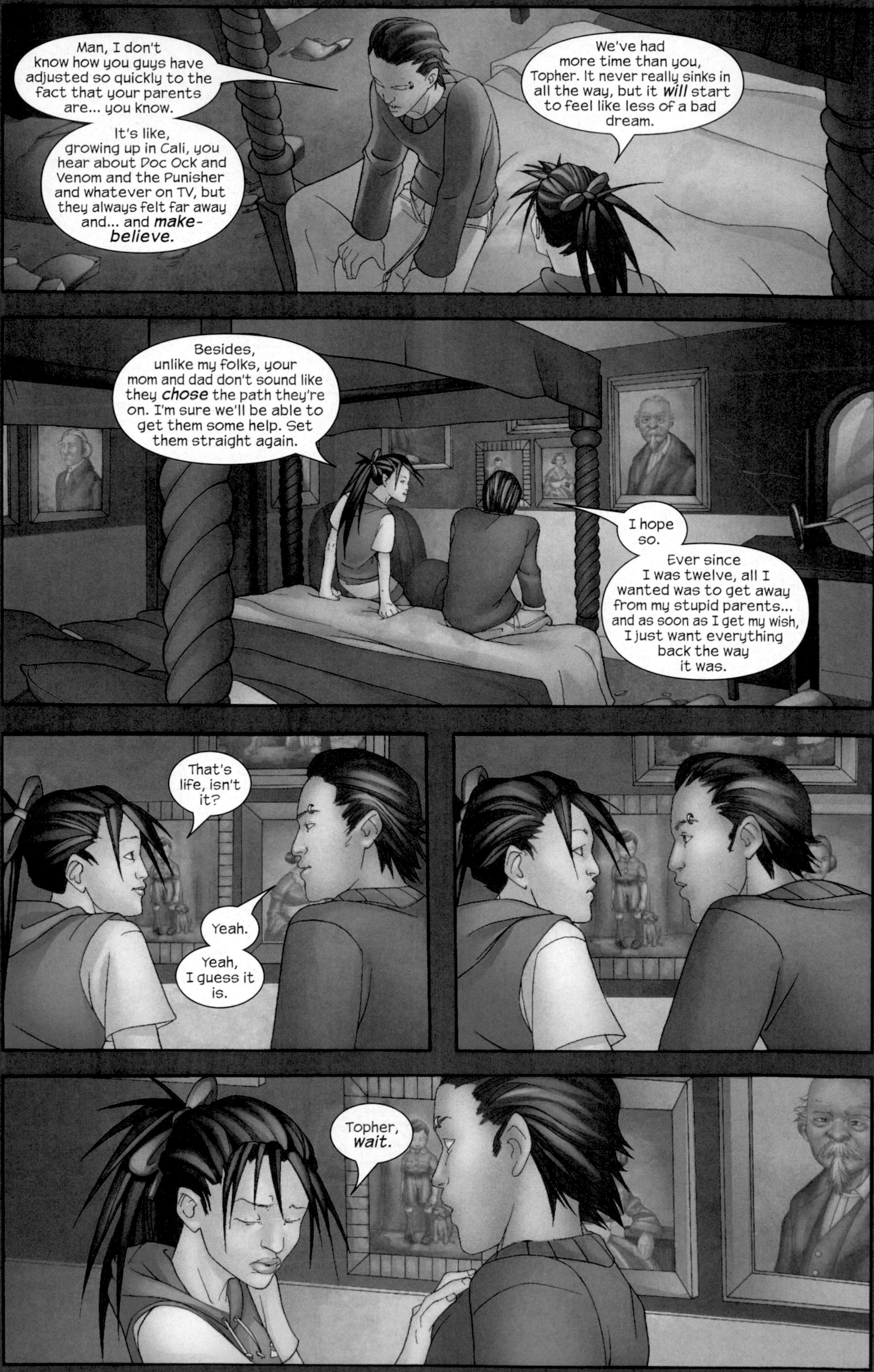
Man, I don't know how you guys have adjusted so quickly to the fact that your parents are... you know.
It's like, growing up in Cali, you hear about Doc Ock and Venom and the Punisher and whatever on TV, but they always felt far away and... and *make-believe.*
We've had more time than you, Topher. It never really sinks in all the way, but it *will* start to feel like less of a bad dream.
Besides, unlike my folks, your mom and dad don't sound like they *chose* the path they're on. I'm sure we'll be able to get them some help. Set them straight again.
I hope so.
Ever since I was twelve, all I wanted was to get away from my stupid parents... and as soon as I get my wish, I just want everything back the way it was.
That's life, isn't it?
Yeah.
Yeah, I guess it is.
Topher, *wait.*

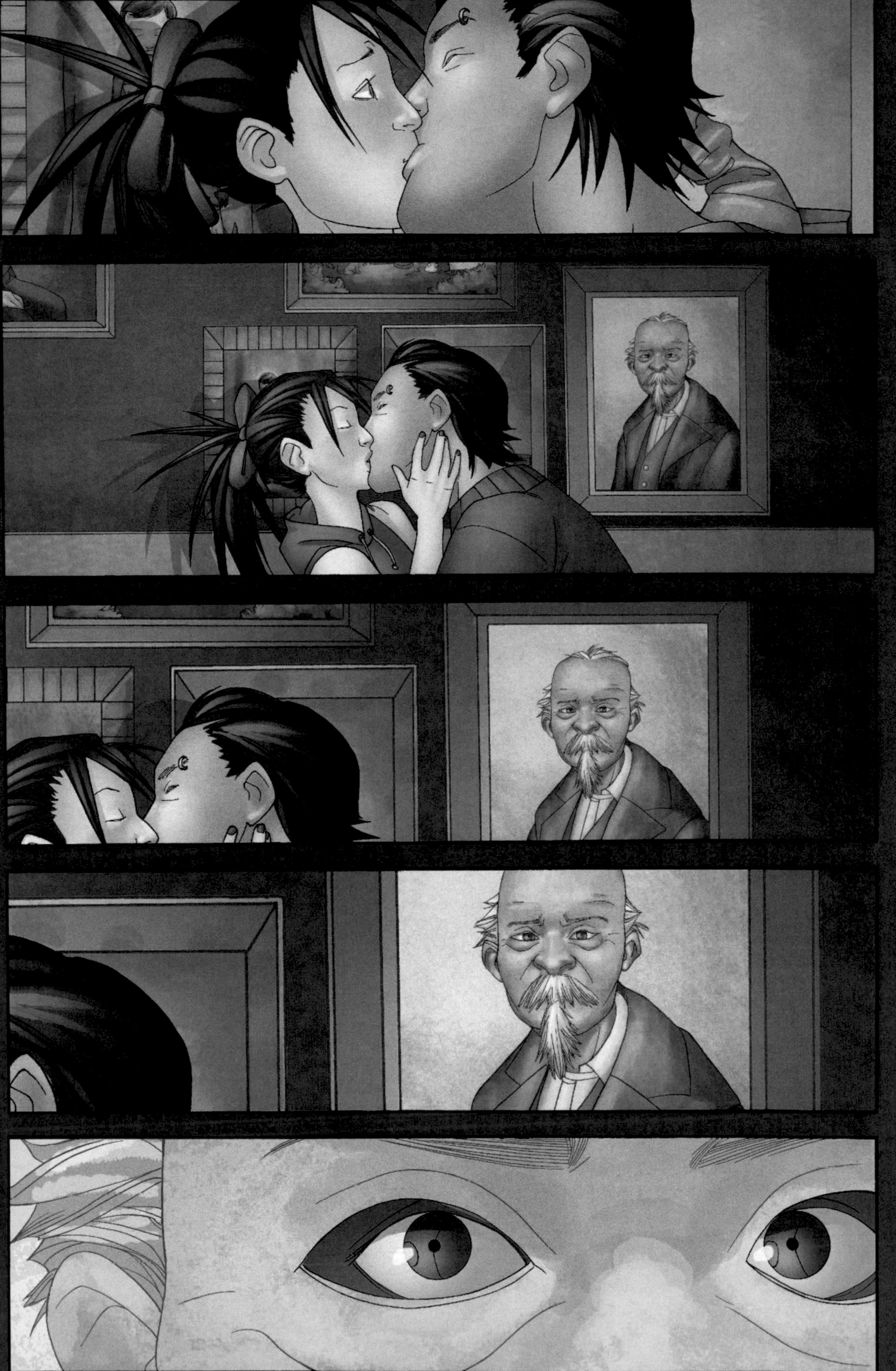

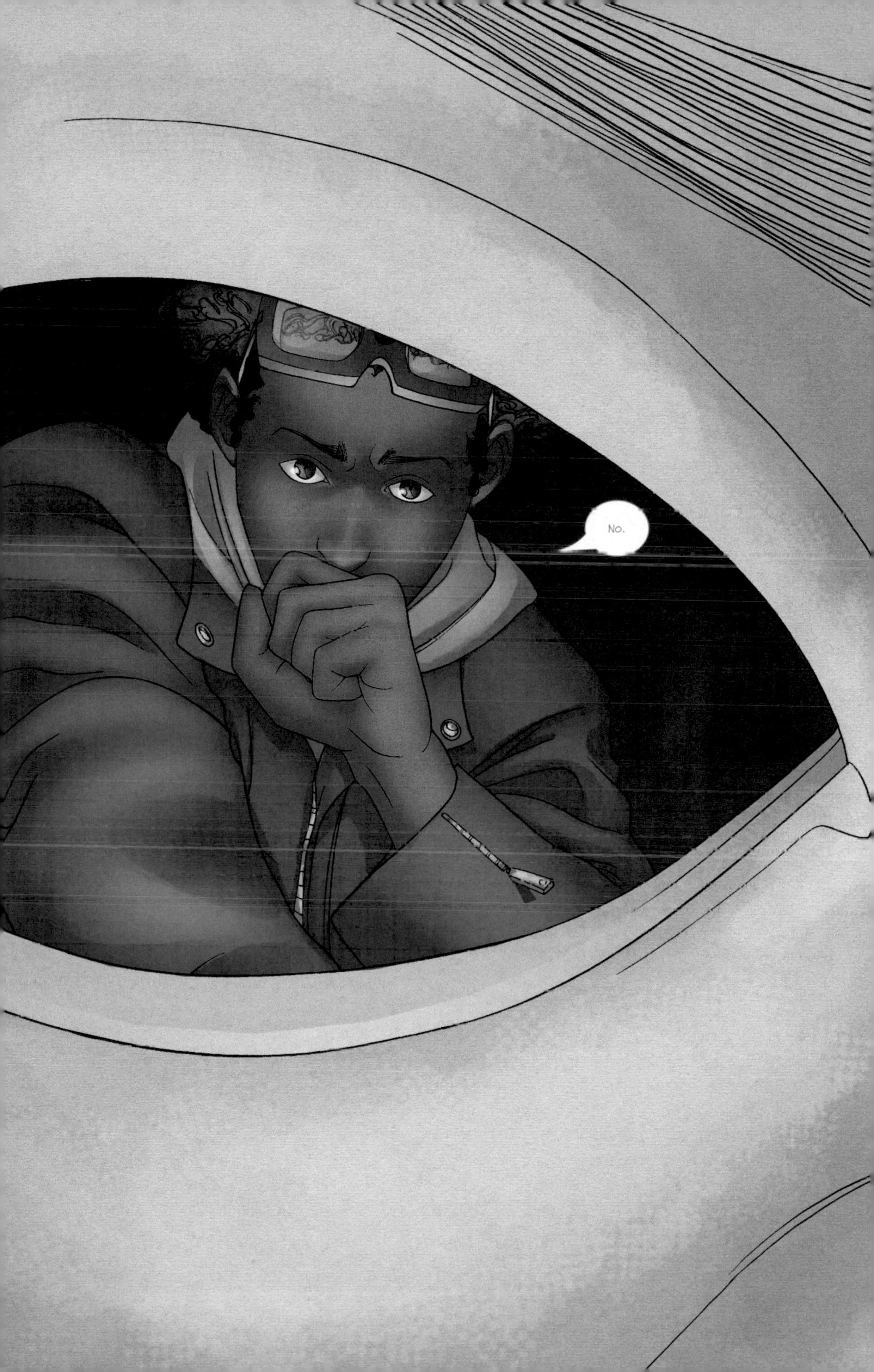
No.

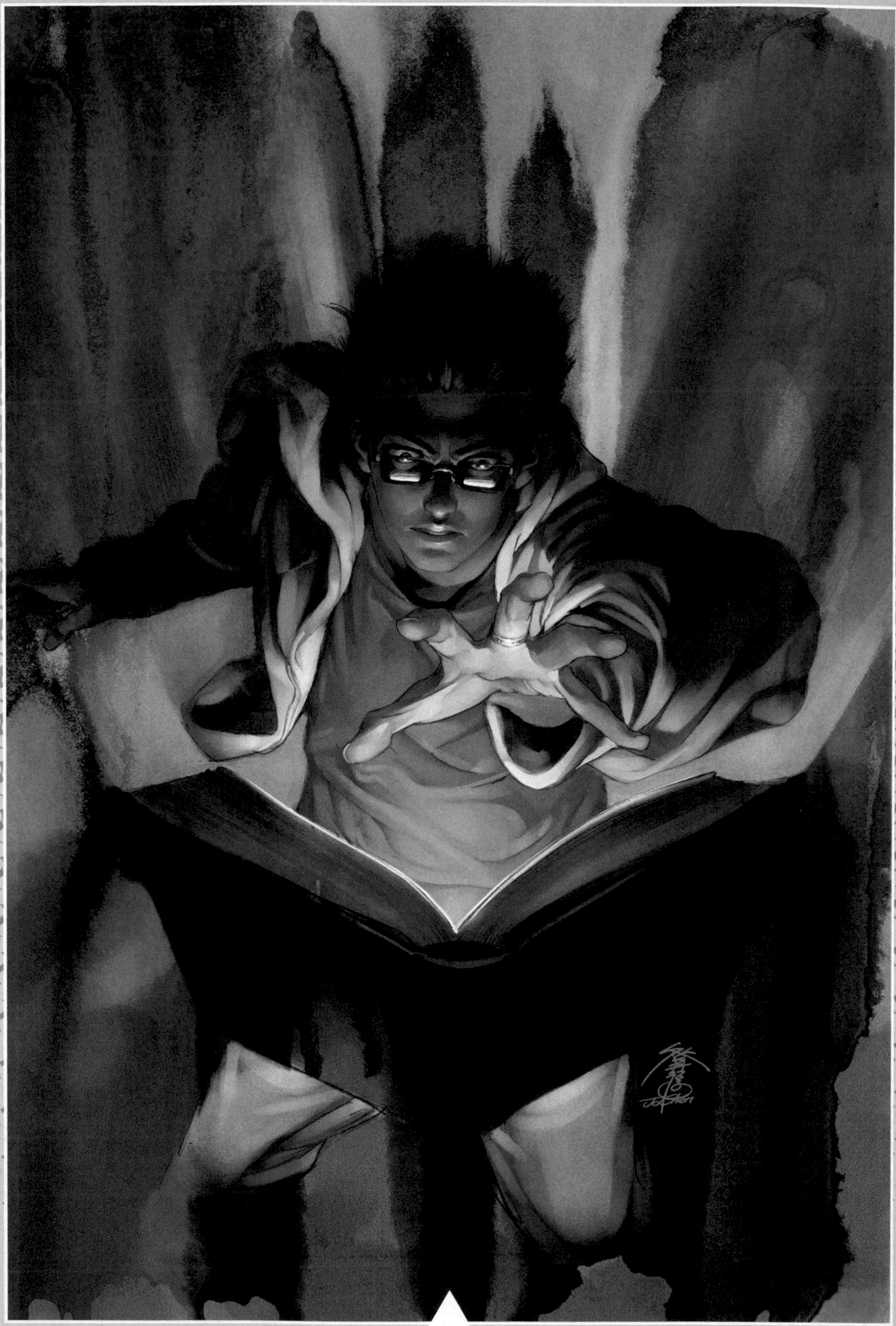

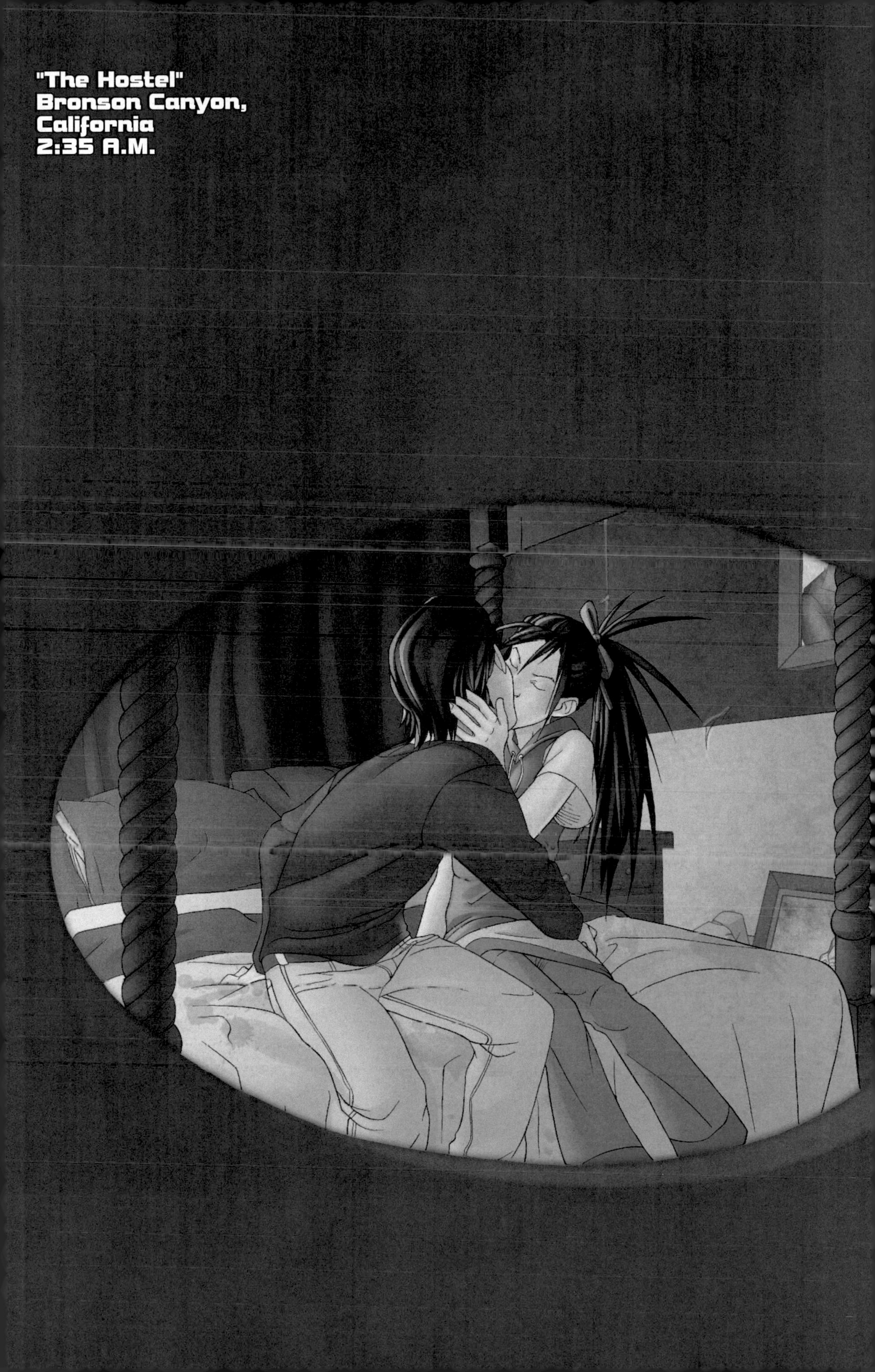
"The Hostel"
Bronson Canyon,
California
2:35 A.M.

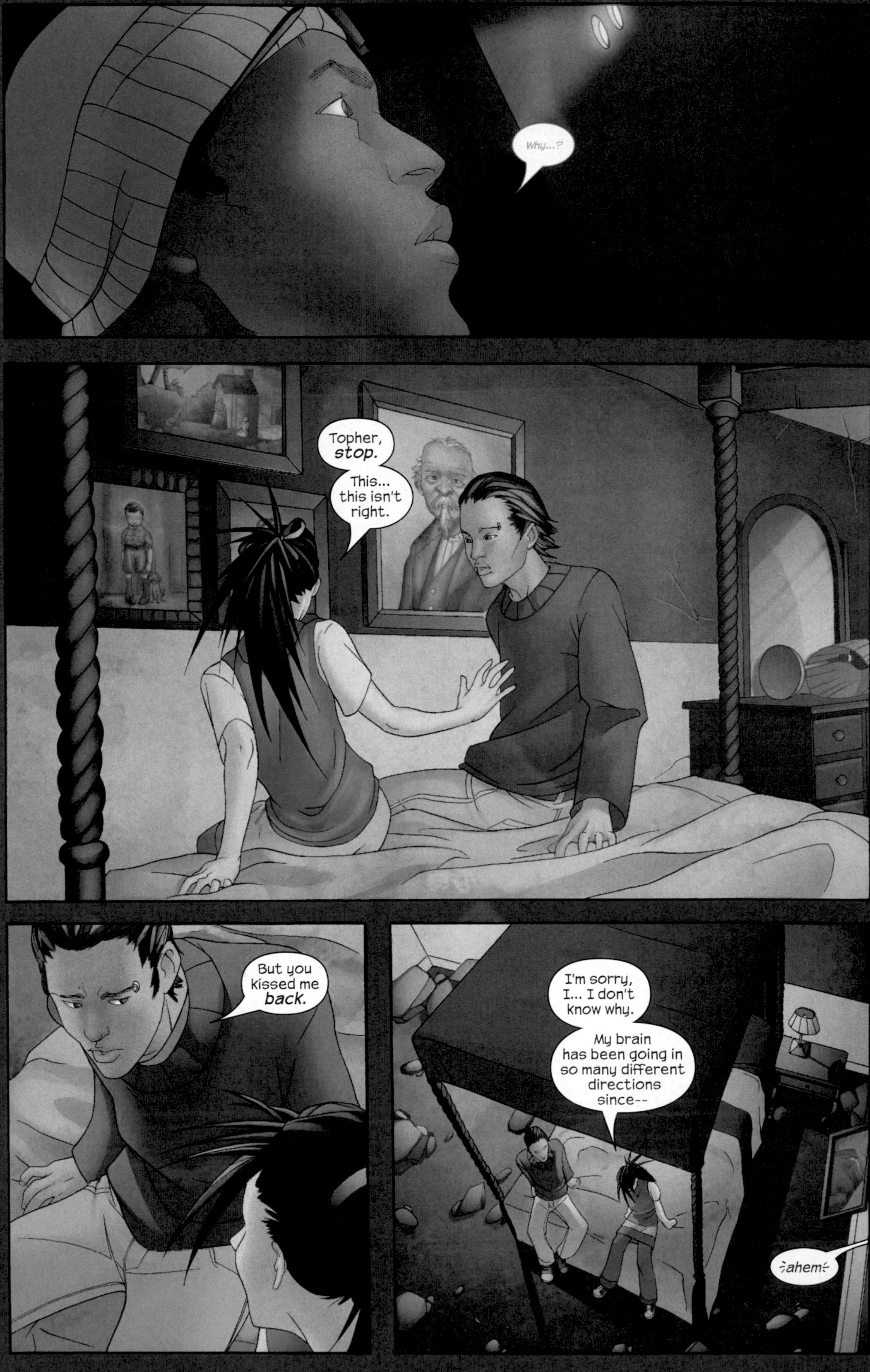
Why...?
Topher, stop.
This... this isn't right.
But you kissed me back.
I'm sorry, I... I don't know why.
My brain has been going in so many different directions since--
ahem

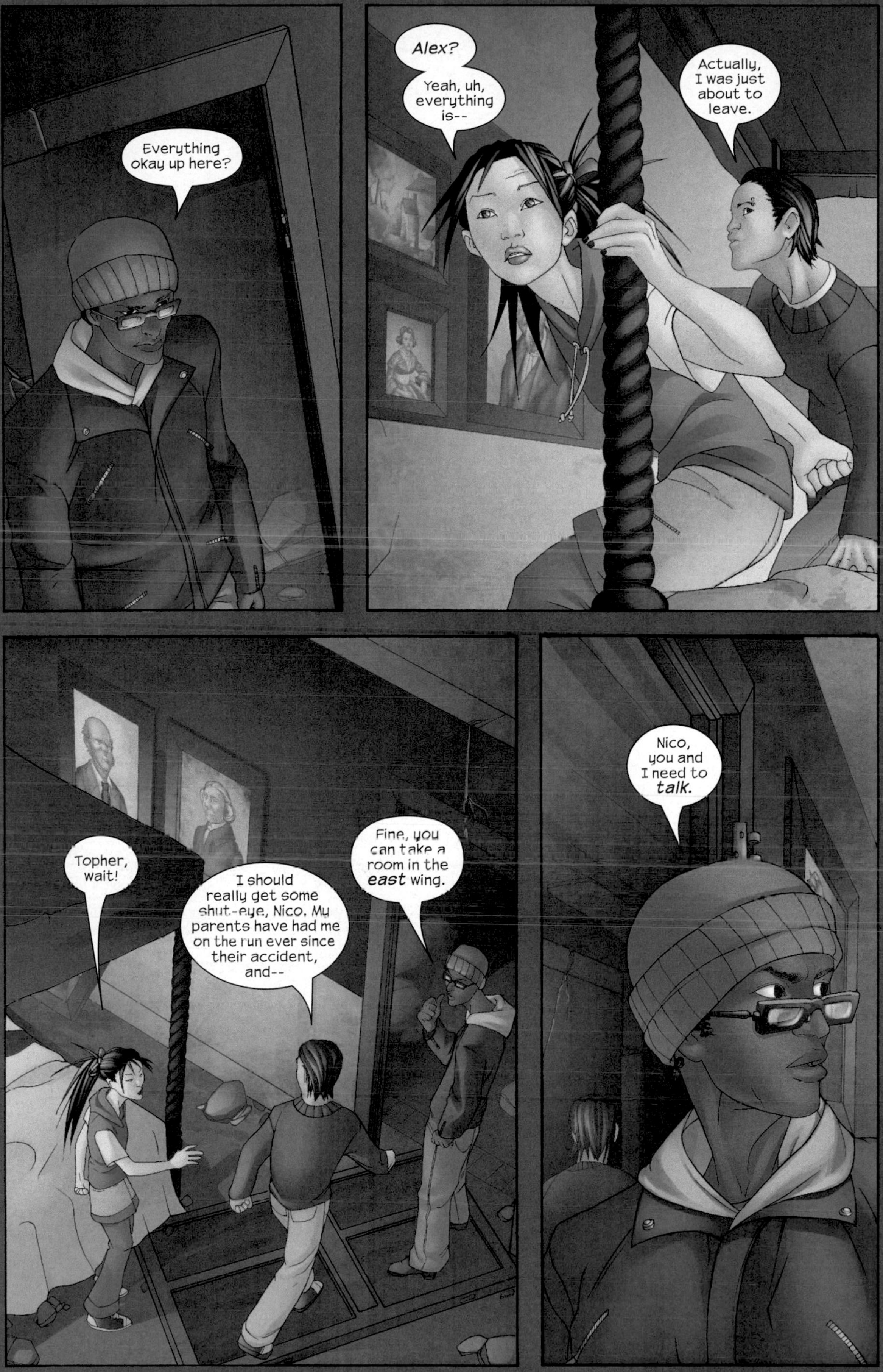
Everything okay up here?
Alex?
Yeah, uh, everything is--
Actually, I was just about to leave.
Topher, wait!
I should really get some shut-eye, Nico. My parents have had me on the run ever since their accident, and--
Fine, you can take a room in the east wing.
Nico, you and I need to talk.

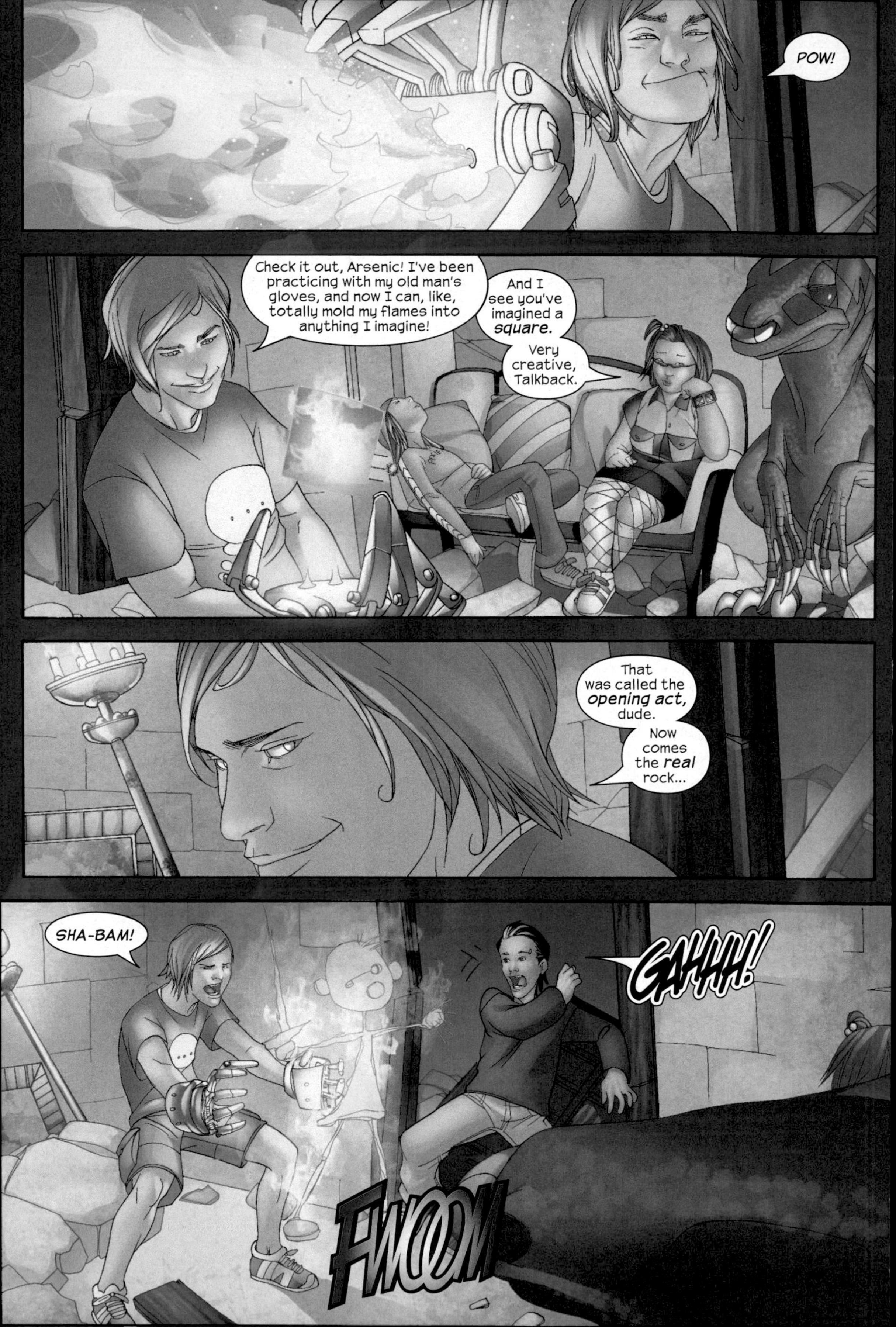
POW!
Check it out, Arsenic! I've been practicing with my old man's gloves, and now I can, like, totally mold my flames into anything I imagine!
And I see you've imagined a *square.*
Very creative, Talkback.
That was called the *opening act,* dude.
Now comes the *real* rock...
SHA-BAM!
GAHHH!
FWOOM

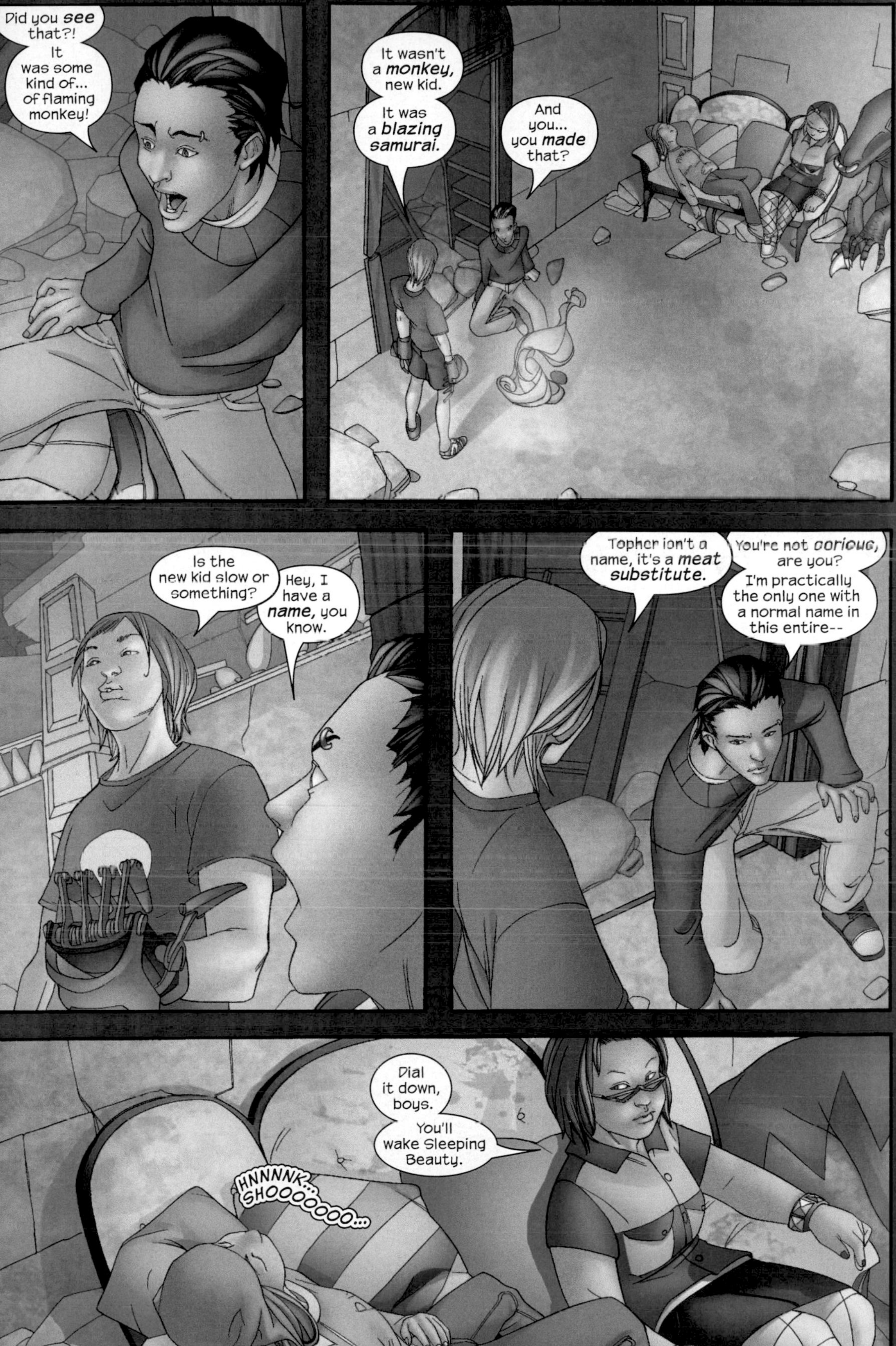

Did you *see* that?! It was some kind of... of flaming monkey!
It wasn't a *monkey,* new kid.
It was a ***blazing samurai.***
And you... you *made* that?
Is the new kid slow or something?
Hey, I have a ***name,*** you know.
Topher isn't a name, it's a ***meat substitute.***
You're not *serious,* are you?
I'm practically the only one with a normal name in this entire--
Dial it down, boys.
You'll wake Sleeping Beauty.
HNNNNK... SHOOOOOOO...

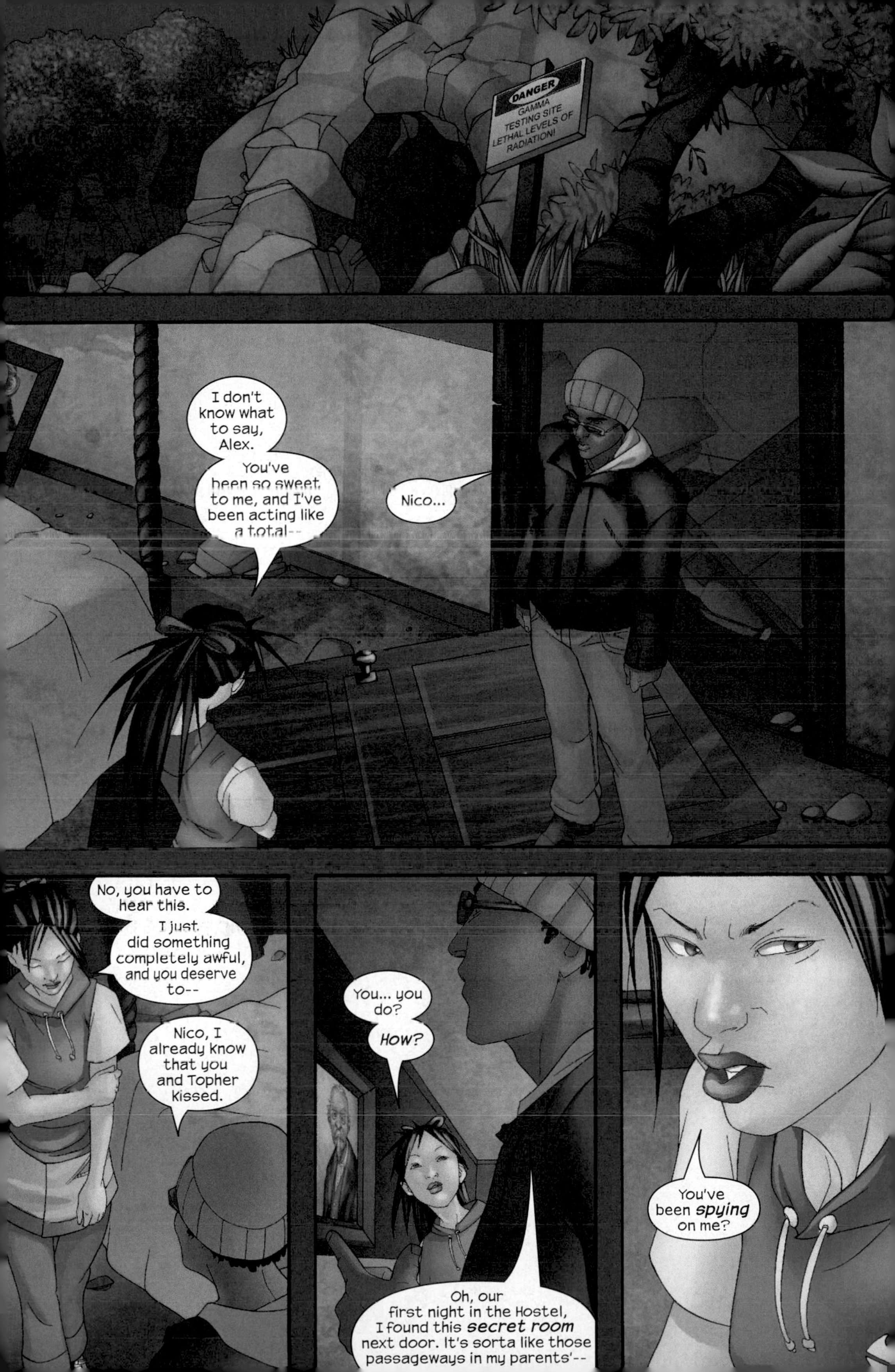
DANGER
GAMMA TESTING SITE LETHAL LEVELS OF RADIATION!
I don't know what to say, Alex.
You've been so sweet to me, and I've been acting like a total--
Nico...
No, you have to hear this.
I just did something completely awful, and you deserve to--
Nico, I already know that you and Topher kissed.
You... you do?
HOW?
Oh, our first night in the Hostel, I found this secret room next door. It's sorta like those passageways in my parents'--
You've been spying on me?

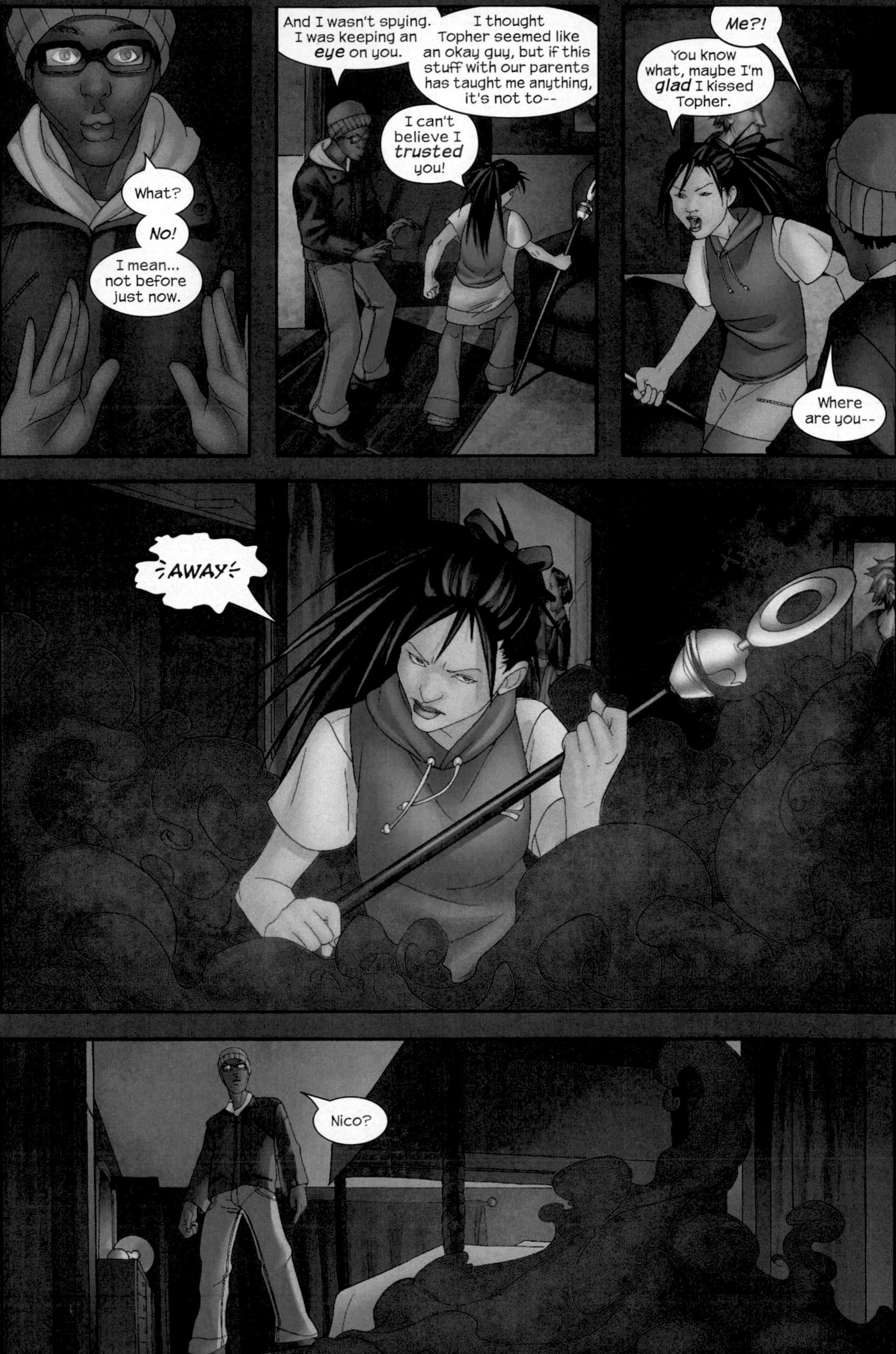
What?
No!
I mean... not before just now.
And I wasn't spying. I was keeping an eye on you.
I thought Topher seemed like an okay guy, but if this stuff with our parents has taught me anything, it's not to--
I can't believe I trusted you!
Me?!
You know what, maybe I'm glad I kissed Topher.
Where are you--
AWAY
Nico?

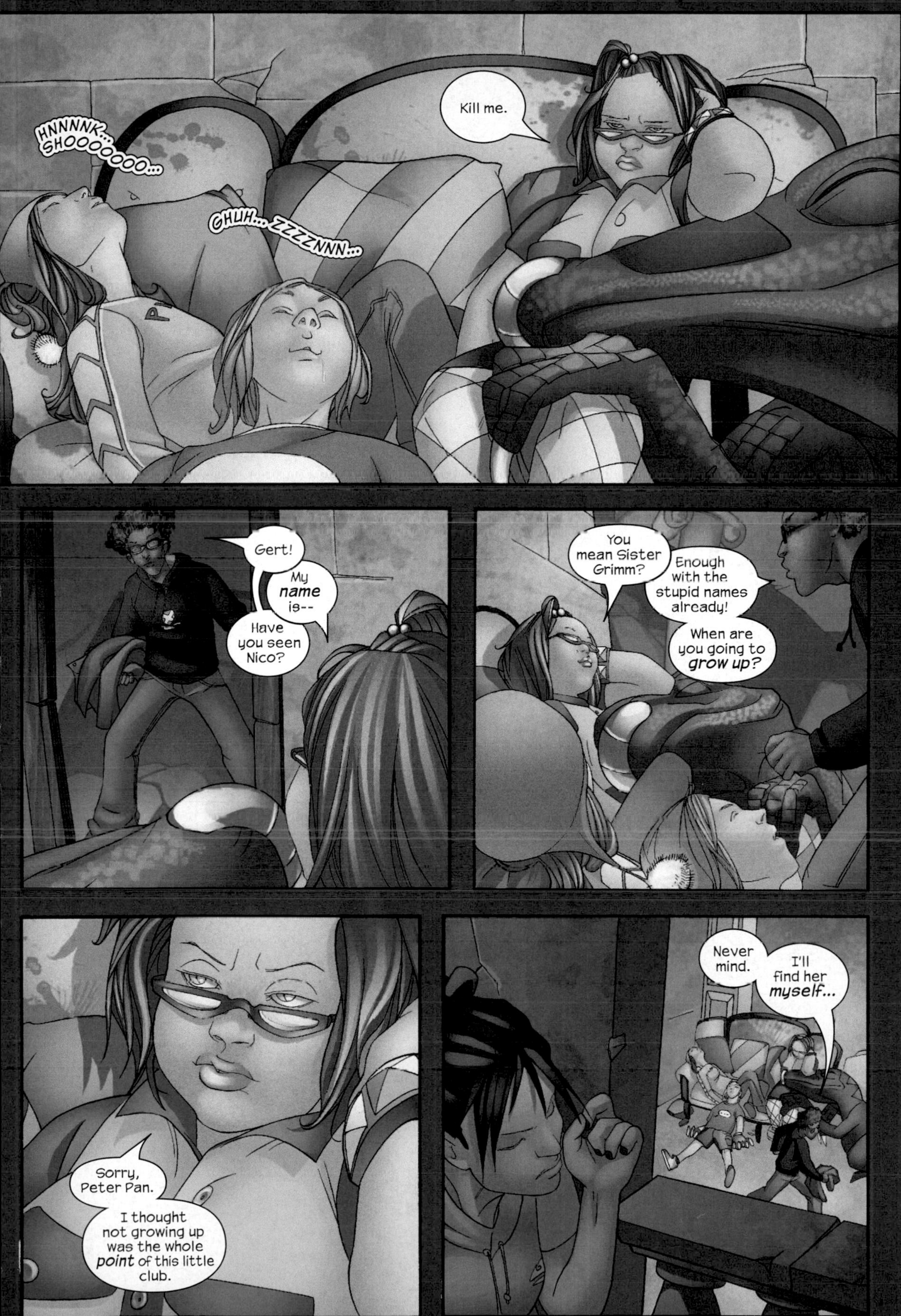
HNNNNK... SHOOOOOOO...
GHUH... ZZZZNNN...
Kill me.
Gert!
My name is--
Have you seen Nico?
You mean Sister Grimm?
Enough with the stupid names already!
When are you going to grow up?
Sorry, Peter Pan.
I thought not growing up was the whole point of this little club.
Never mind.
I'll find her myself...

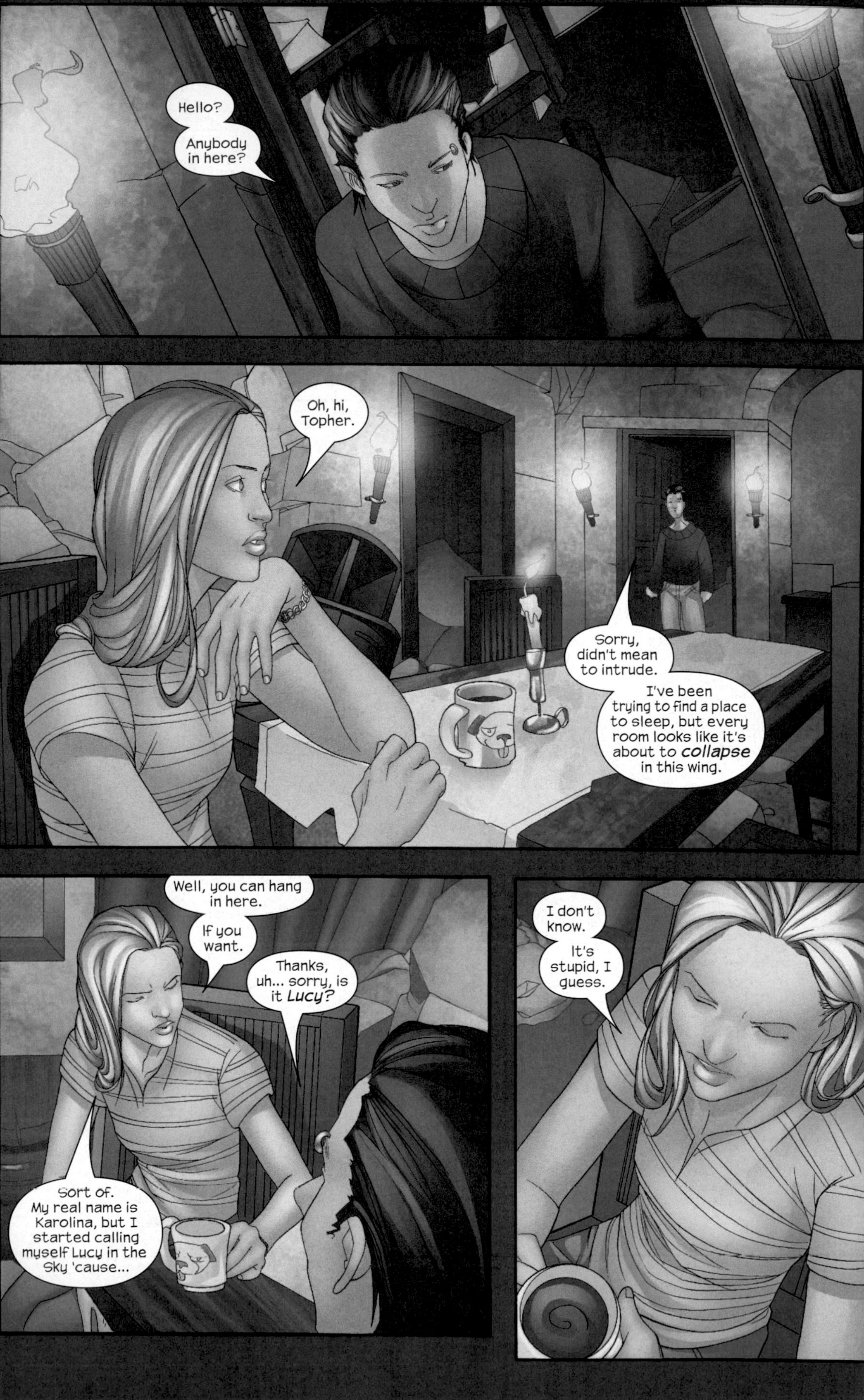
Hello?
Anybody in here?
Oh, hi, Topher.
Sorry, didn't mean to intrude.
I've been trying to find a place to sleep, but every room looks like it's about to *collapse* in this wing.
Well, you can hang in here.
If you want.
Thanks, uh... sorry, is it *Lucy*?
Sort of. My real name is Karolina, but I started calling myself Lucy in the Sky 'cause...
I don't know.
It's stupid, I guess.

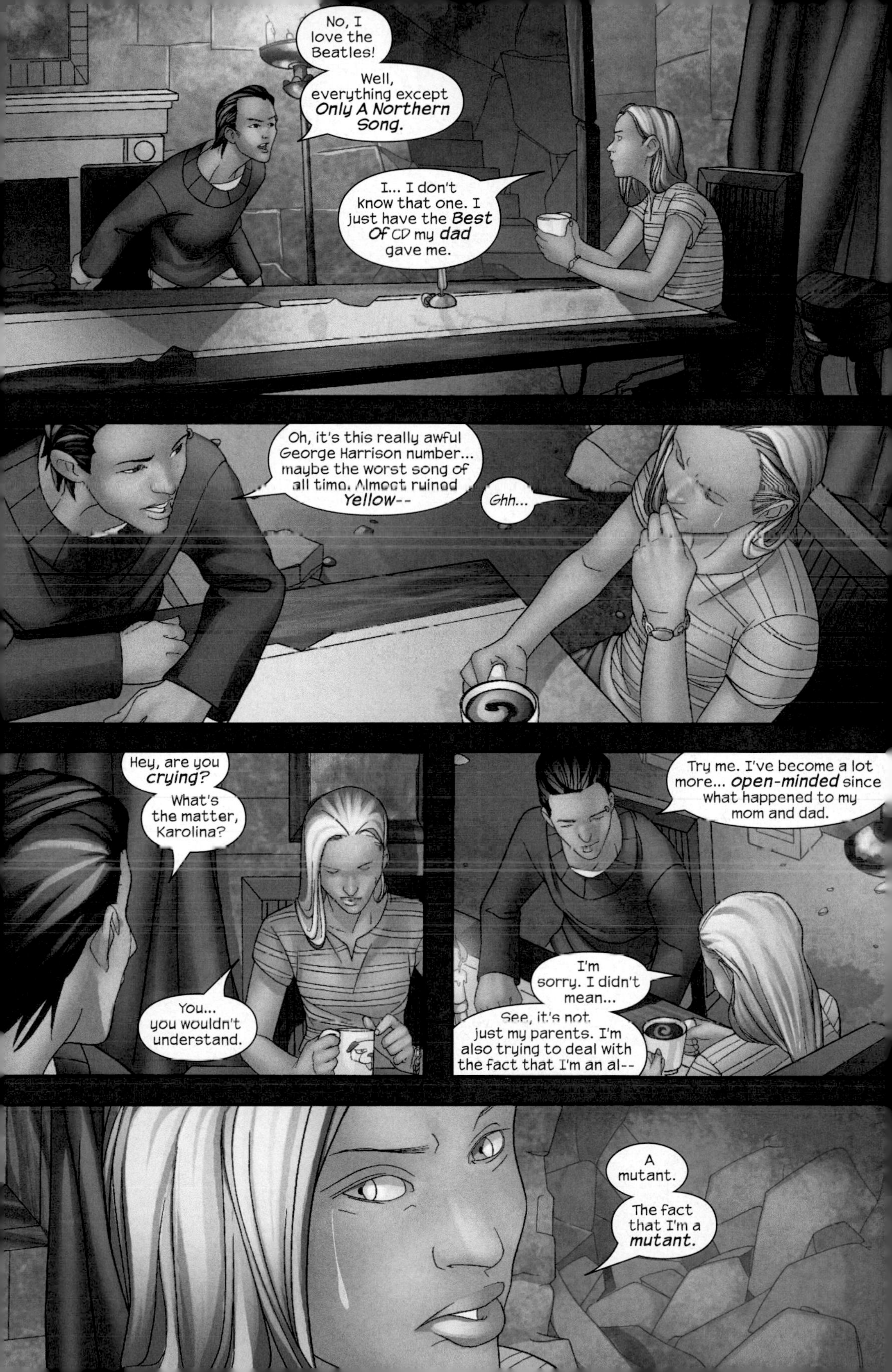
No, I love the Beatles!
Well, everything except *Only A Northern Song.*
I... I don't know that one. I just have the ***Best Of*** CD my ***dad*** gave me.
Oh, it's this really awful George Harrison number... maybe the worst song of all time. Almost ruined ***Yellow***--
Ghh...
Hey, are you ***crying?***
What's the matter, Karolina?
You... you wouldn't understand.
Try me. I've become a lot more... ***open-minded*** since what happened to my mom and dad.
I'm sorry. I didn't mean...
See, it's not just my parents. I'm also trying to deal with the fact that I'm an al--
A mutant.
The fact that I'm a ***mutant.***

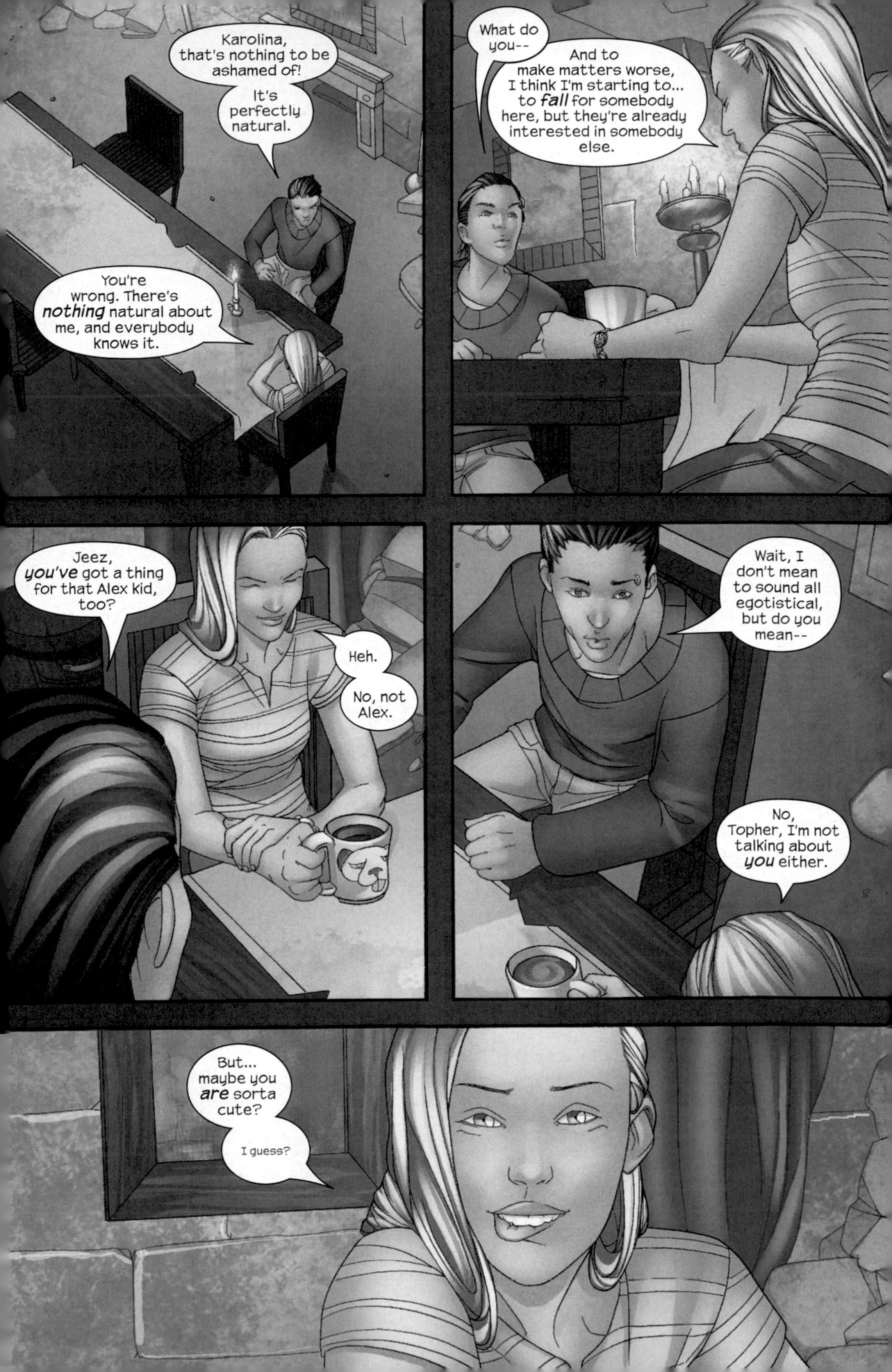
Karolina, that's nothing to be ashamed of!
It's perfectly natural.
You're wrong. There's nothing natural about me, and everybody knows it.
What do you--
And to make matters worse, I think I'm starting to... to fall for somebody here, but they're already interested in somebody else.
Jeez, you've got a thing for that Alex kid, too?
Heh.
No, not Alex.
Wait, I don't mean to sound all egotistical, but do you mean--
No, Topher, I'm not talking about you either.
But... maybe you are sorta cute?
I guess?

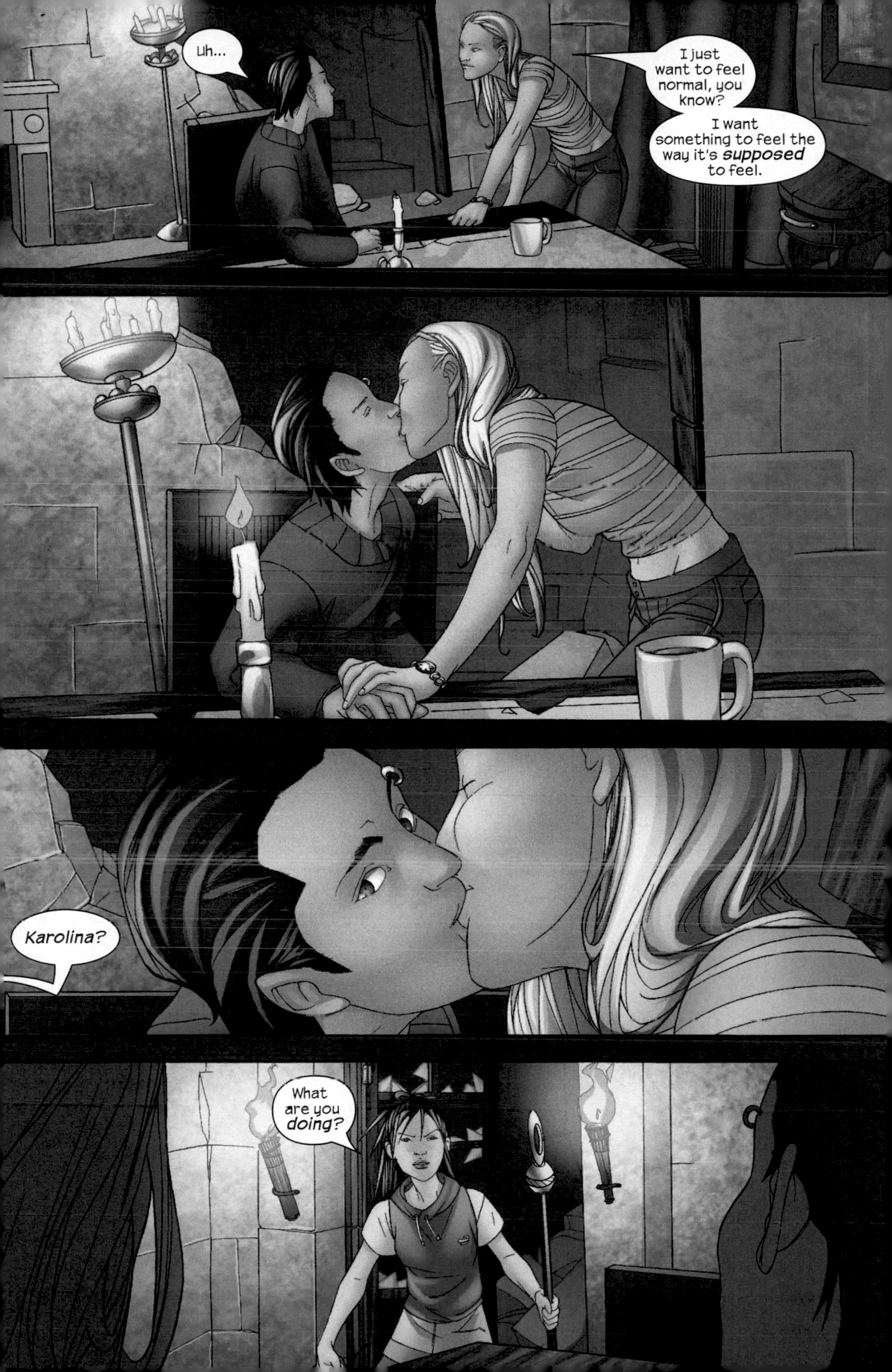

Uh...
I just want to feel normal, you know?
I want something to feel the way it's *supposed* to feel.
Karolina?
What are you *doing*?

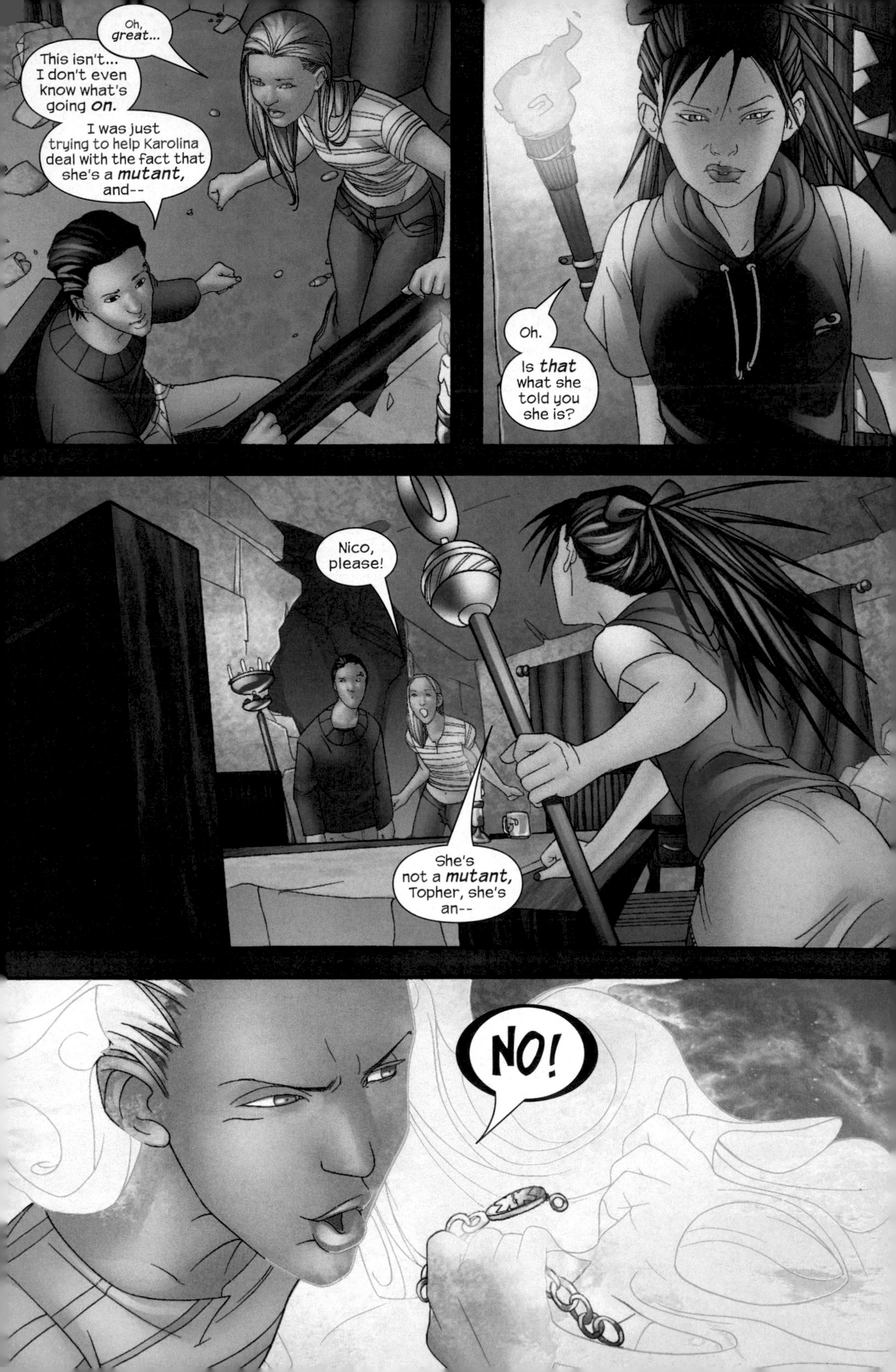
Oh, great...
This isn't... I don't even know what's going on.
I was just trying to help Karolina deal with the fact that she's a mutant, and--
Oh.
Is that what she told you she is?
Nico, please!
She's not a mutant, Topher, she's an--
NO!

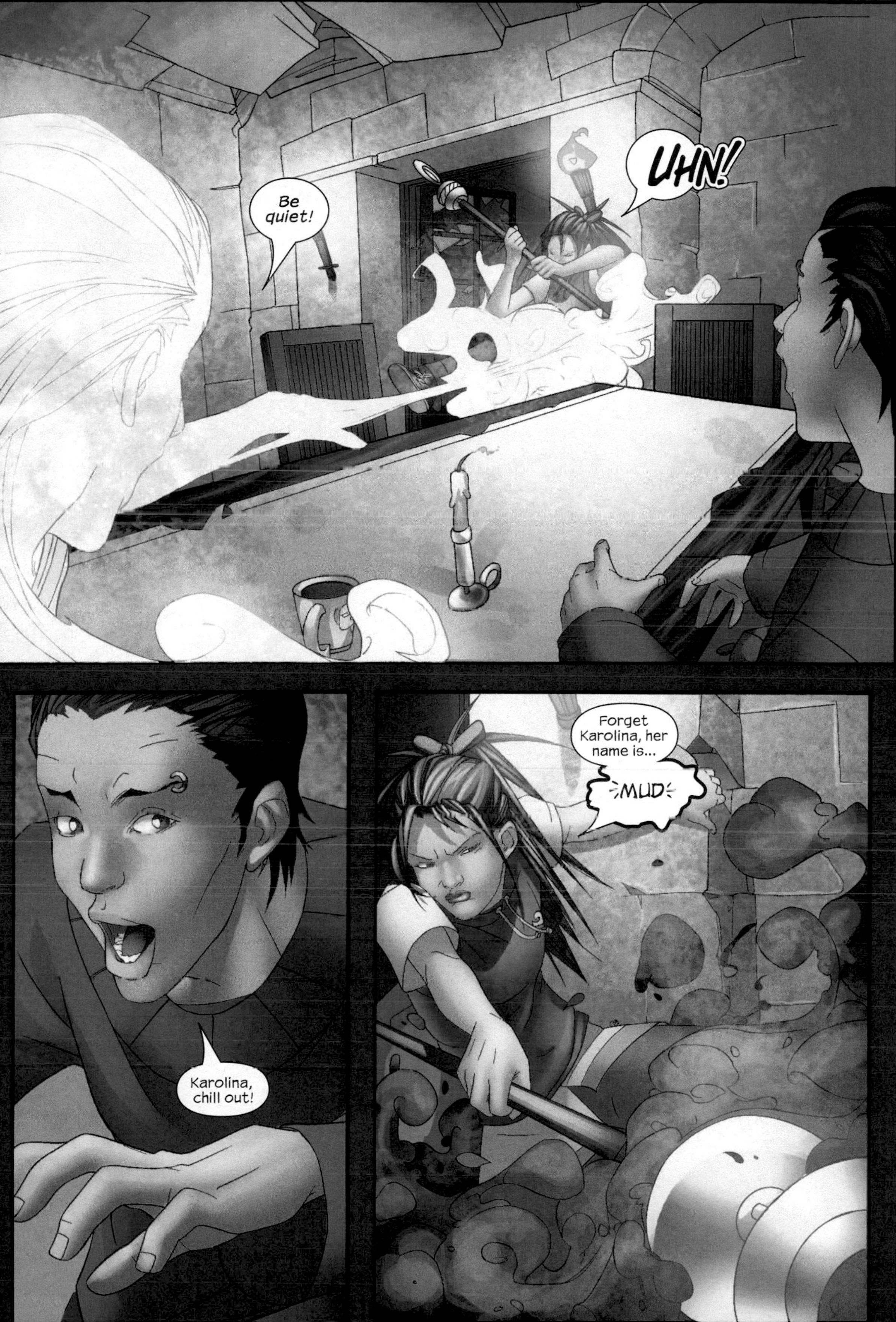
Be quiet!
UHN!
Karolina, chill out!
Forget Karolina, her name is...
MUD

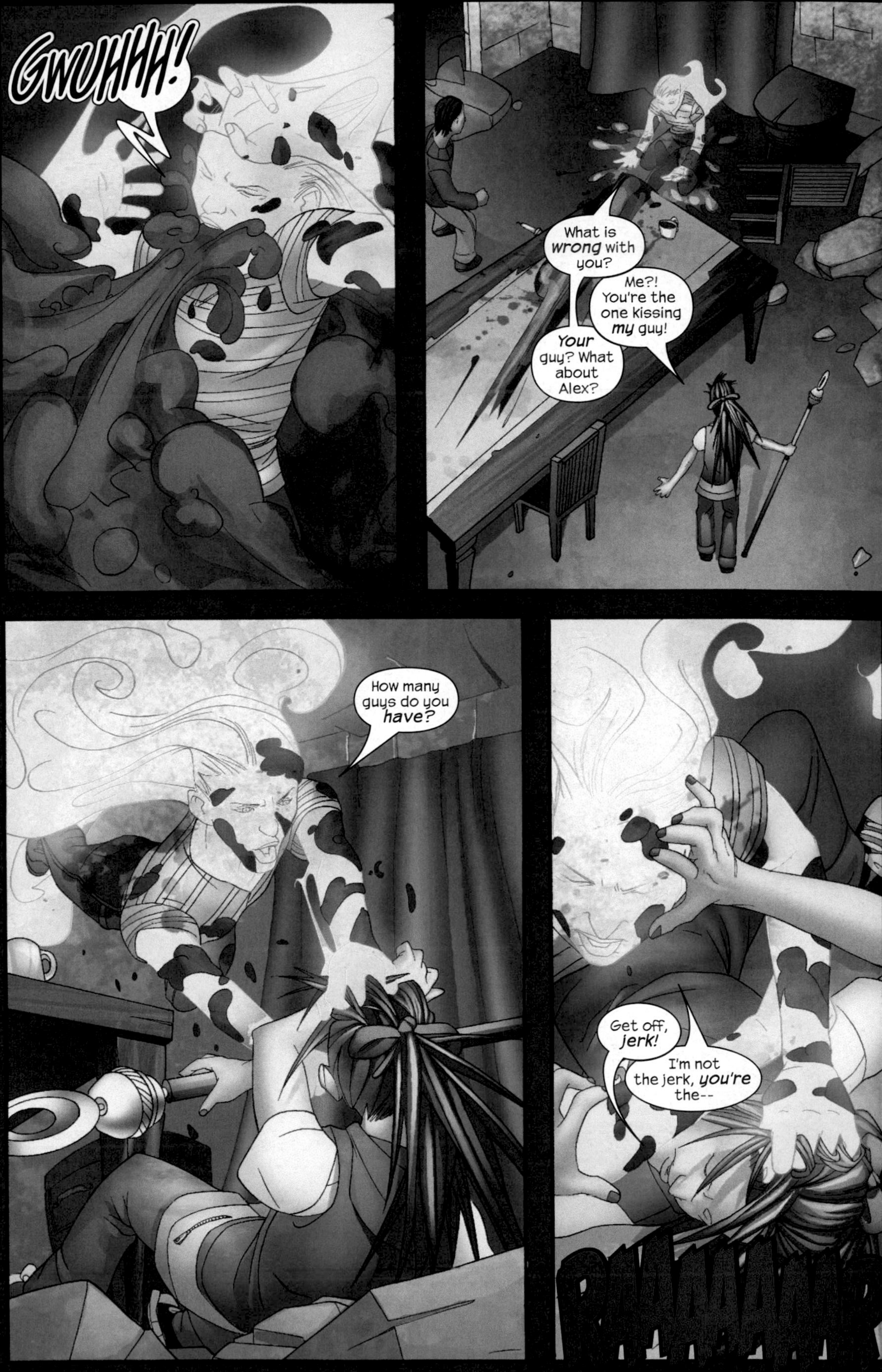
GWUHHH!
What is wrong with you?
Me?! You're the one kissing my guy!
Your guy? What about Alex?
How many guys do you have?
Get off, jerk!
I'm not the jerk, you're the--

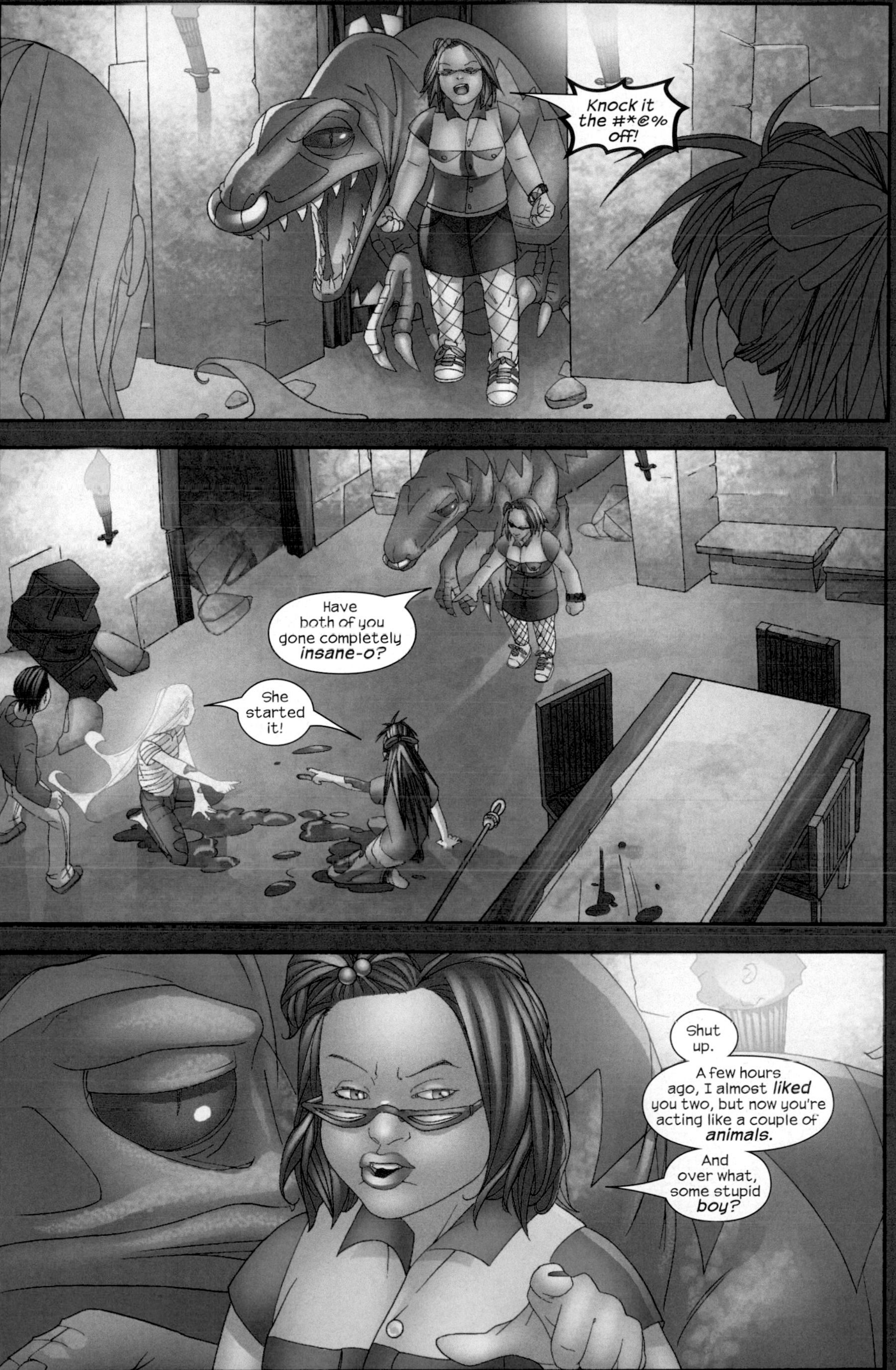
Knock it the #*@% off!
Have both of you gone completely insane-o?
She started it!
Shut up.
A few hours ago, I almost liked you two, but now you're acting like a couple of animals.
And over what, some stupid boy?

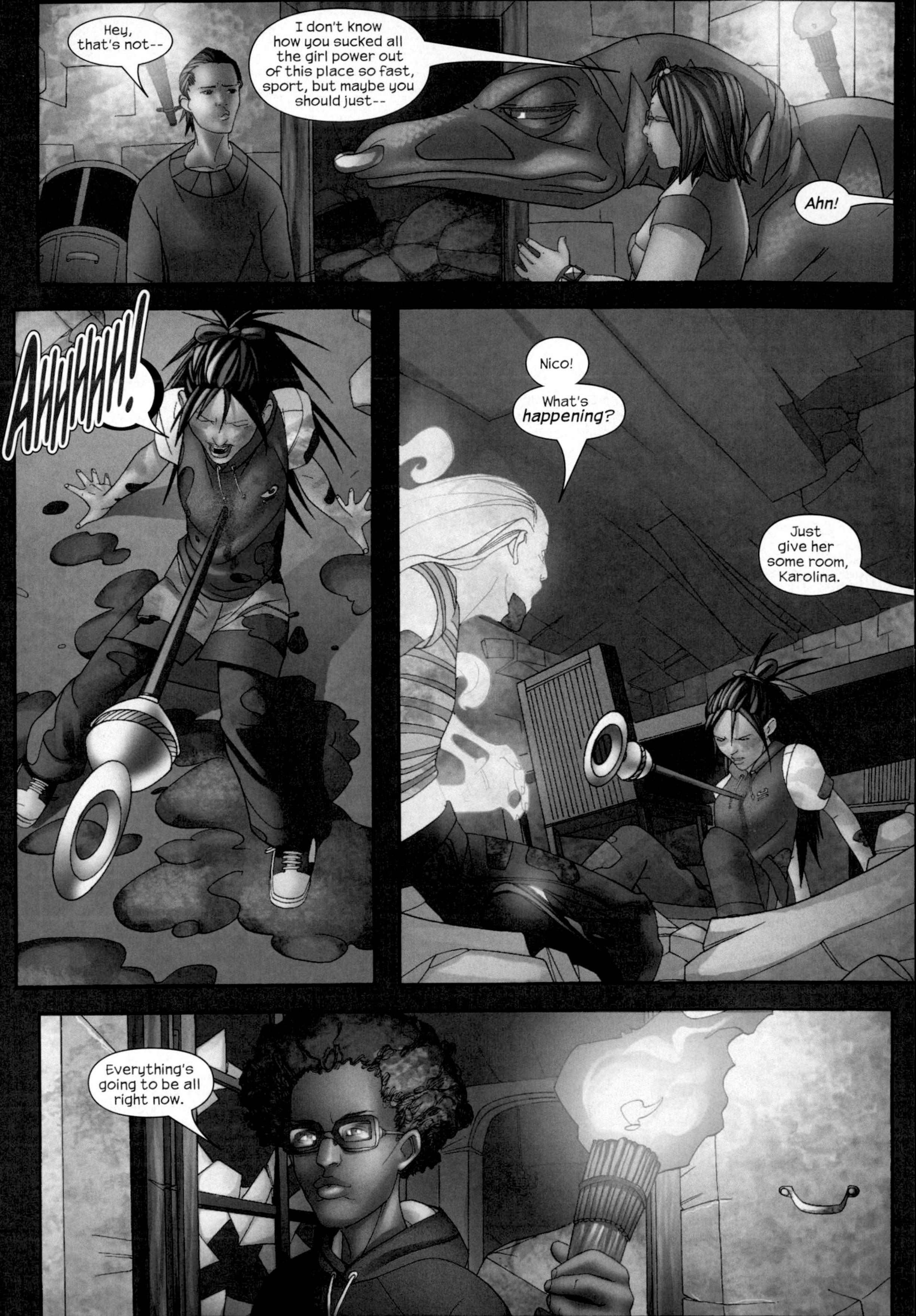
Hey, that's not--
I don't know how you sucked all the girl power out of this place so fast, sport, but maybe you should just--
Ahn!
AHHHHH!
Nico!
What's *happening*?
Just give her some room, Karolina.
Everything's going to be all right now.

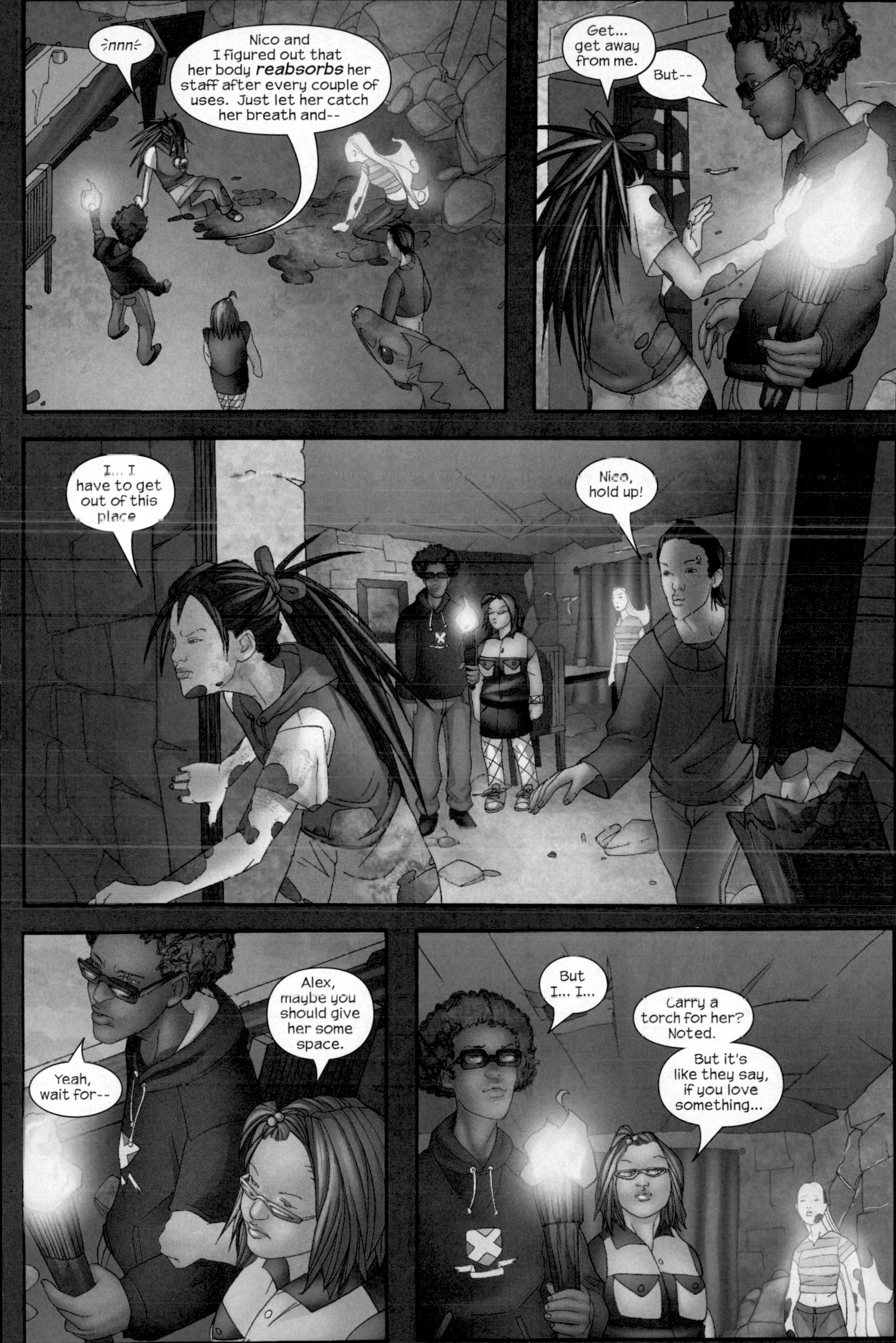

nnn
Nico and I figured out that her body **reabsorbs** her staff after every couple of uses. Just let her catch her breath and--
Get... get away from me.
But--
I... I have to get out of this place
Nico, hold up!
Yeah, wait for--
Alex, maybe you should give her some space.
But I... I...
Carry a torch for her? Noted.
But it's like they say, if you love something...

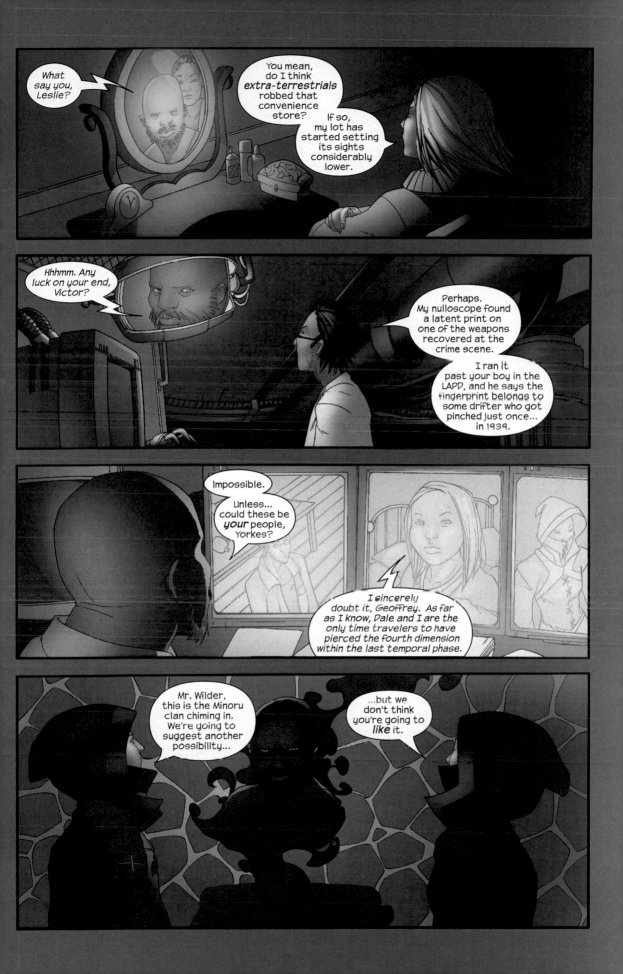

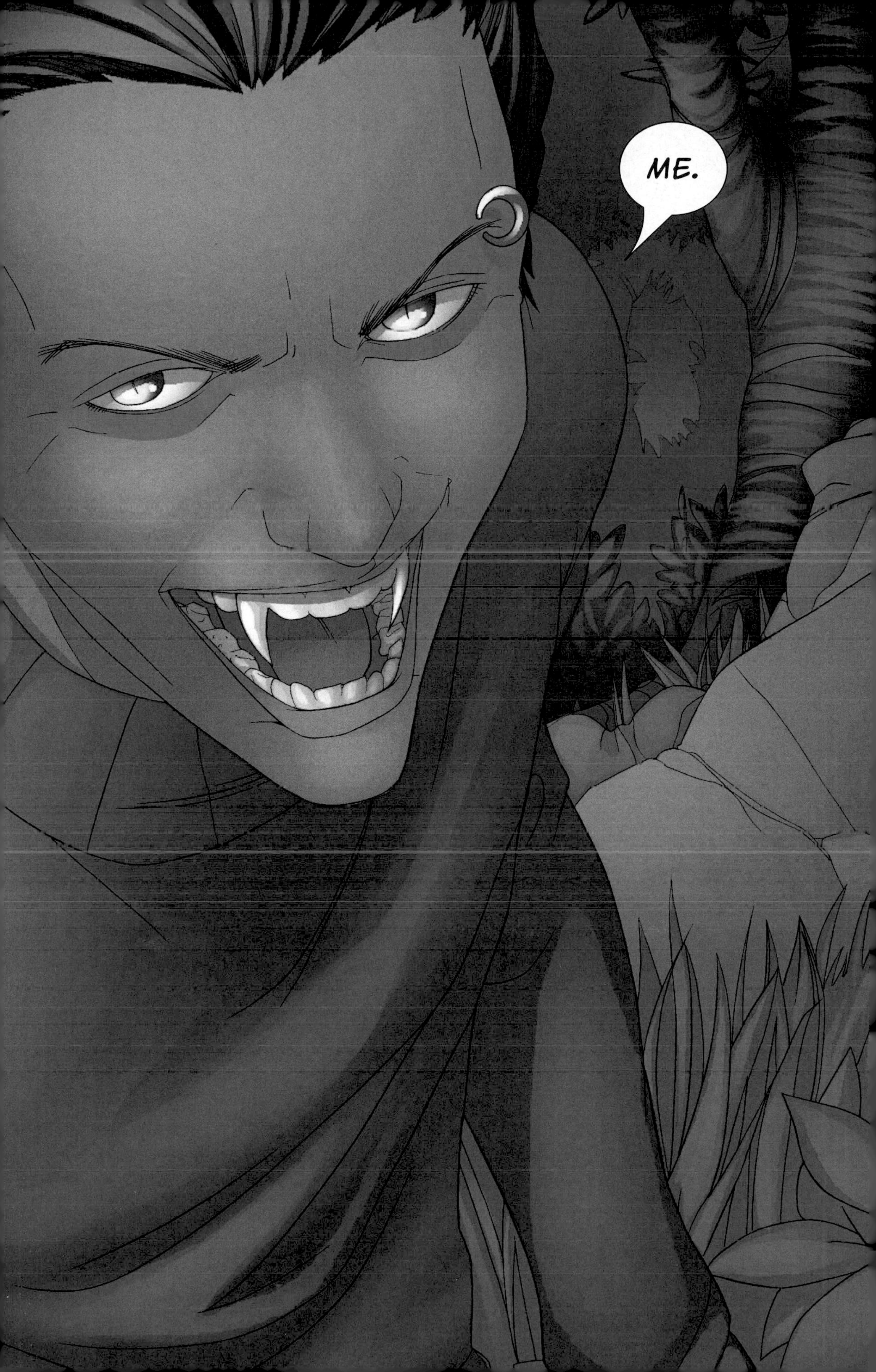
ME.

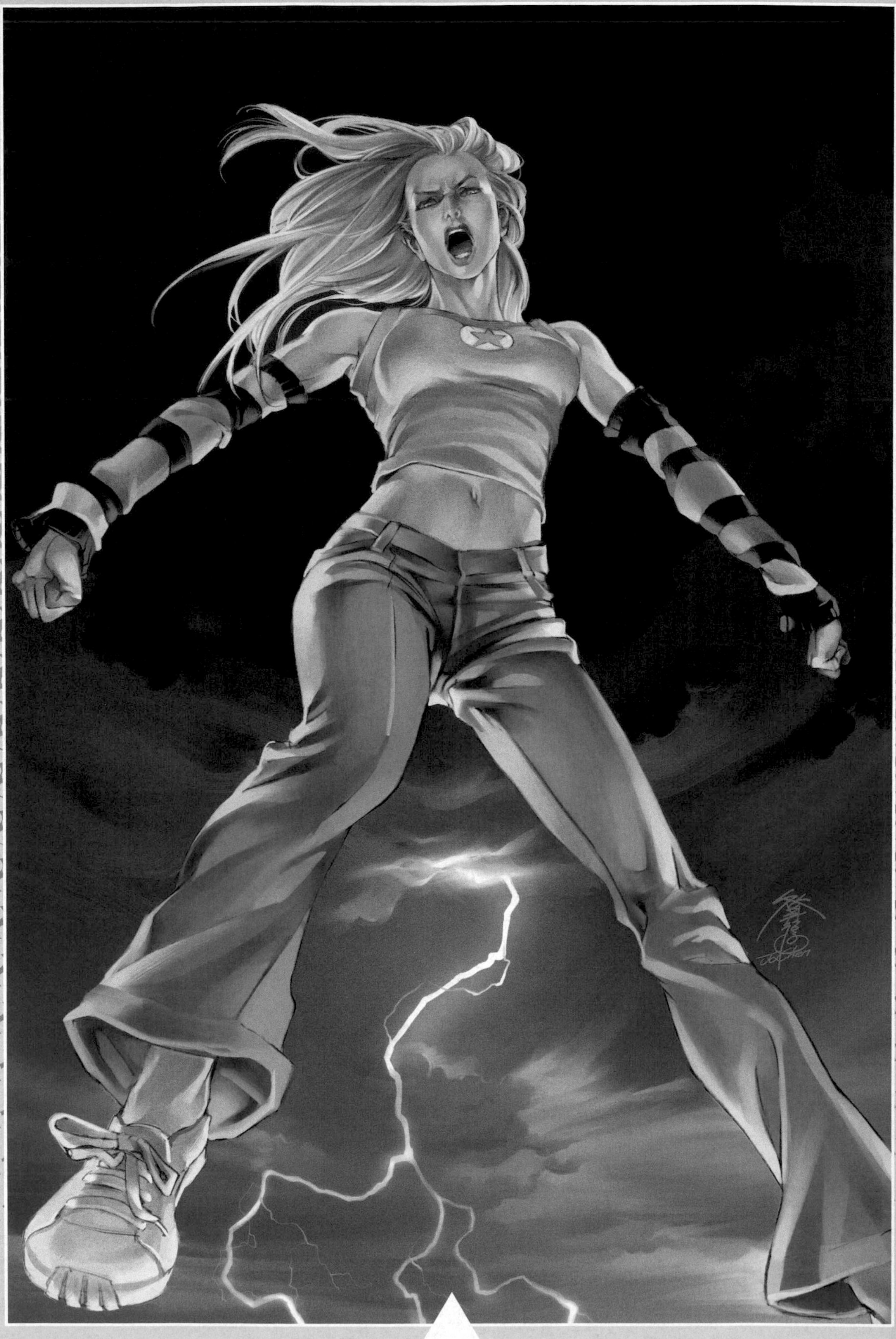

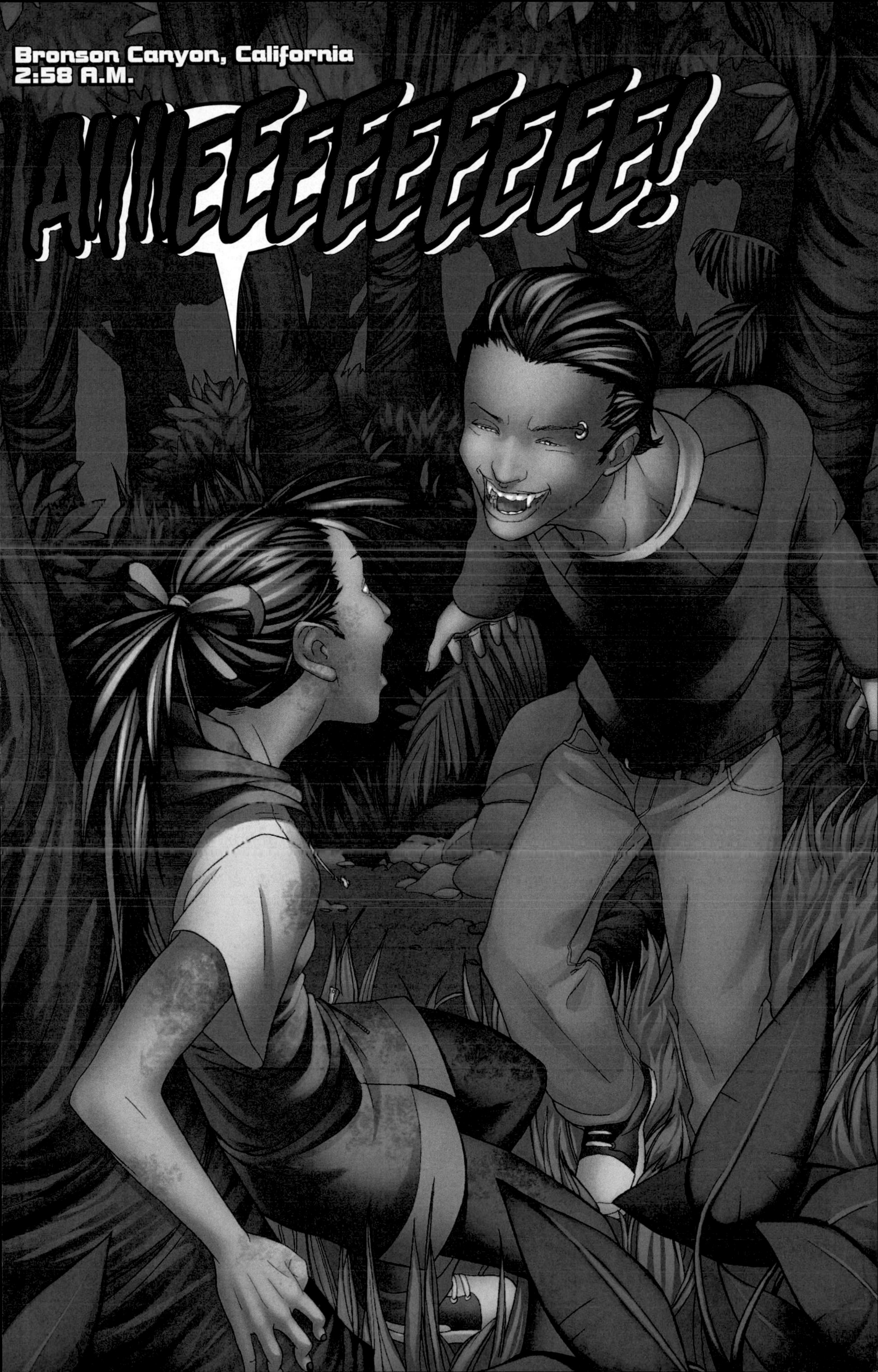
Bronson Canyon, California
2:58 A.M.
AIIIEEEEEEEEEE!

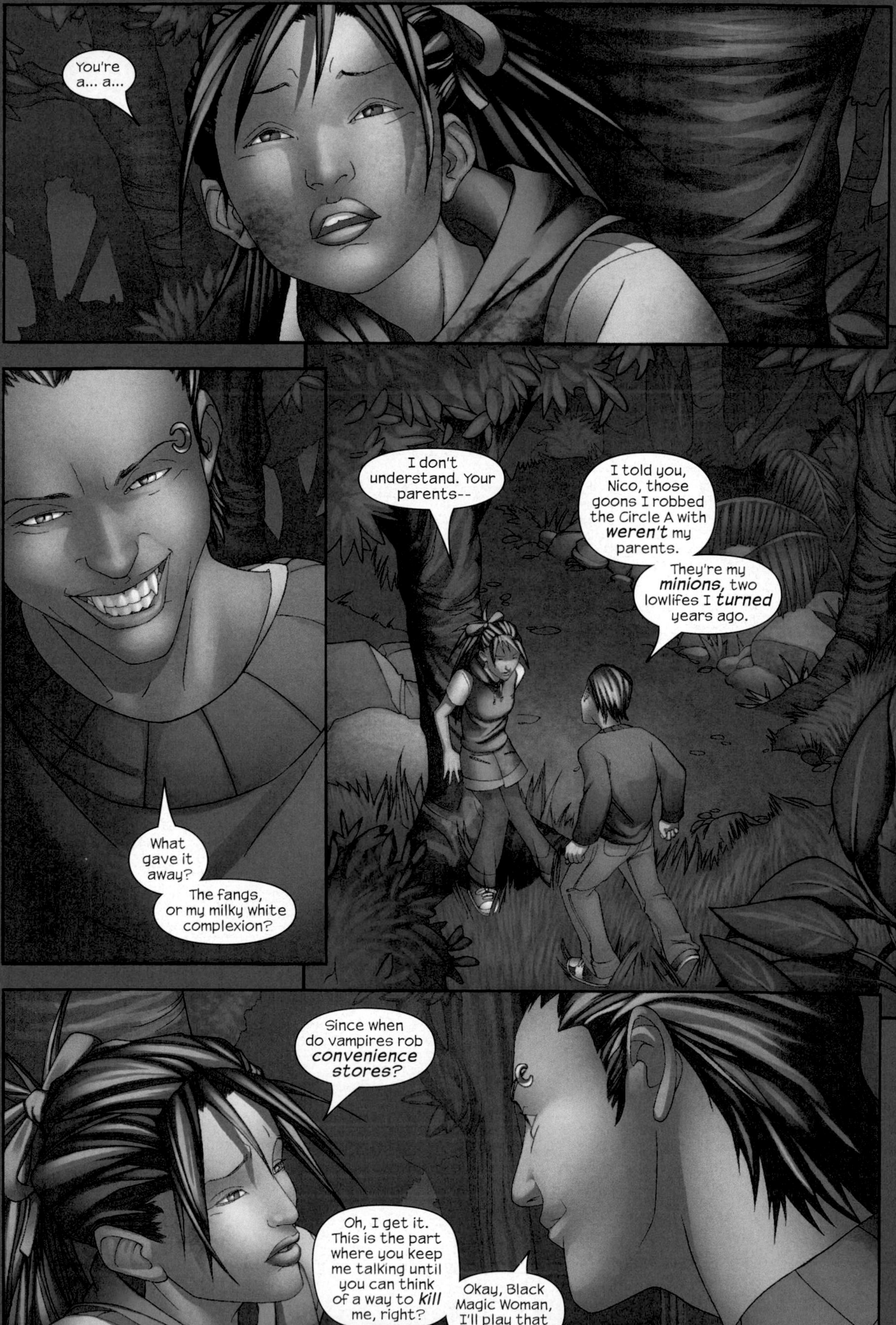
You're a... a...
What gave it away?
The fangs, or my milky white complexion?
I don't understand. Your parents--
I told you, Nico, those goons I robbed the Circle A with *weren't* my parents.
They're my *minions,* two lowlifes I *turned* years ago.
Since when do vampires rob *convenience stores?*
Oh, I get it. This is the part where you keep me talking until you can think of a way to *kill* me, right?
Okay, Black Magic Woman, I'll play that game...

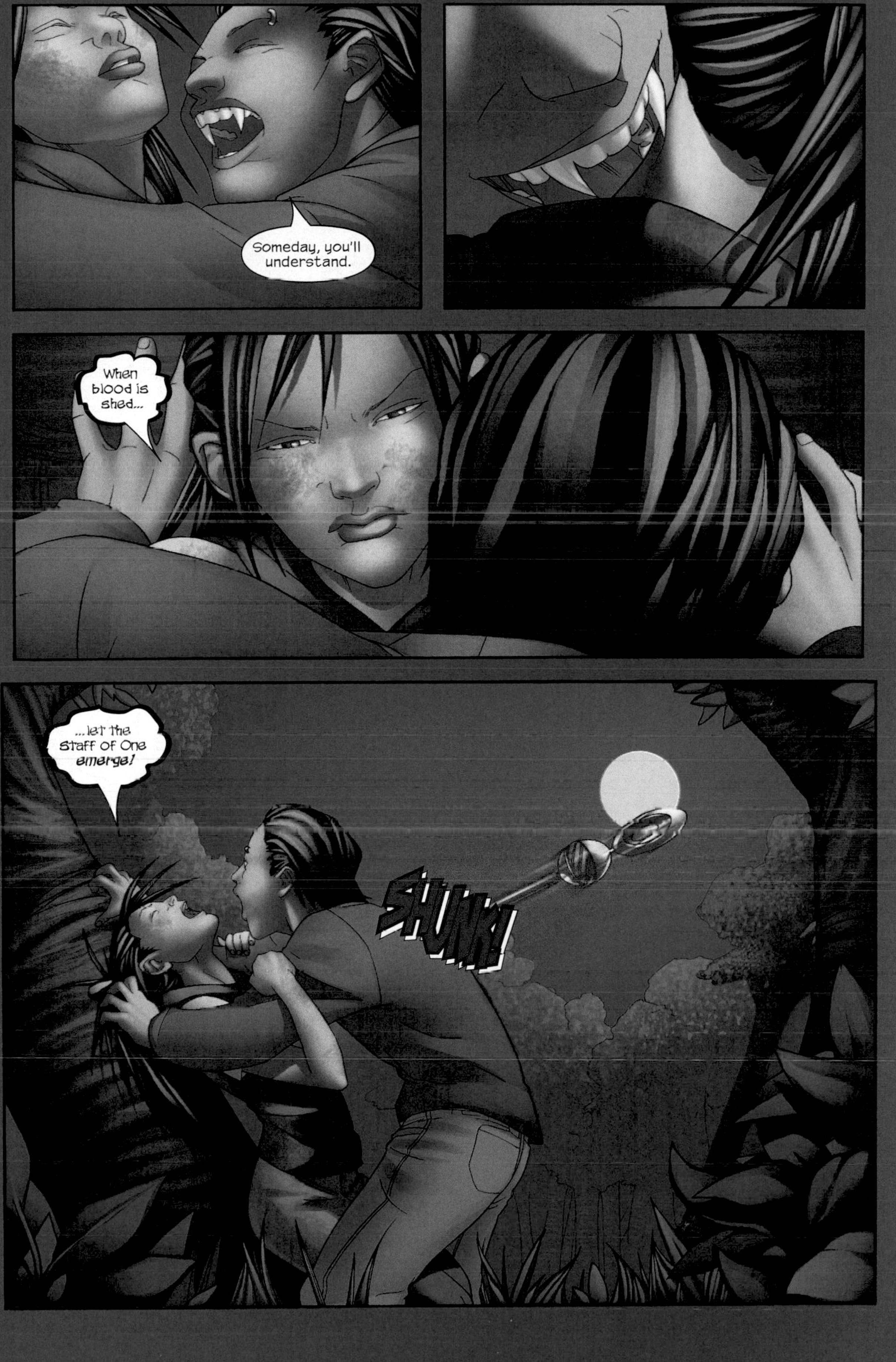
Someday, you'll understand.
When blood is shed...
...let the Staff of One emerge!
SHUNK!

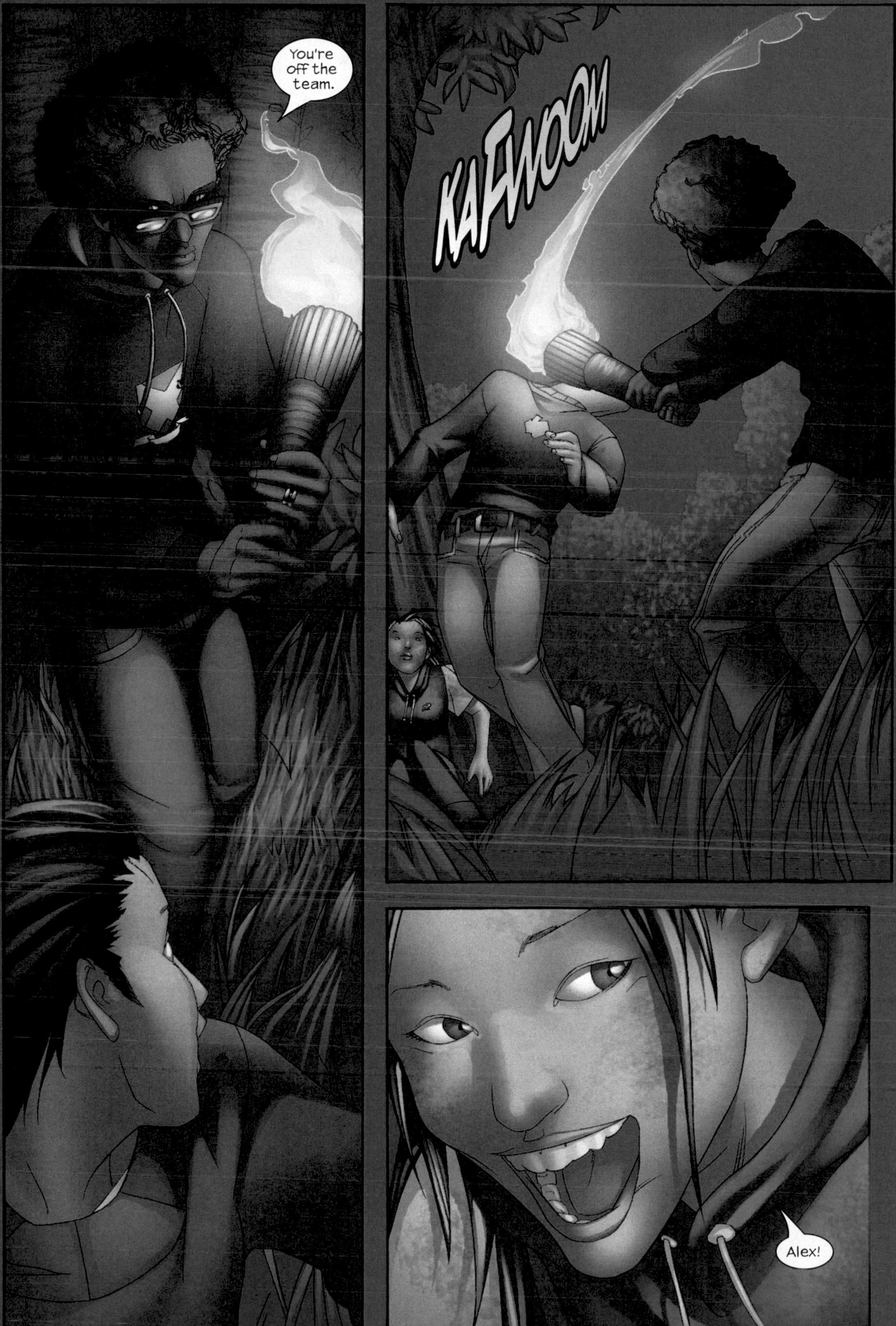
You're off the team.
KAFWOOM
Alex!

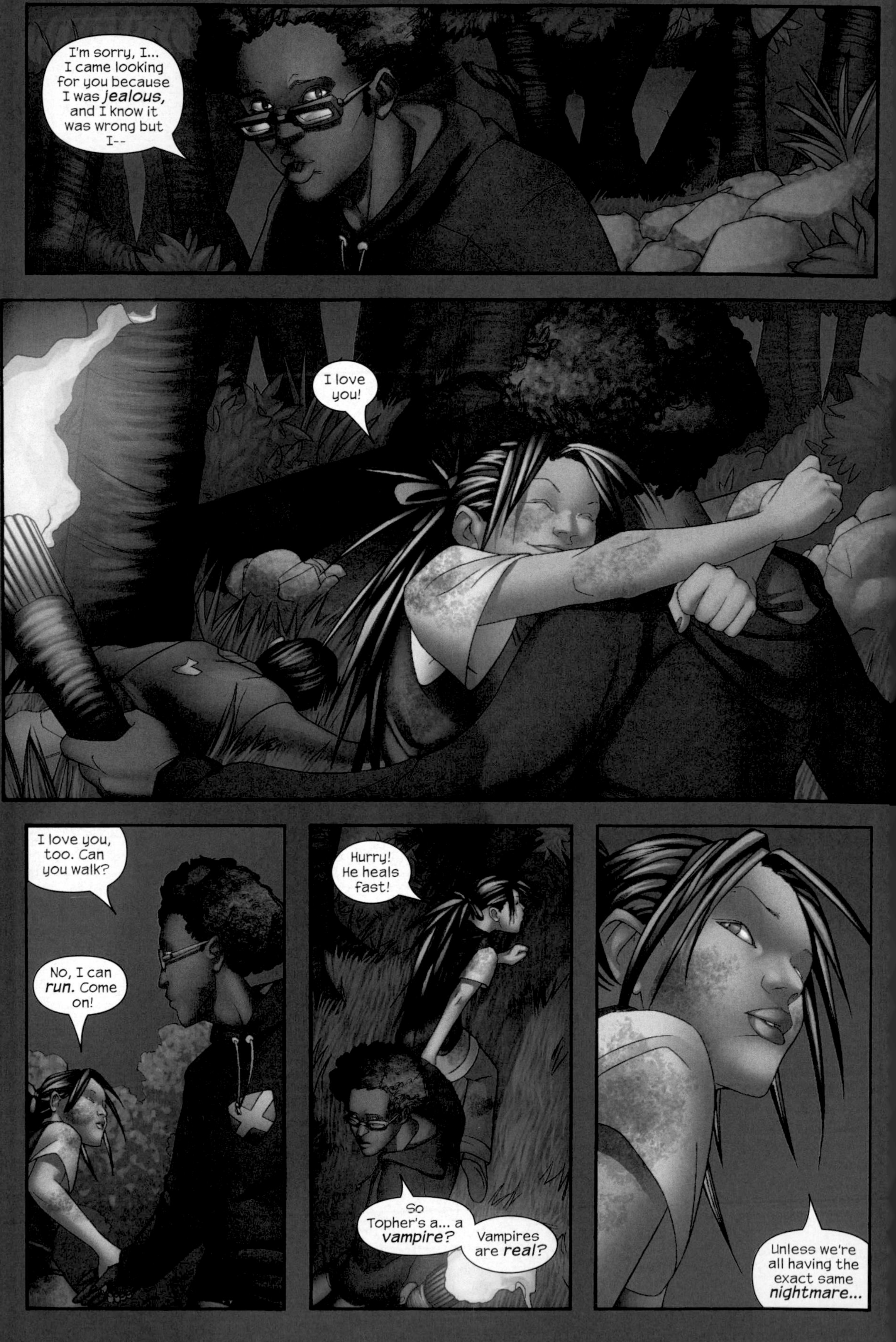
I'm sorry, I... I came looking for you because I was *jealous,* and I know it was wrong but I--
I love you!
I love you, too. Can you walk?
No, I can *run.* Come on!
Hurry! He heals fast!
So Topher's a... a *vampire?*
Vampires are *real?*
Unless we're all having the exact same *nightmare...*

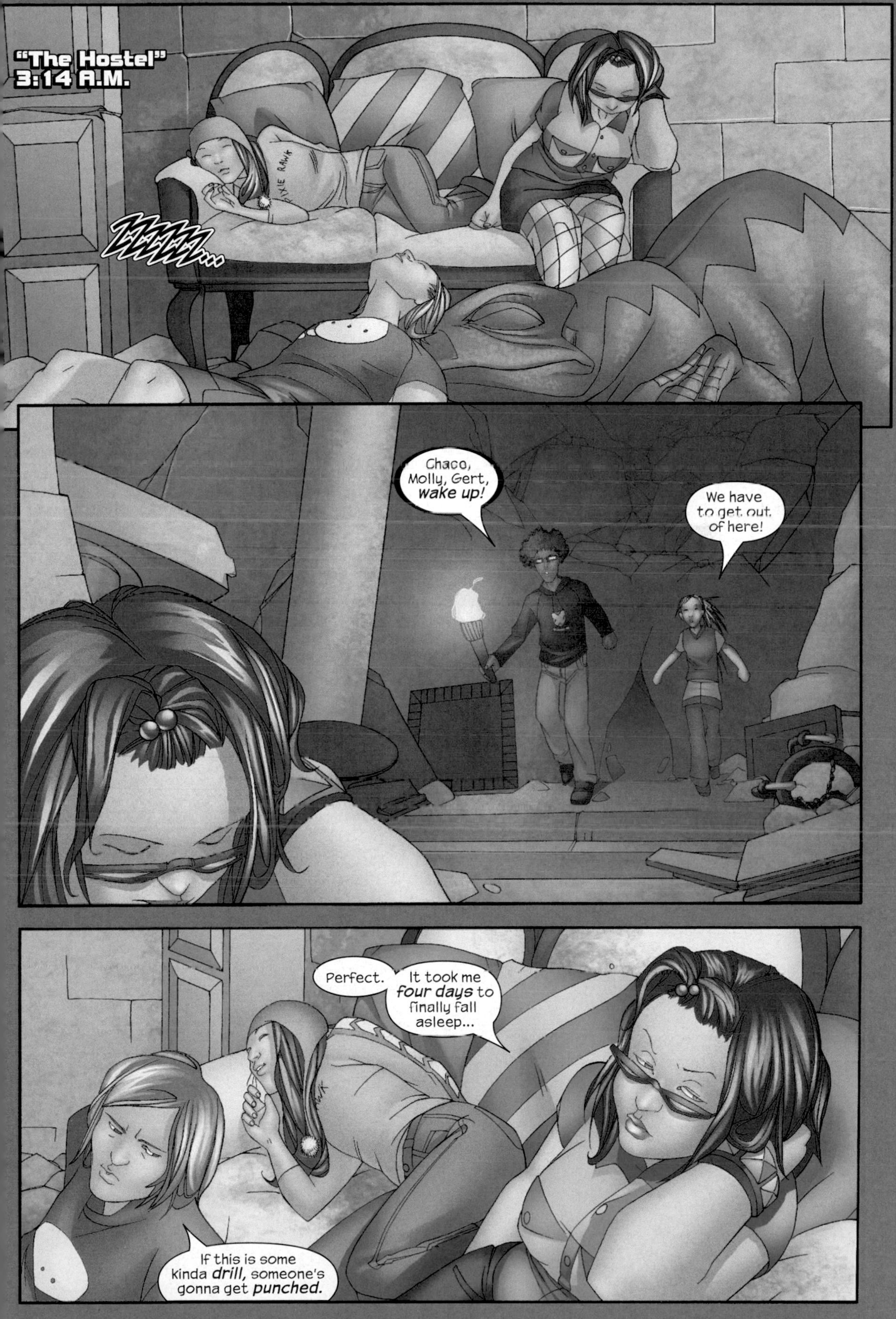
"The Hostel"
3:14 A.M.
PIXIE RAWK
Chaco, Molly, Gert, *wake up!*
We have to get out of here!
Perfect.
It took me *four days* to finally fall asleep...
If this is some kinda *drill,* someone's gonna get *punched.*

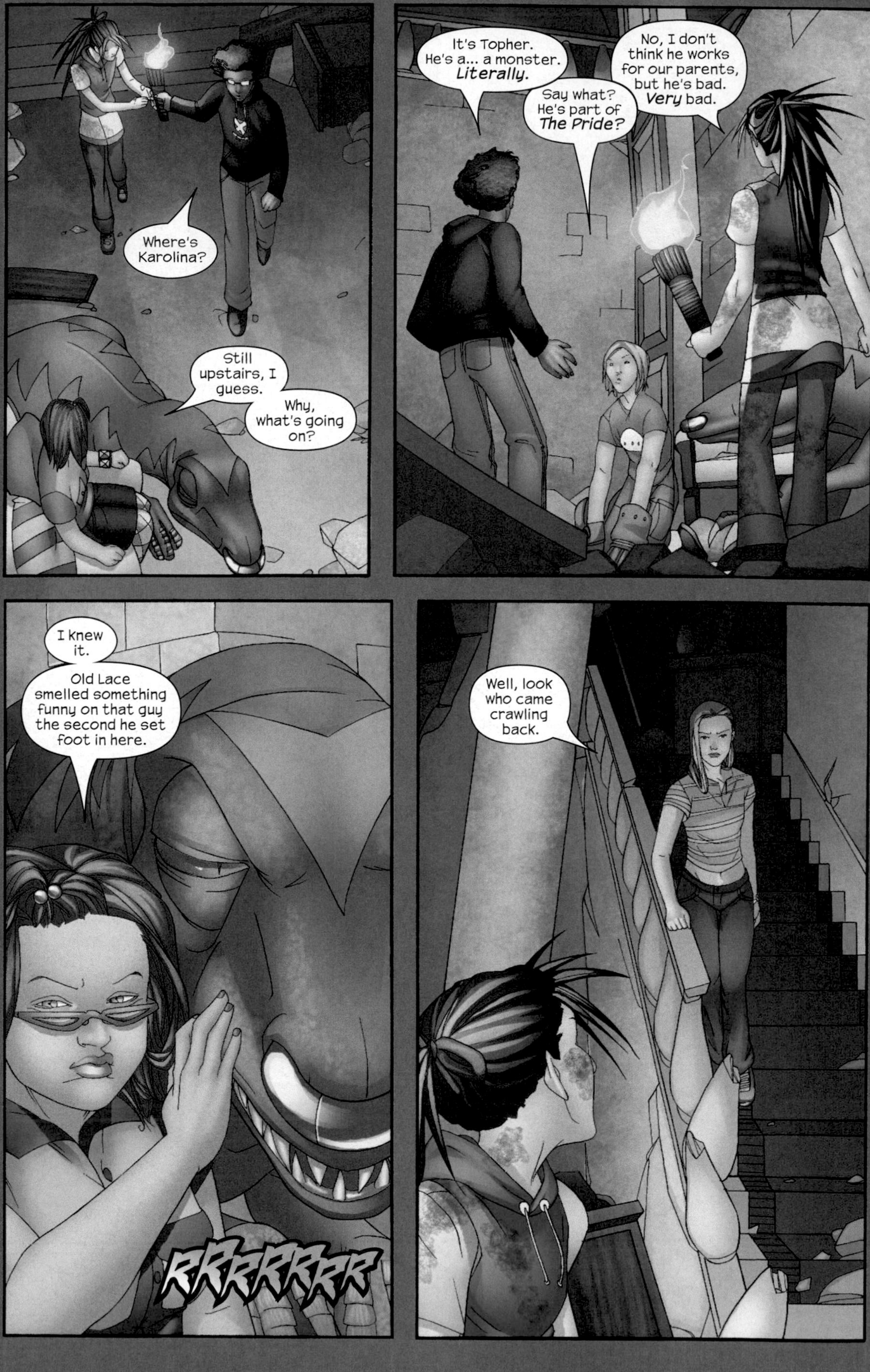
Where's Karolina?
Still upstairs, I guess.
Why, what's going on?
It's Topher. He's a... a monster. *Literally.*
Say what? He's part of *The Pride?*
No, I don't think he works for our parents, but he's bad. *Very* bad.
I knew it.
Old Lace smelled something funny on that guy the second he set foot in here.
RRRRRRR
Well, look who came crawling back.

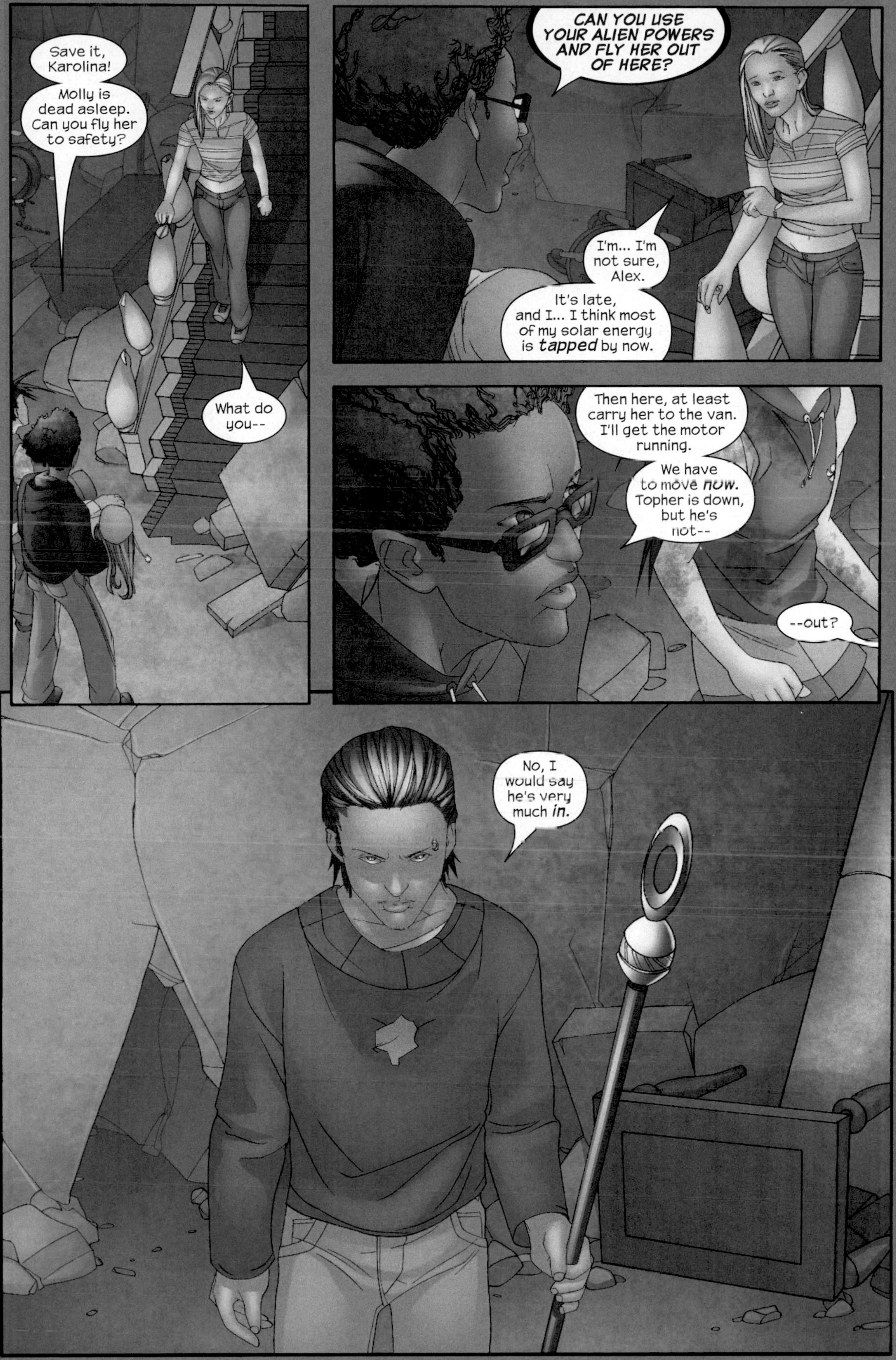
Save it, Karolina!
Molly is dead asleep. Can you fly her to safety?
What do you--
CAN YOU USE YOUR ALIEN POWERS AND FLY HER OUT OF HERE?
I'm... I'm not sure, Alex.
It's late, and I... I think most of my solar energy is *tapped* by now.
Then here, at least carry her to the van. I'll get the motor running.
We have to move *now.* Topher is down, but he's not--
--out?
No, I would say he's very much *in.*

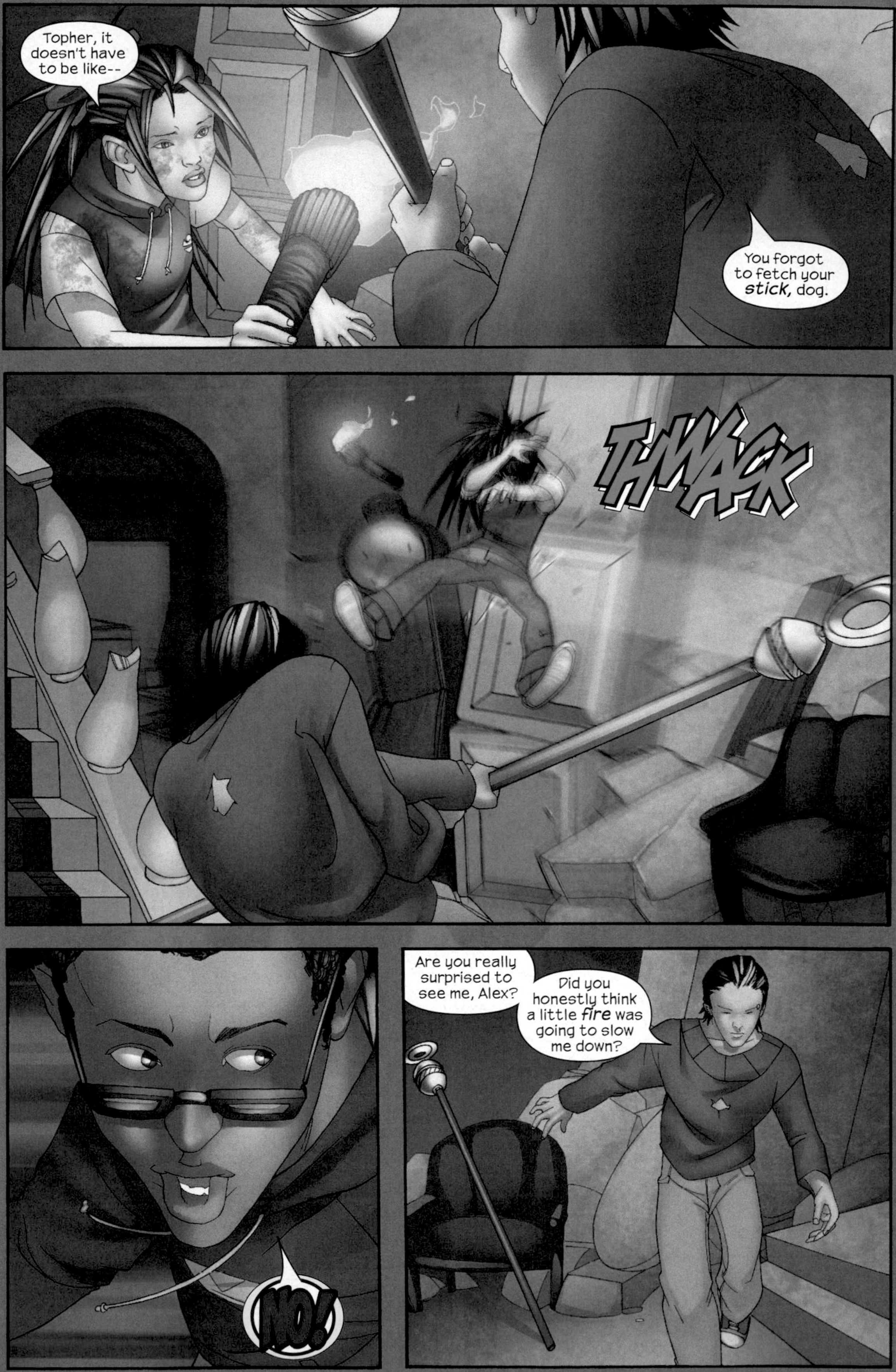

Topher, it doesn't have to be like--
You forgot to fetch your stick, dog.
THWACK
NO!
Are you really surprised to see me, Alex?
Did you honestly think a little fire was going to slow me down?

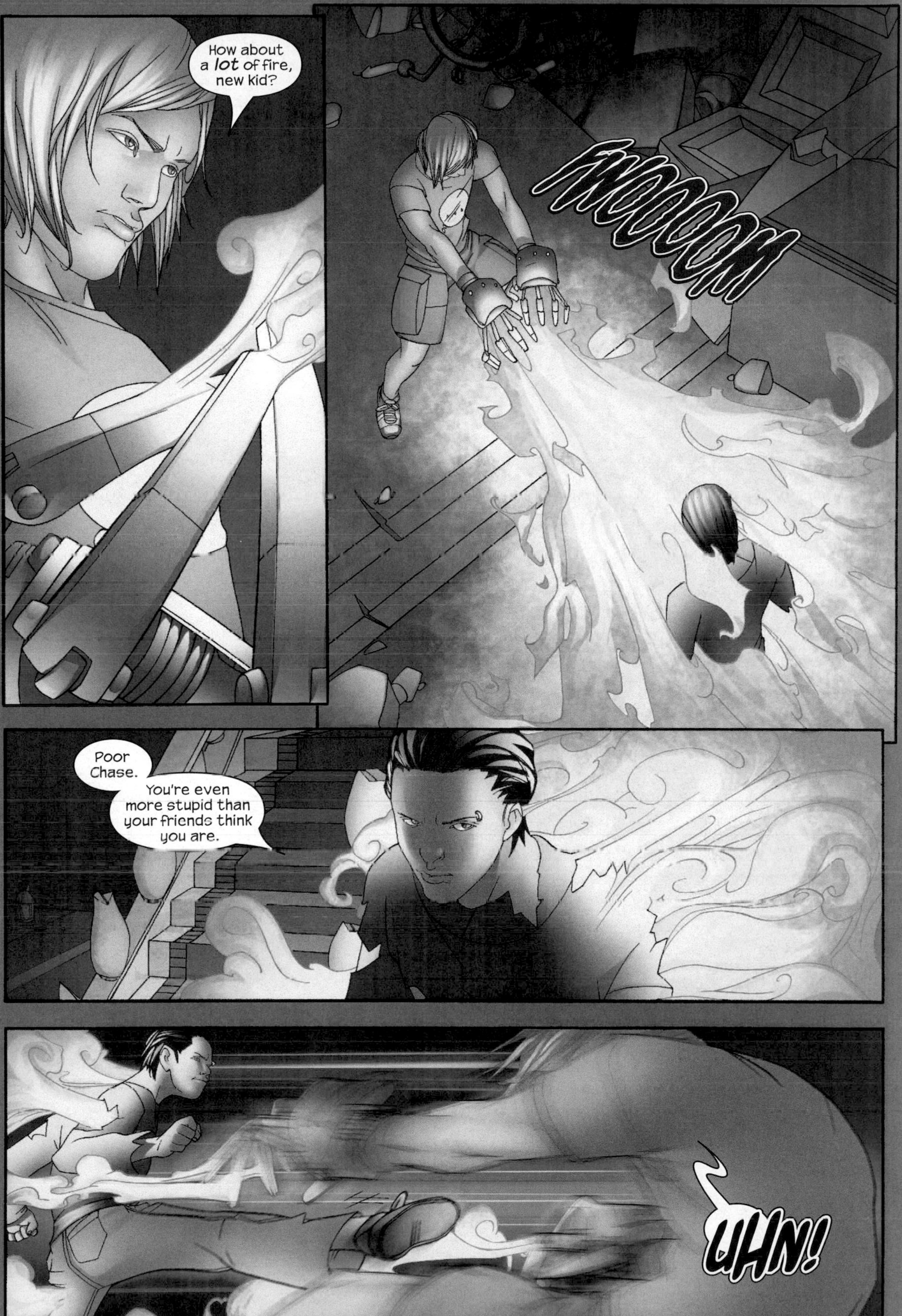
How about a *lot* of fire, new kid?
FWOOOOM
Poor Chase.
You're even more stupid than your friends think you are.
UHN!

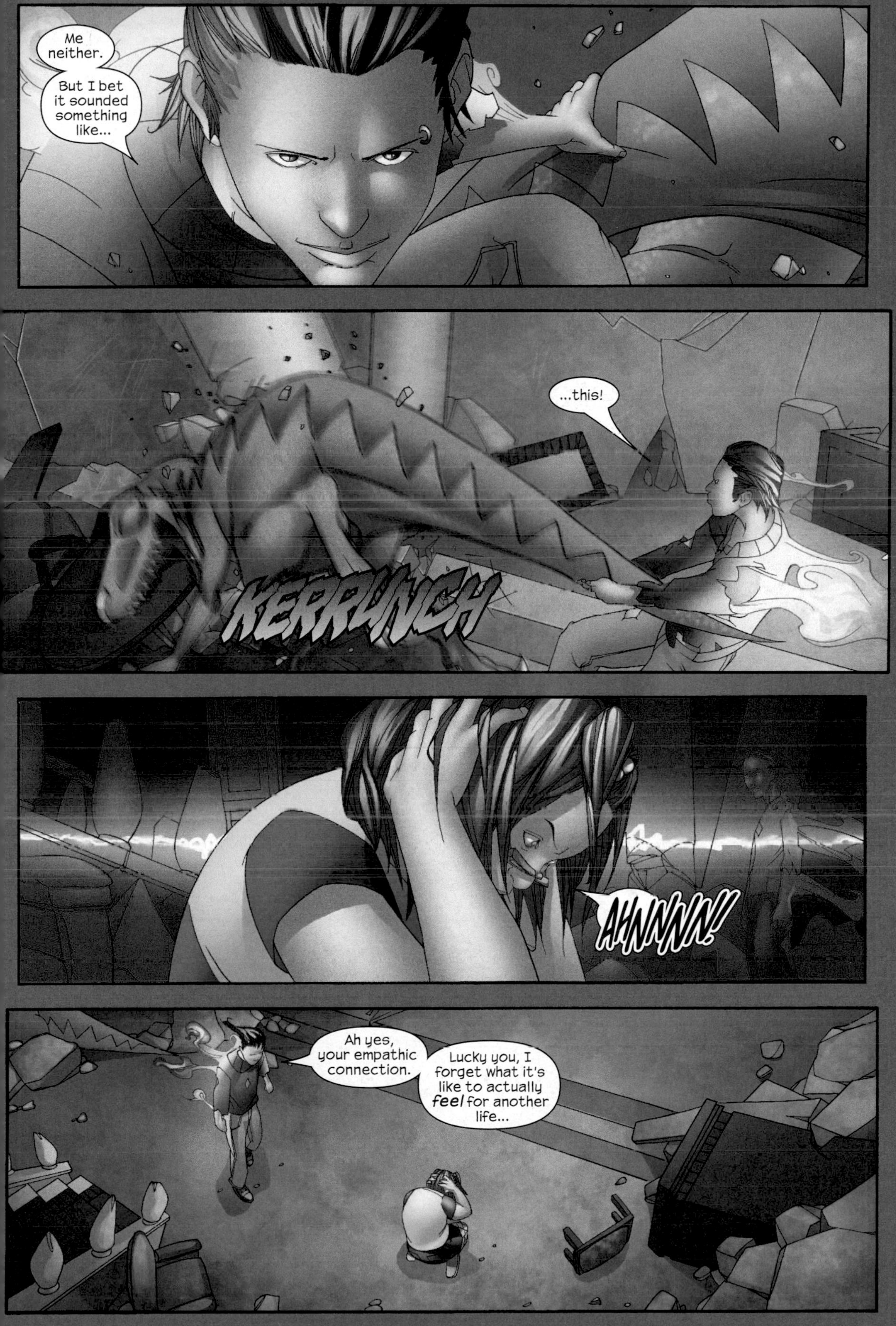
Me neither.
But I bet it sounded something like...
...this!
KERRUNCH
AHNNNN!
Ah yes, your empathic connection.
Lucky you, I forget what it's like to actually *feel* for another life...

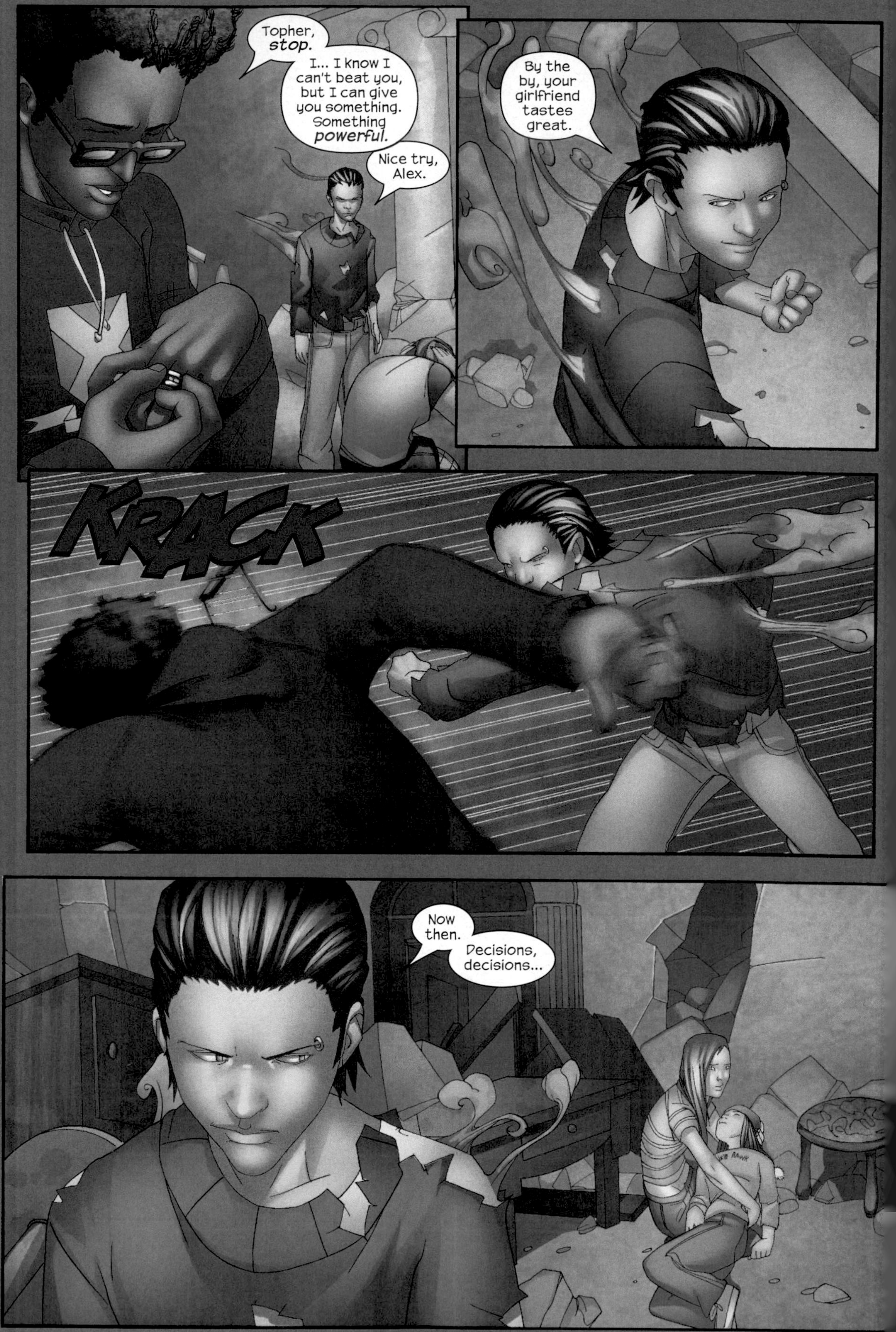
Topher, stop.
I... I know I can't beat you, but I can give you something. Something powerful.
Nice try, Alex.
By the by, your girlfriend tastes great.
KRACK
Now then.
Decisions, decisions...

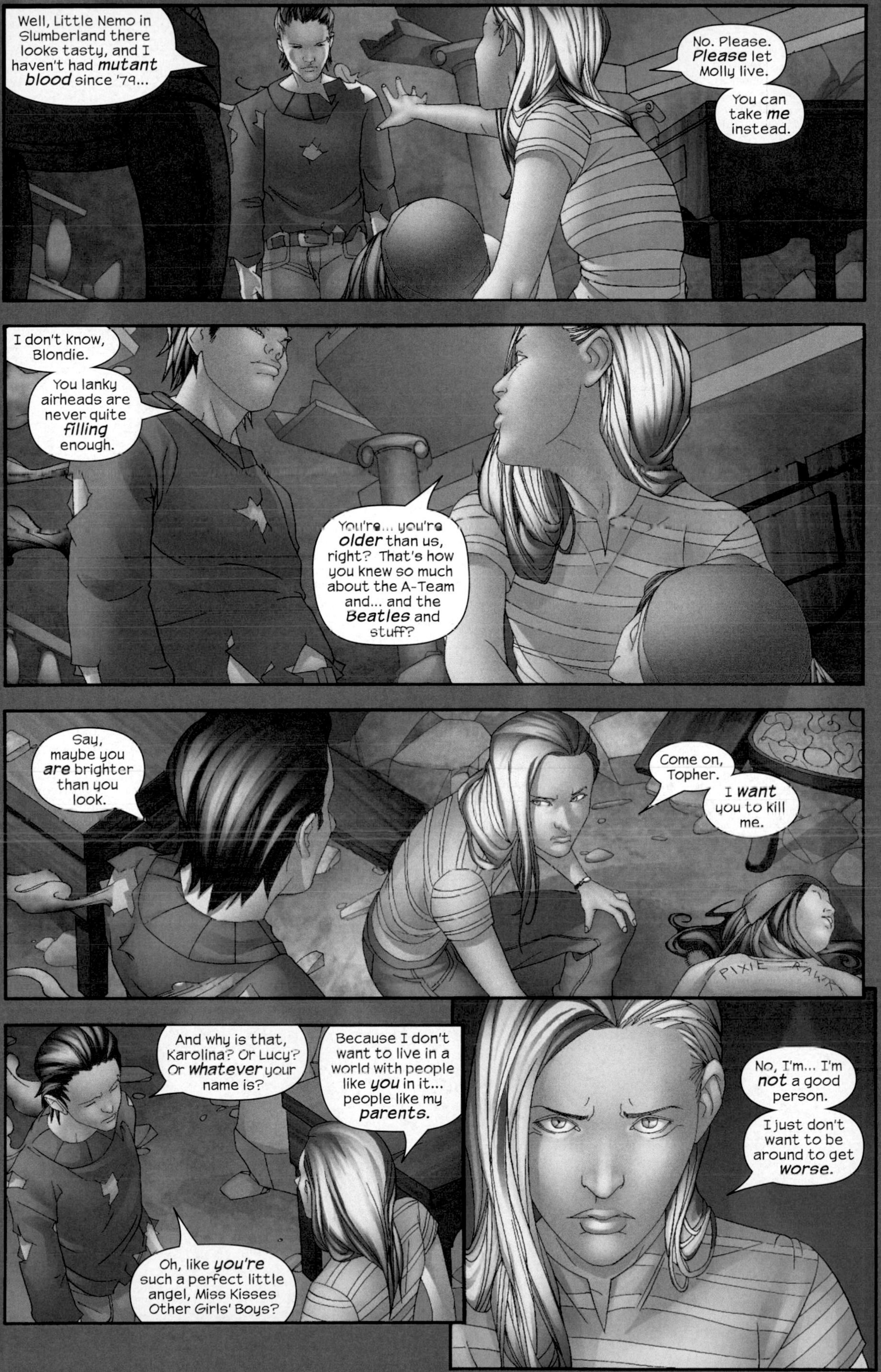
Well, Little Nemo in Slumberland there looks tasty, and I haven't had mutant blood since '79...
No. Please. Please let Molly live.
You can take me instead.
I don't know, Blondie.
You lanky airheads are never quite filling enough.
You're... you're older than us, right? That's how you knew so much about the A-Team and... and the Beatles and stuff?
Say, maybe you are brighter than you look.
Come on, Topher.
I want you to kill me.
PIXIE RAWR
And why is that, Karolina? Or Lucy? Or whatever your name is?
Because I don't want to live in a world with people like you in it... people like my parents.
Oh, like you're such a perfect little angel, Miss Kisses Other Girls' Boys?
No, I'm... I'm not a good person.
I just don't want to be around to get worse.

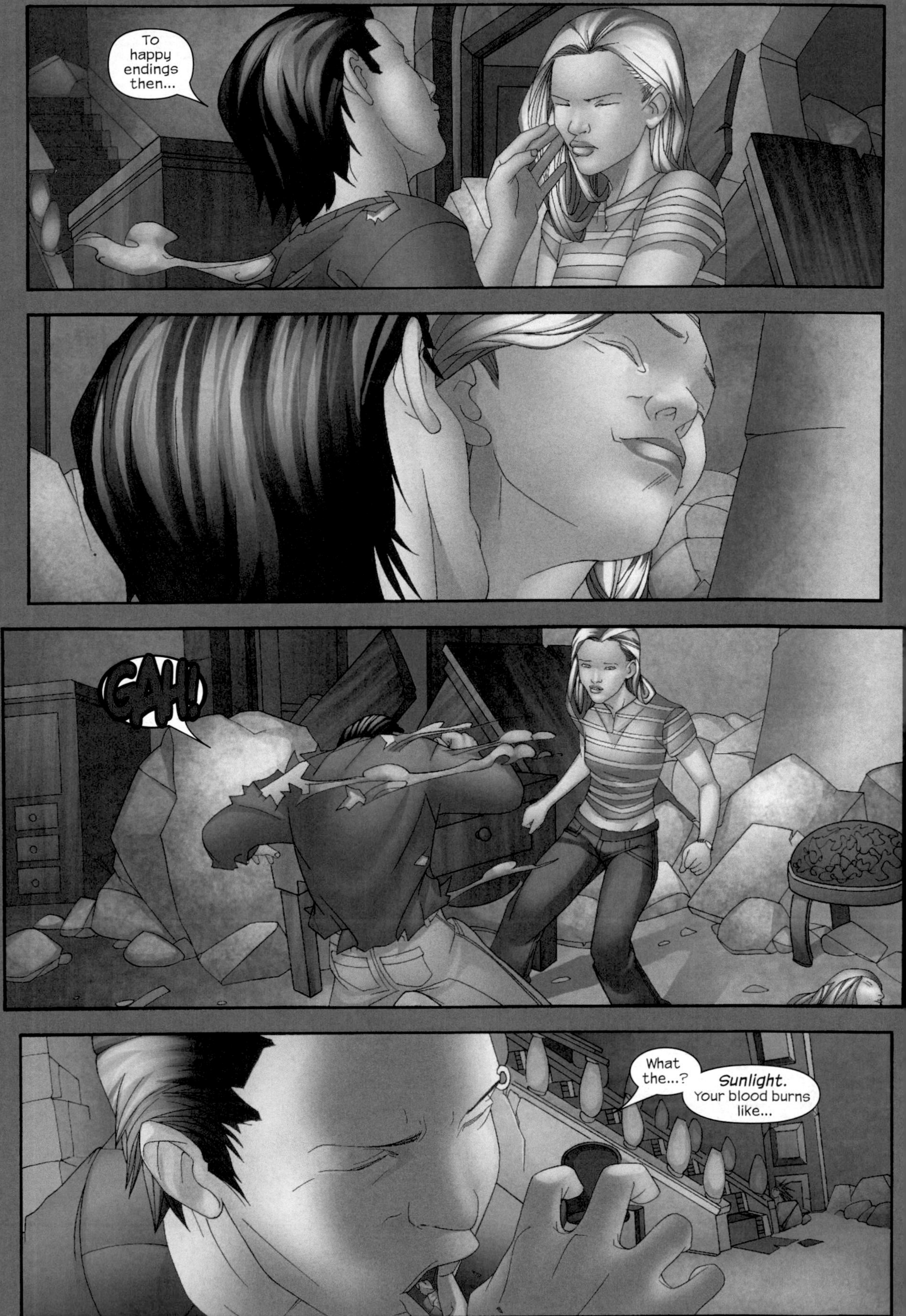
To happy endings then...
GAH!
What the...?
Sunlight. Your blood burns like...

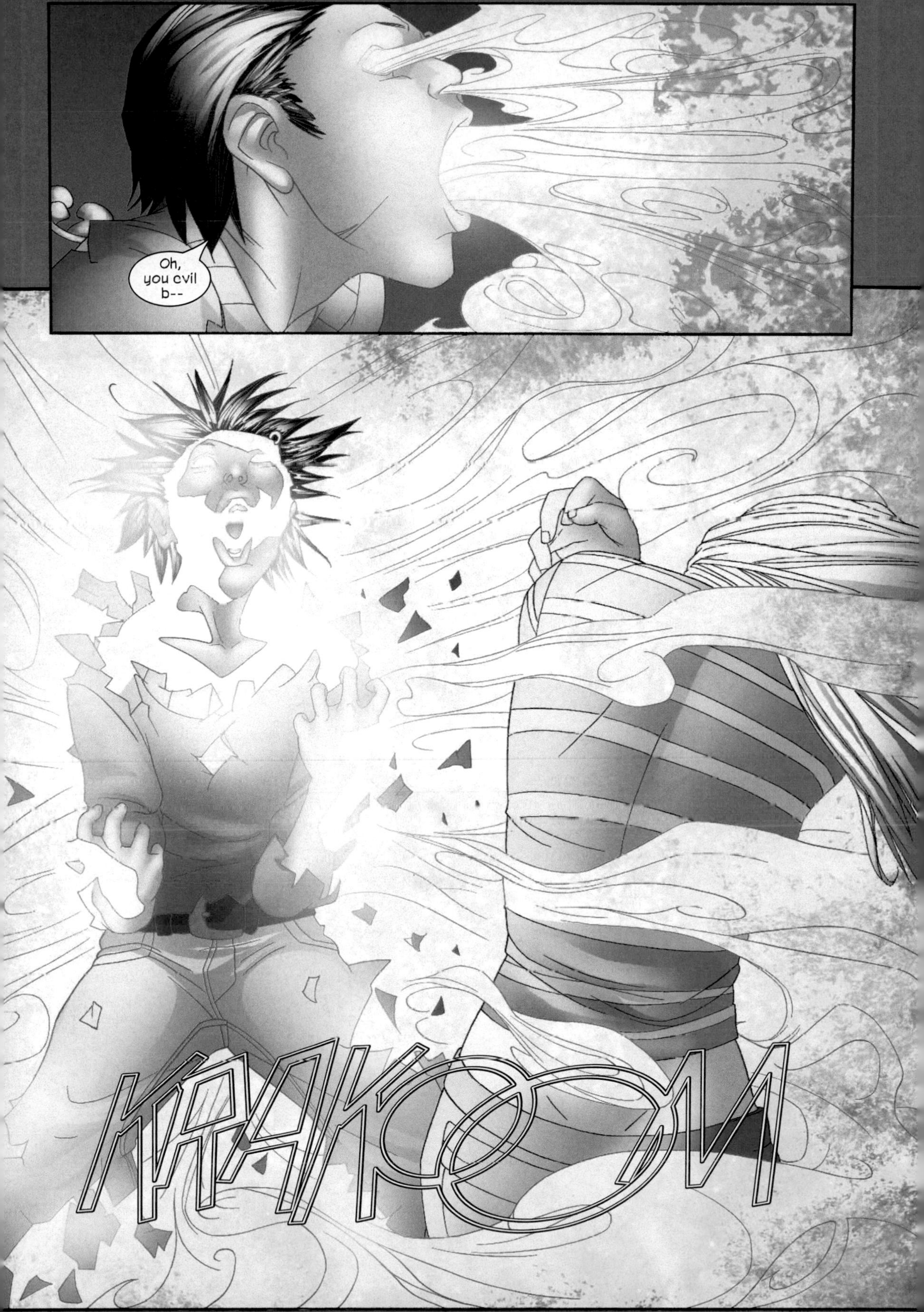
Oh, you evil b--
KRAKOOM

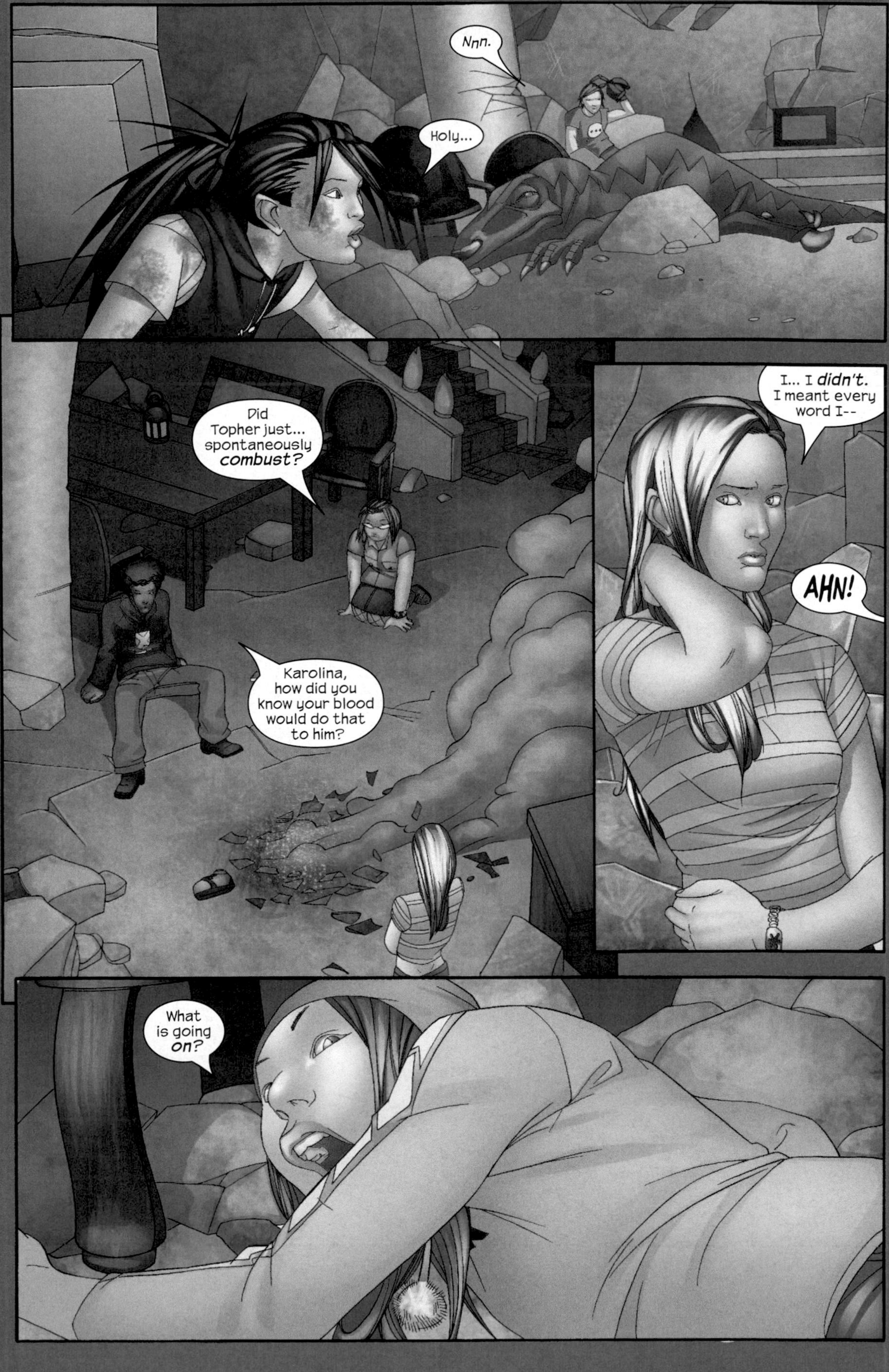
Nnn.
Holy...
Did Topher just... spontaneously *combust?*
Karolina, how did you know your blood would do that to him?
I... I *didn't.* I meant every word I--
AHN!
What is going *on?*

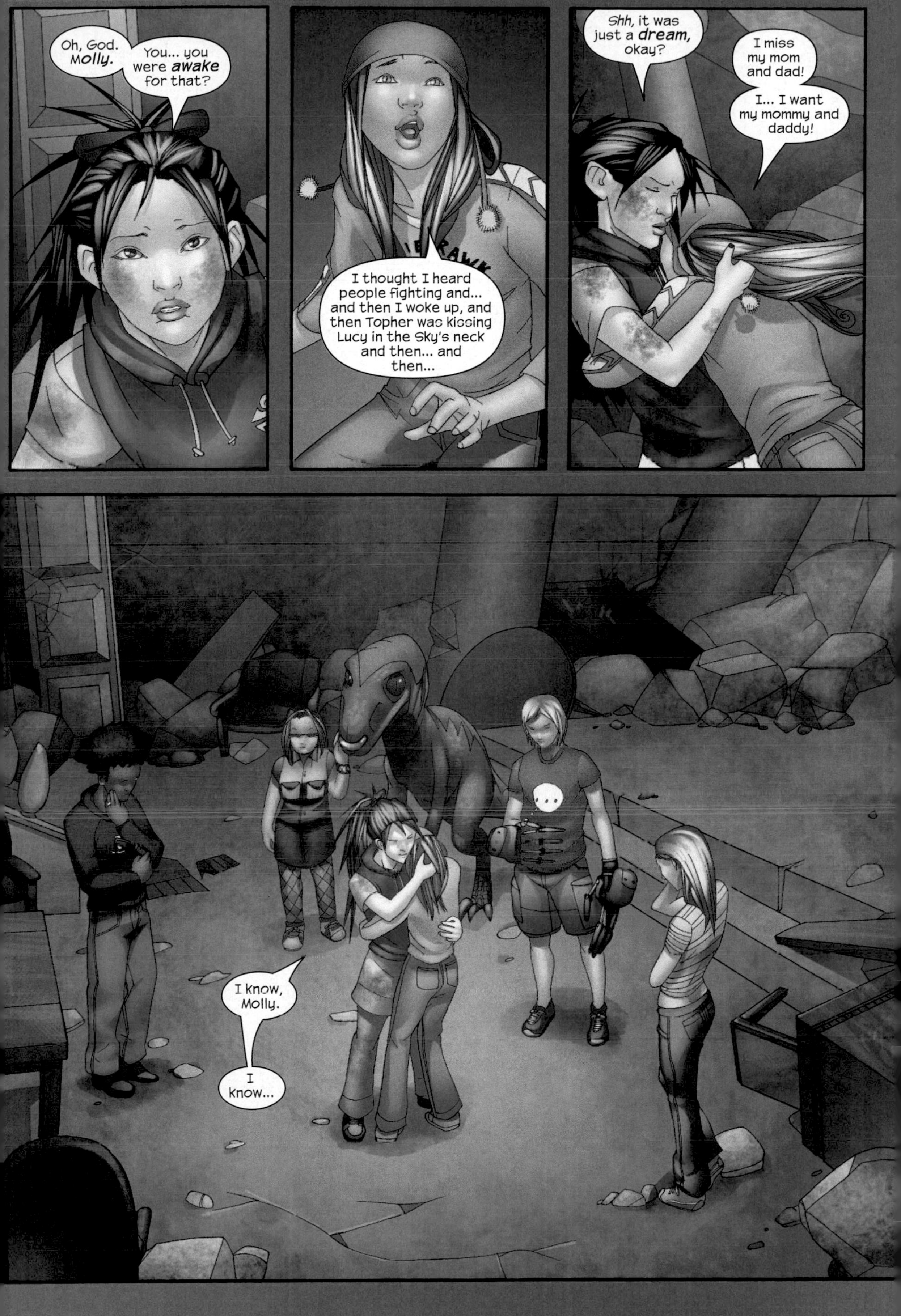
Oh, God. Molly.
You... you were *awake* for that?
I thought I heard people fighting and... and then I woke up, and then Topher was kissing Lucy in the Sky's neck and then... and then...
Shh, it was just a *dream,* okay?
I miss my mom and dad!
I... I want my mommy and daddy!
I know, Molly.
I know...

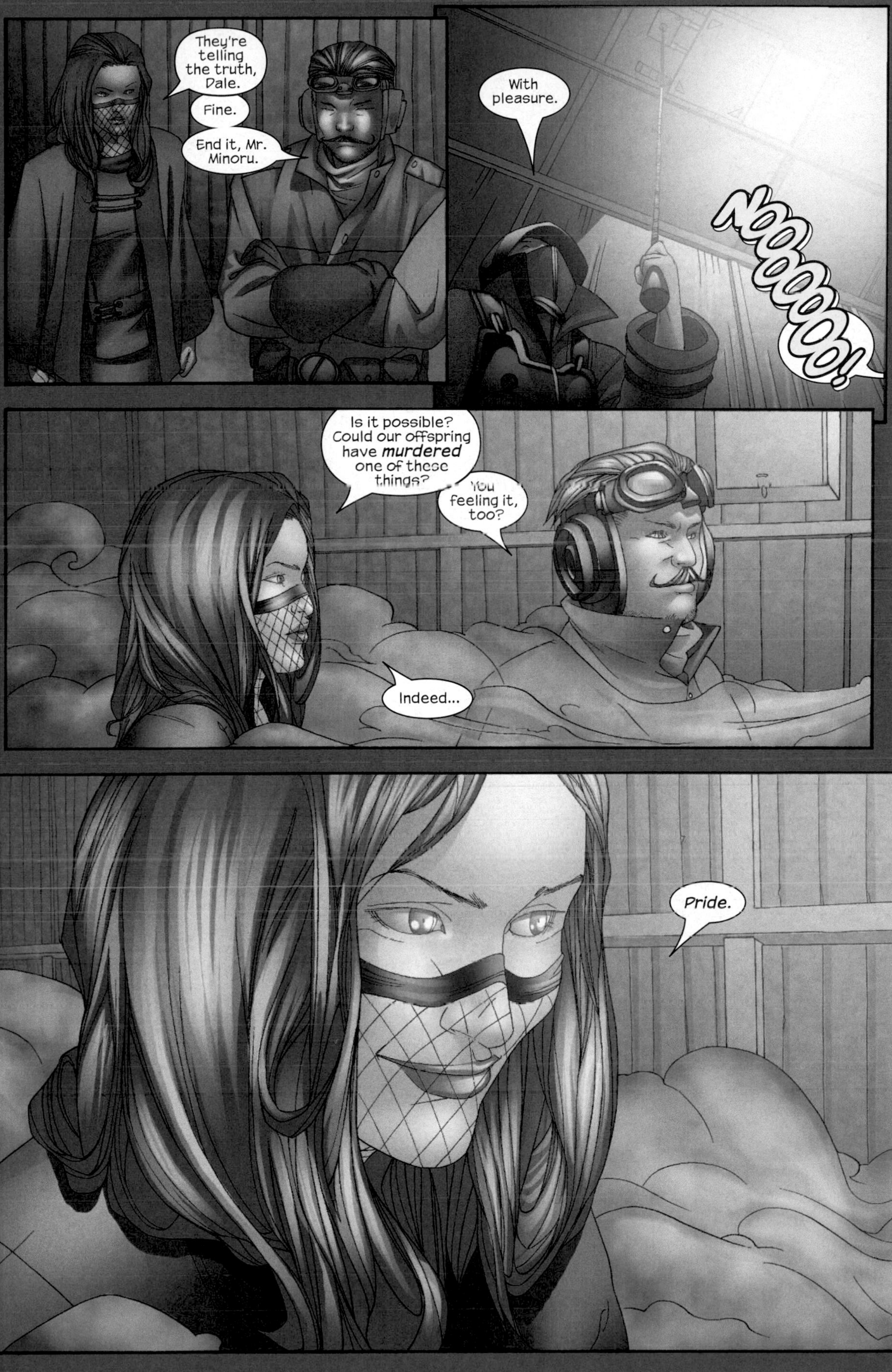
They're telling the truth, Dale.
Fine.
End it, Mr. Minoru.
With pleasure.
NOOOOOOO!
Is it possible? Could our offspring have *murdered* one of these things?
You feeling it, too?
Indeed...
Pride.

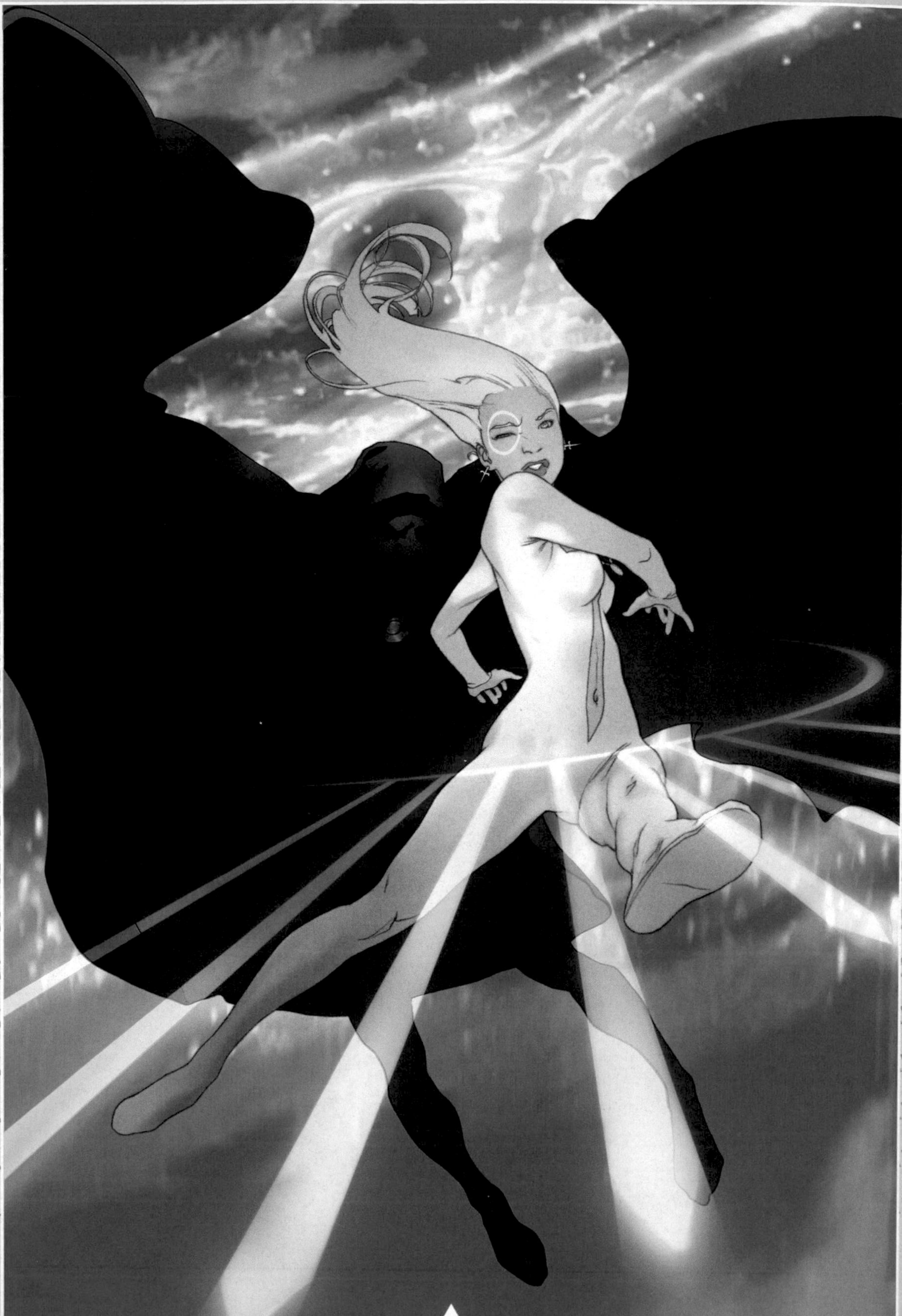

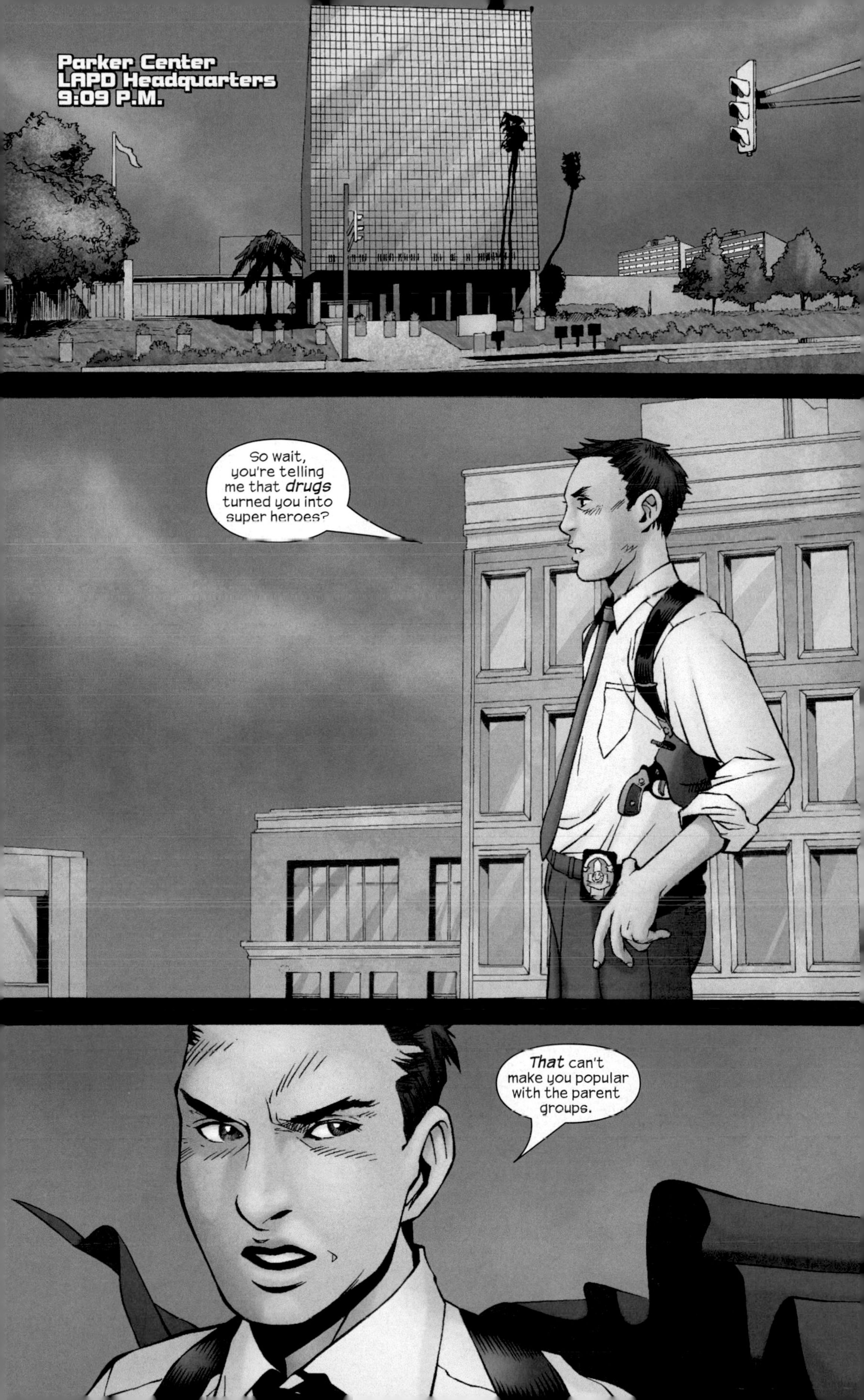
Parker Center
LAPD Headquarters
9:09 P.M.
So wait, you're telling me that drugs turned you into super heroes?
That can't make you popular with the parent groups.

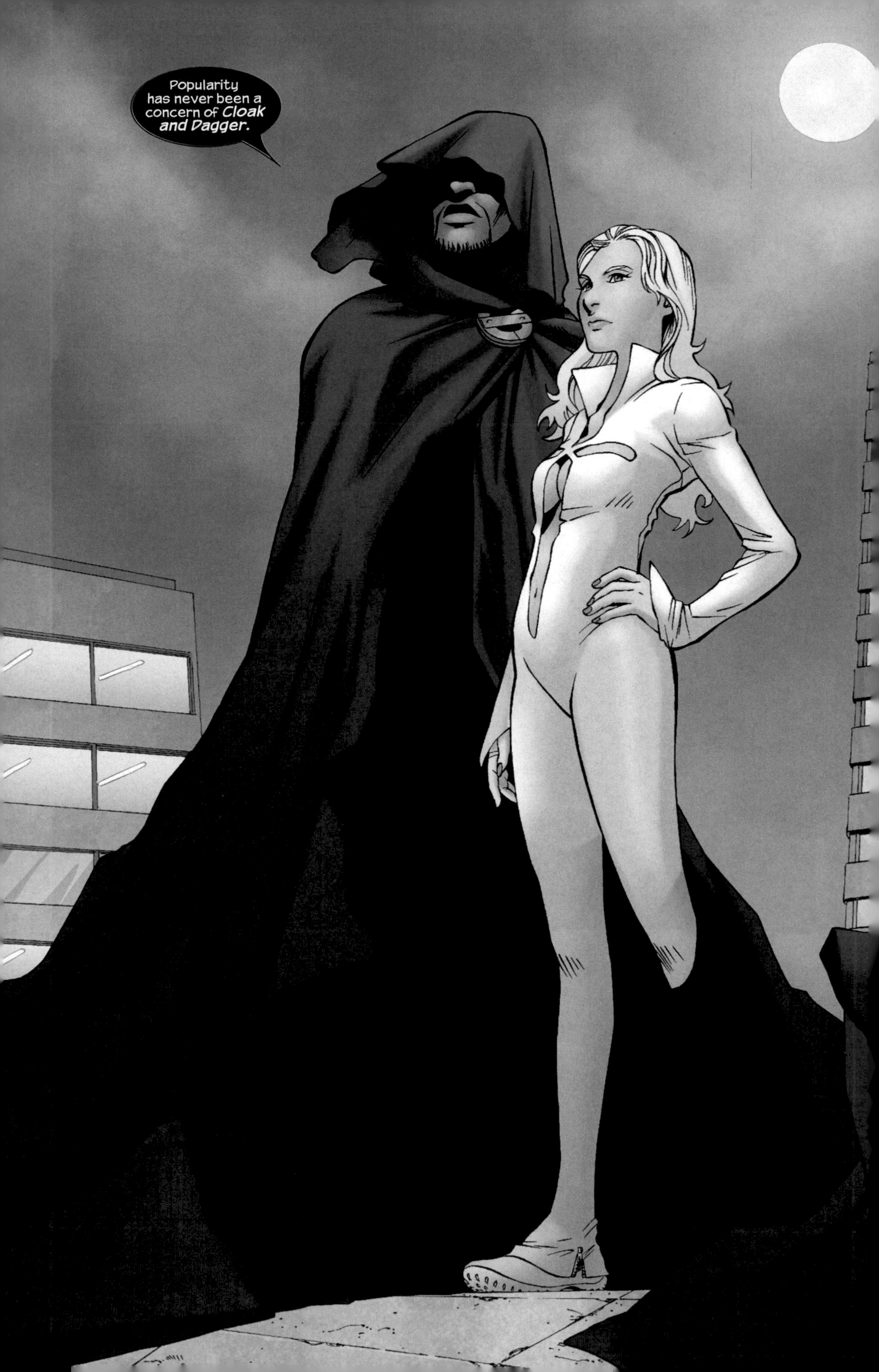
Popularity has never been a concern of *Cloak and Dagger.*

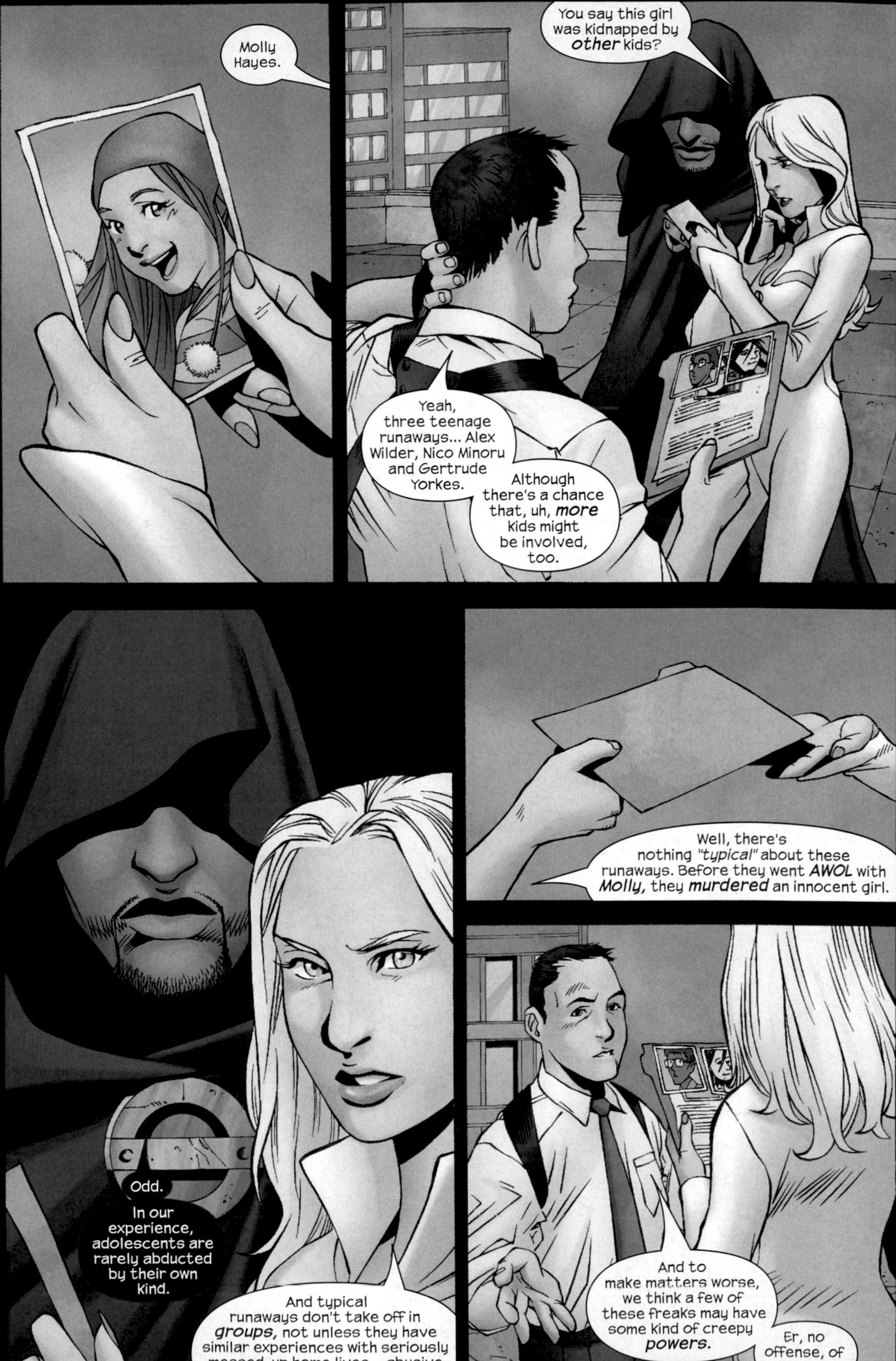

Molly Hayes.
You say this girl was kidnapped by *other* kids?
Yeah, three teenage runaways... Alex Wilder, Nico Minoru and Gertrude Yorkes.
Although there's a chance that, uh, *more* kids might be involved, too.
Odd.
In our experience, adolescents are rarely abducted by their own kind.
And typical runaways don't take off in *groups,* not unless they have similar experiences with seriously messed-up home lives... abusive parents and stuff like that.
Well, there's nothing *"typical"* about these runaways. Before they went *AWOL* with *Molly,* they *murdered* an innocent girl.
And to make matters worse, we think a few of these freaks may have some kind of creepy *powers.*
Er, no offense, of course...

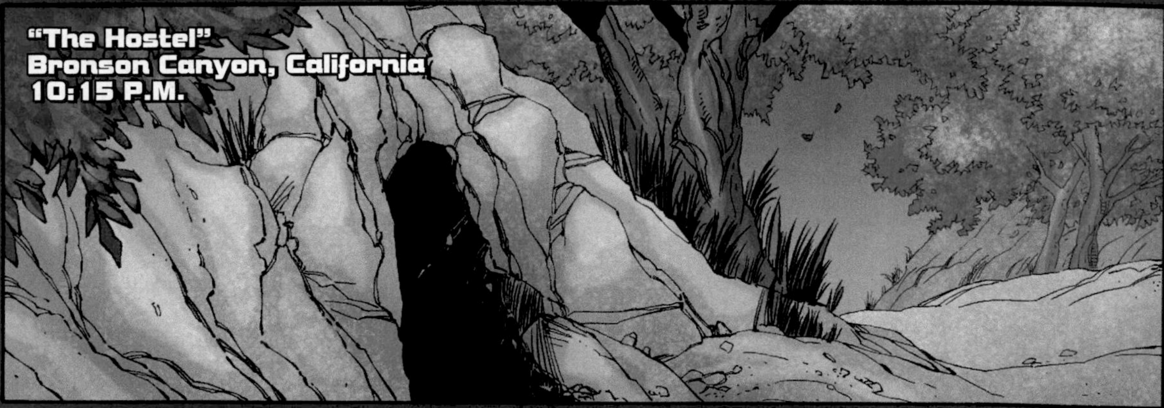
"The Hostel"
Bronson Canyon, California
10:15 P.M.

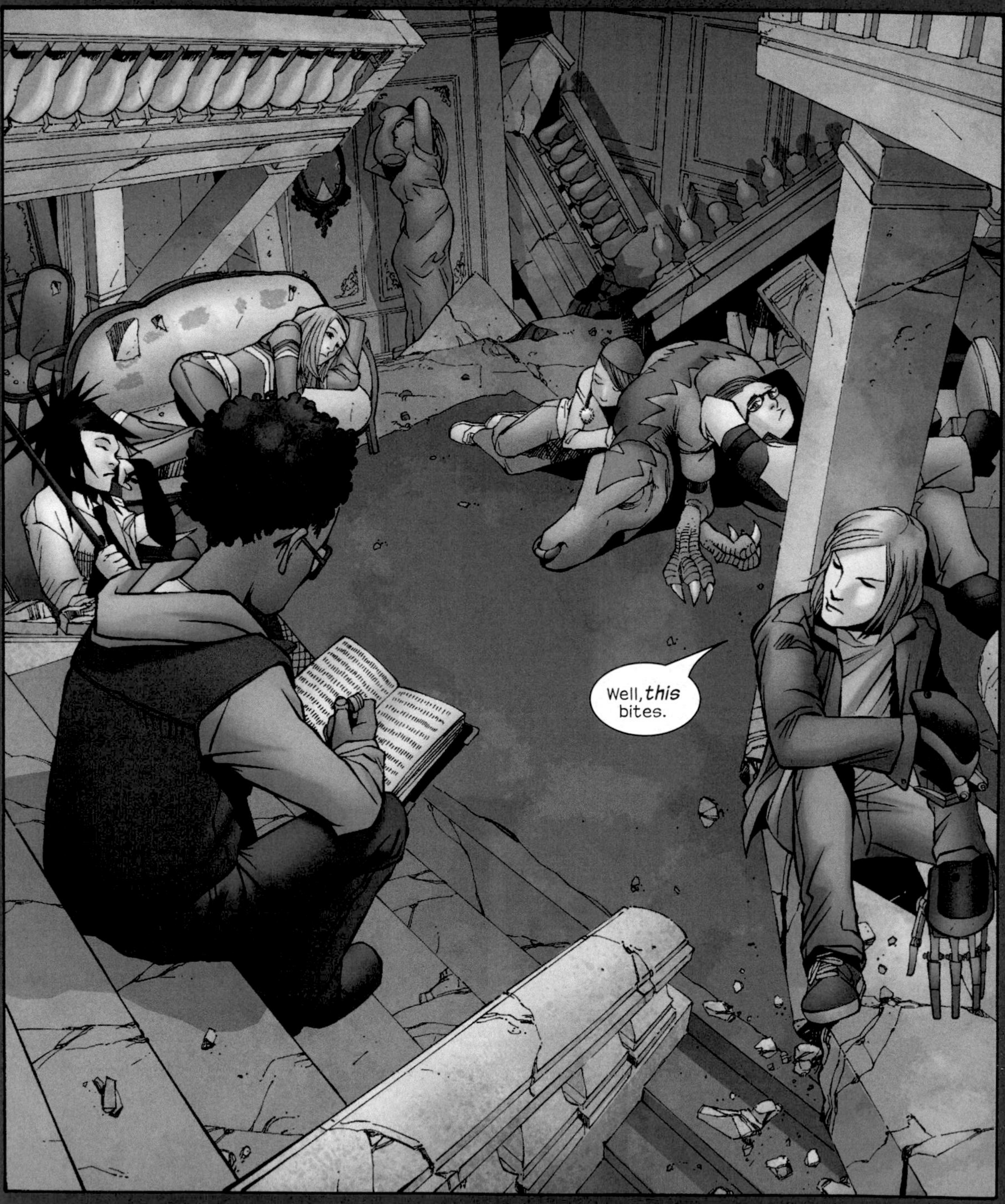
Well, *this* bites.

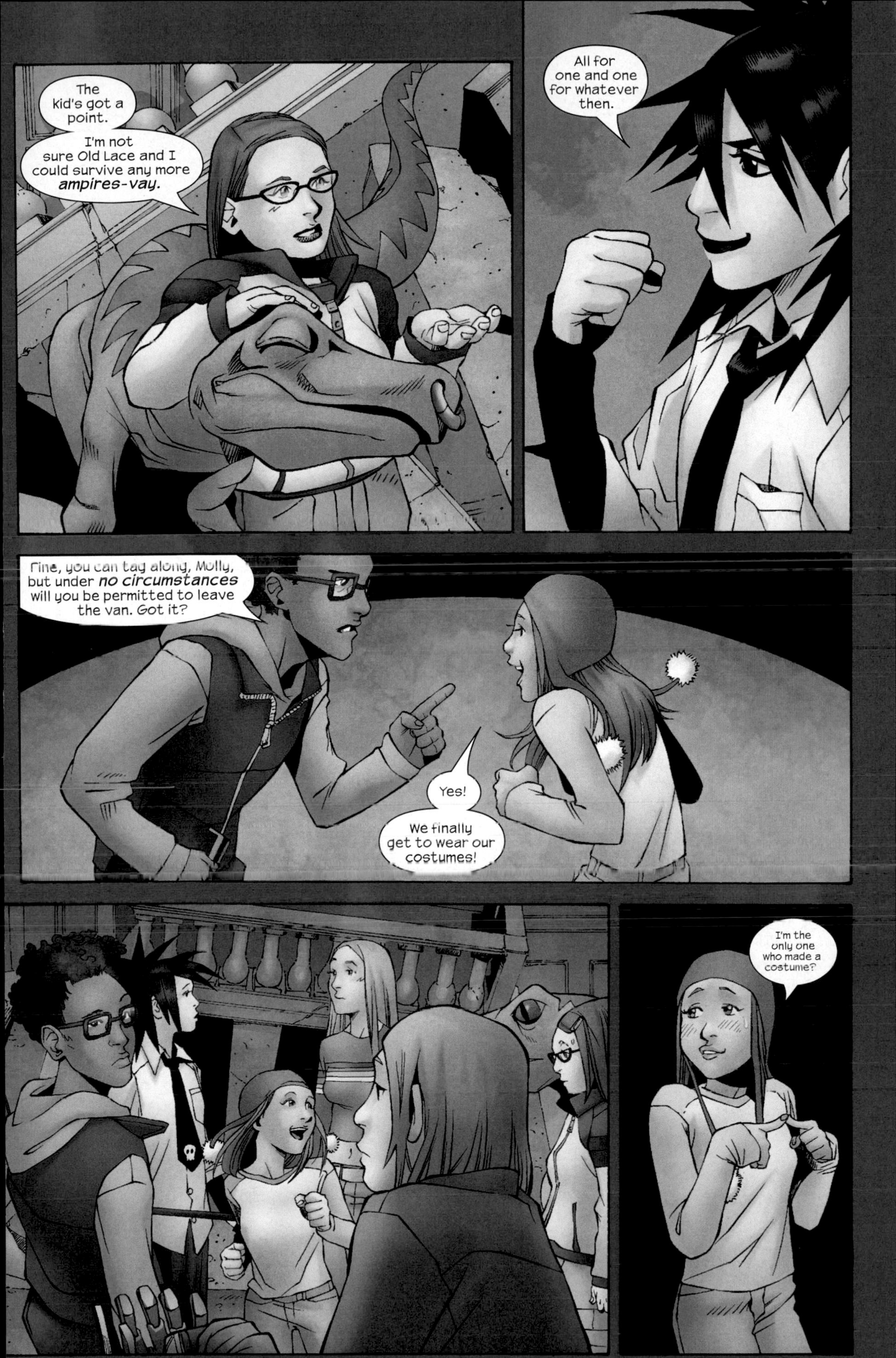
The kid's got a point.
I'm not sure Old Lace and I could survive any more *ampires-vay.*
All for one and one for whatever then.
Fine, you can tag along, Molly, but under *no circumstances* will you be permitted to leave the van. Got it?
Yes!
We finally get to wear our costumes!
I'm the only one who made a costume?

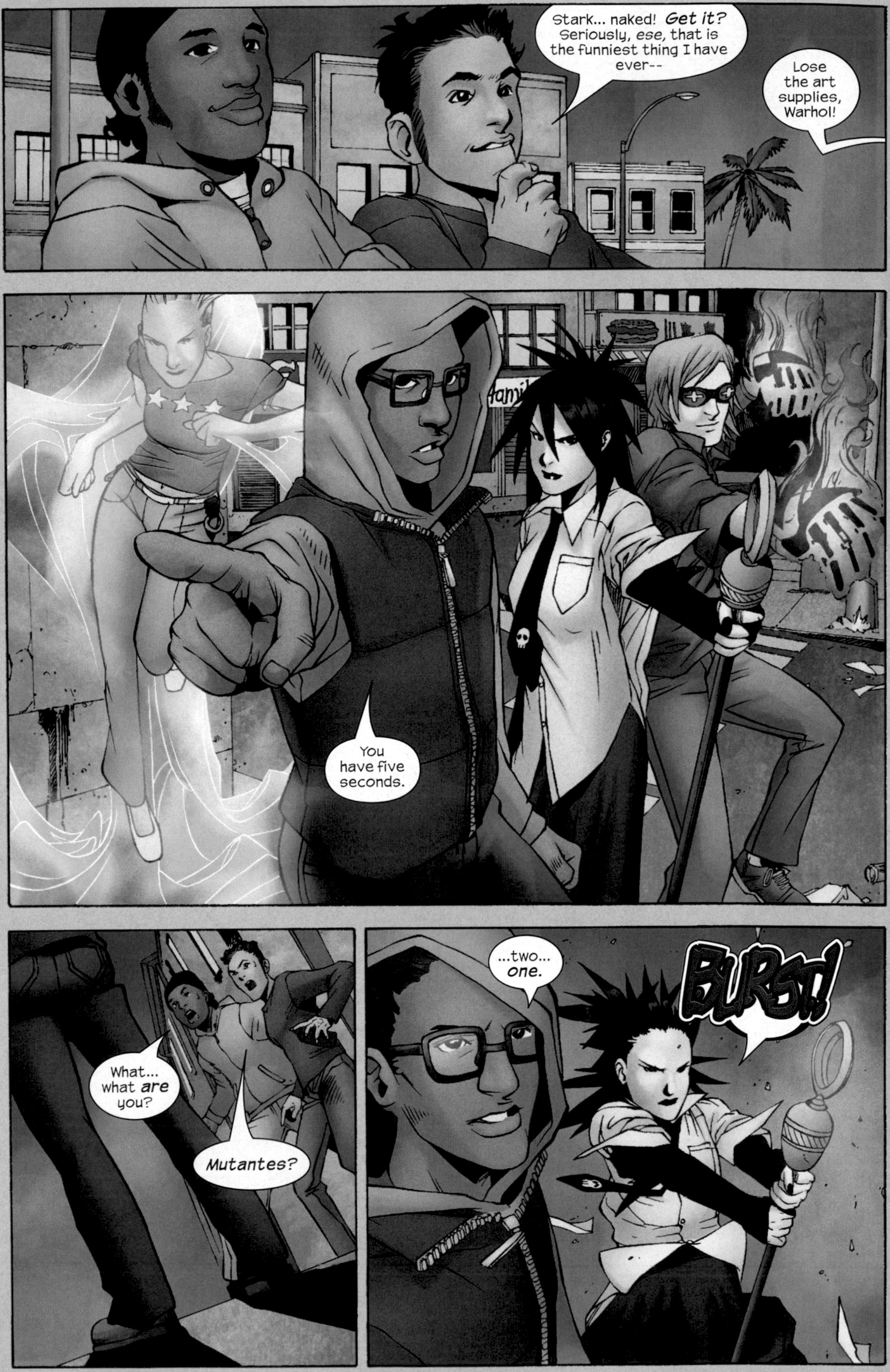

Stark... naked! *Get it?* Seriously, *ese,* that is the funniest thing I have ever--
Lose the art supplies, Warhol!
You have five seconds.
What... what *are* you?
Mutantes?
...two... *one.*
BURST!

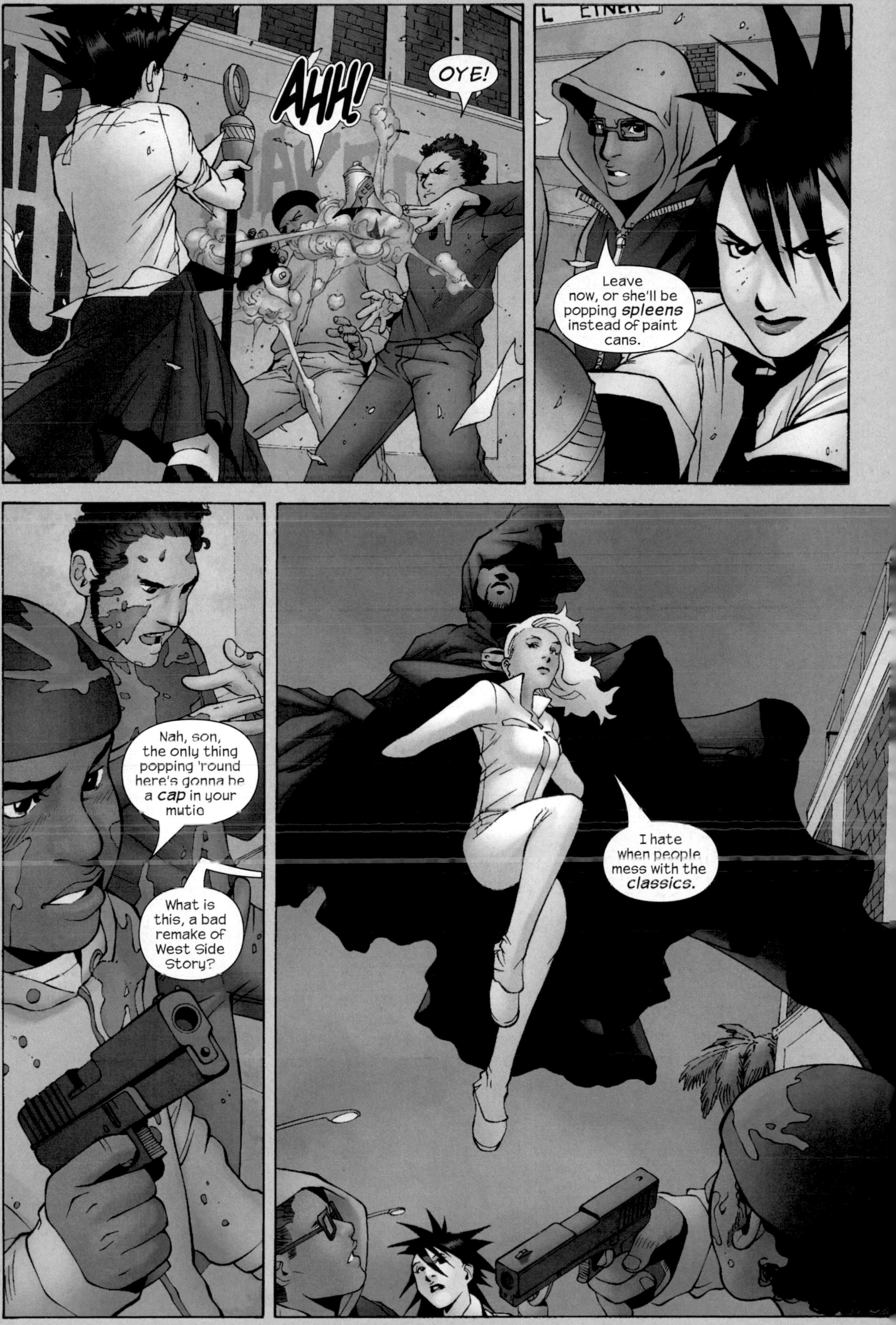
AHH!
OYE!
Leave now, or she'll be popping spleens instead of paint cans.
Nah, son, the only thing popping 'round here's gonna be a cap in your mutie
What is this, a bad remake of West Side Story?
I hate when people mess with the classics.

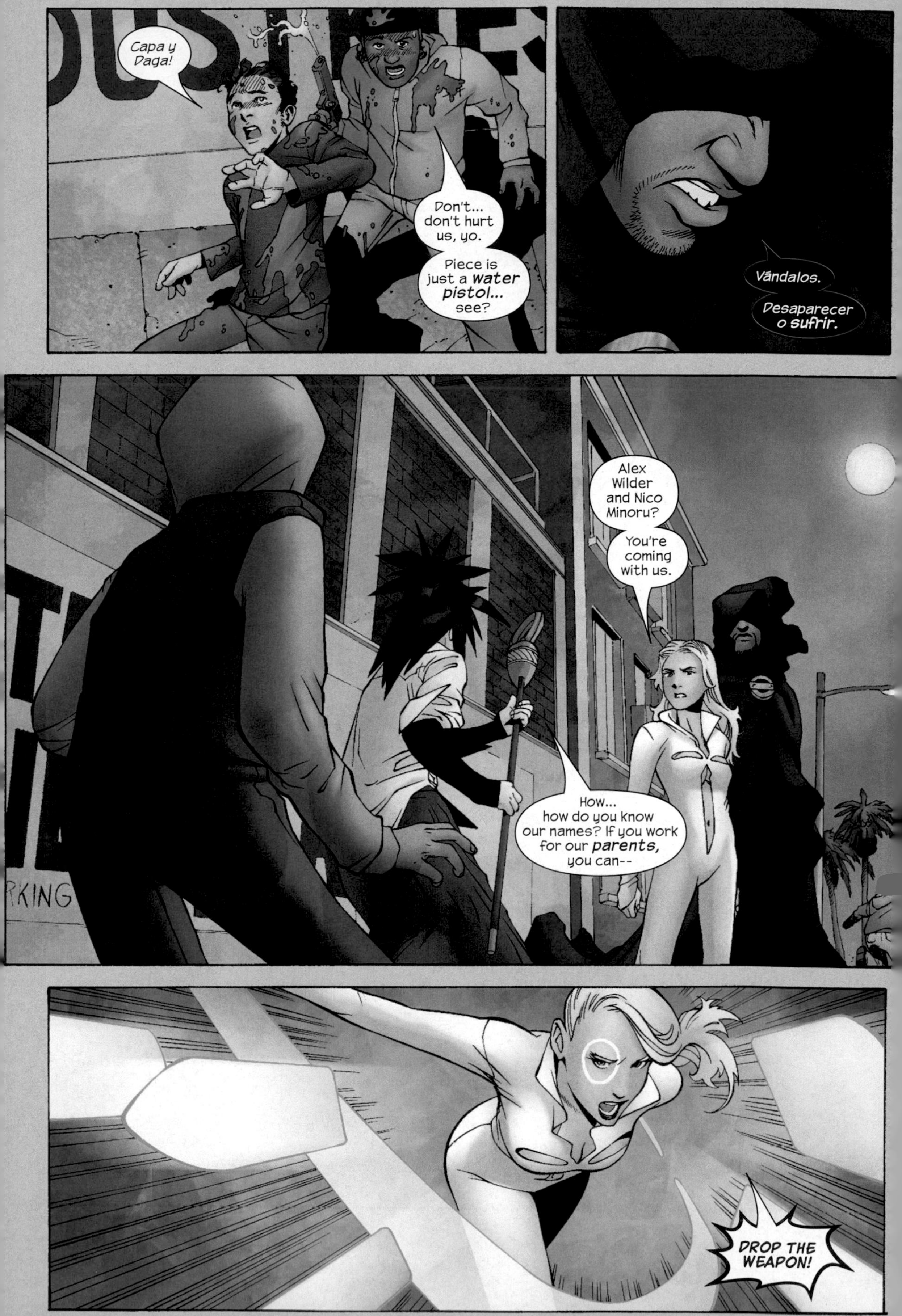

Capa y Daga!
Don't... don't hurt us, yo.
Piece is just a water pistol... see?
Vándalos.
Desaparecer o sufrir.
Alex Wilder and Nico Minoru?
You're coming with us.
How... how do you know our names? If you work for our parents, you can--
DROP THE WEAPON!

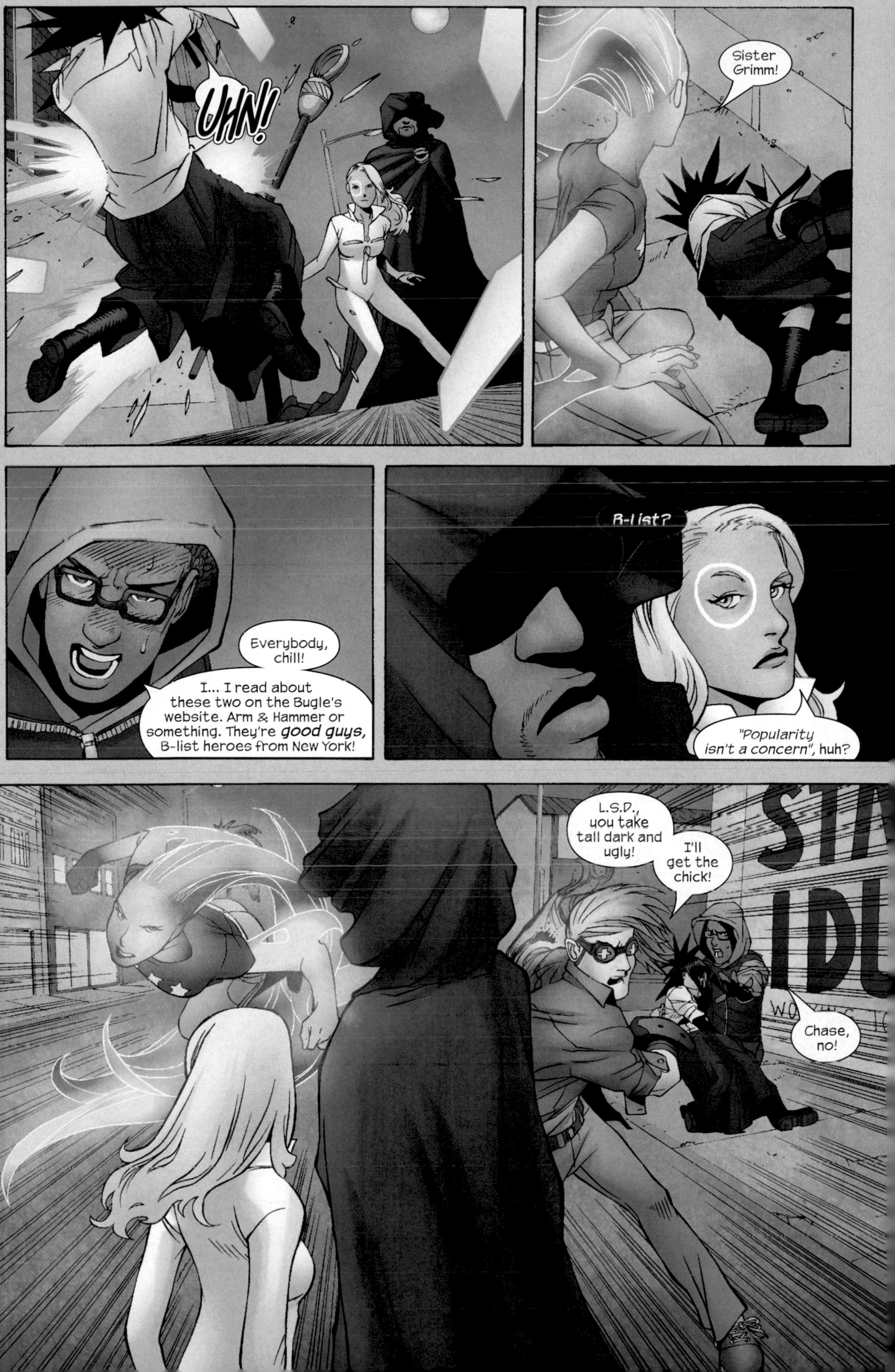
UHN!
Sister Grimm!
Everybody, chill!
I... I read about these two on the Bugle's website. Arm & Hammer or something. They're good guys, B-list heroes from New York!
B-list?
"Popularity isn't a concern", huh?
L.S.D., you take tall dark and ugly!
I'll get the chick!
Chase, no!

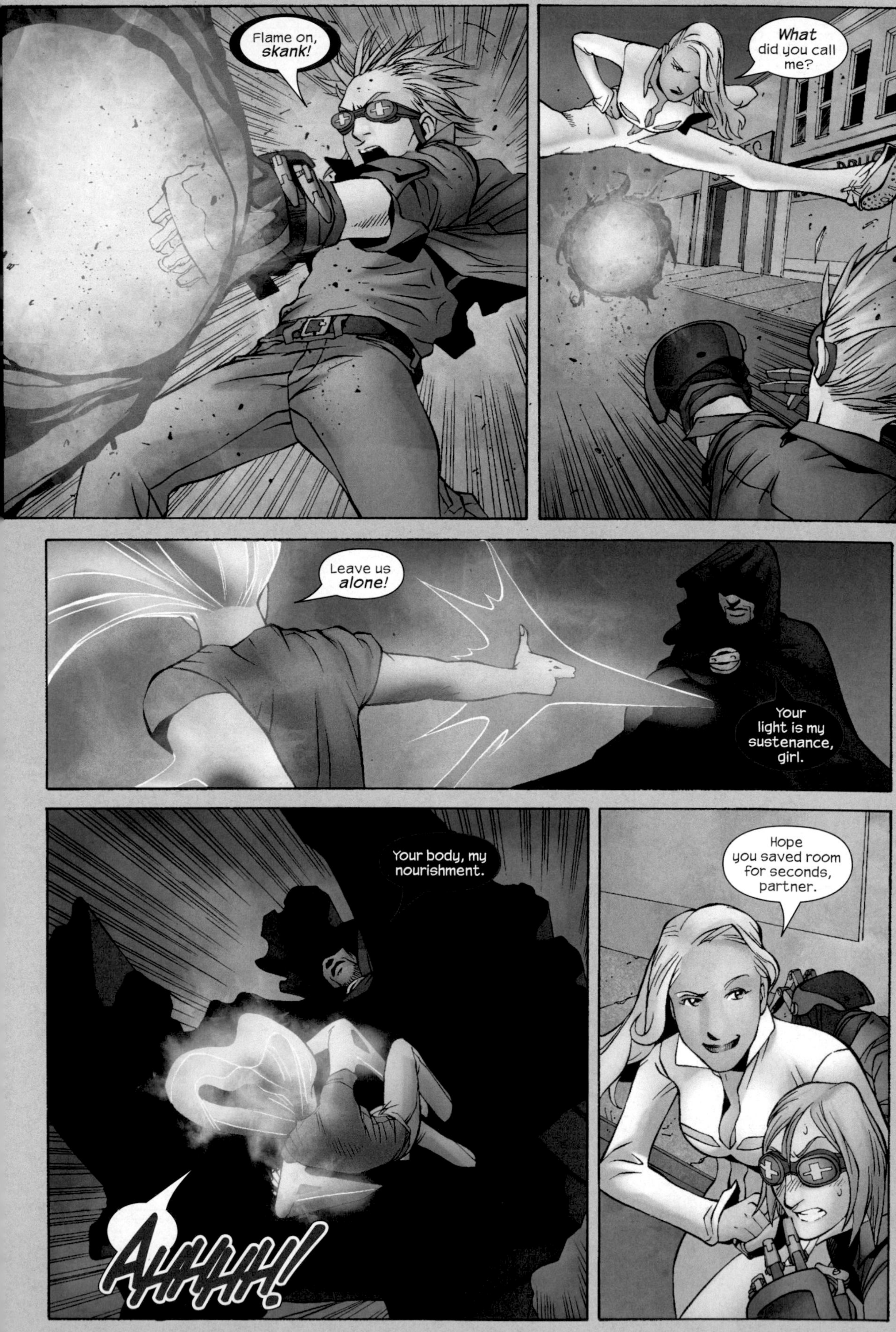

Flame on, skank!
What did you call me?
Leave us alone!
Your light is my sustenance, girl.
Your body, my nourishment.
AHHHH!
Hope you saved room for seconds, partner.

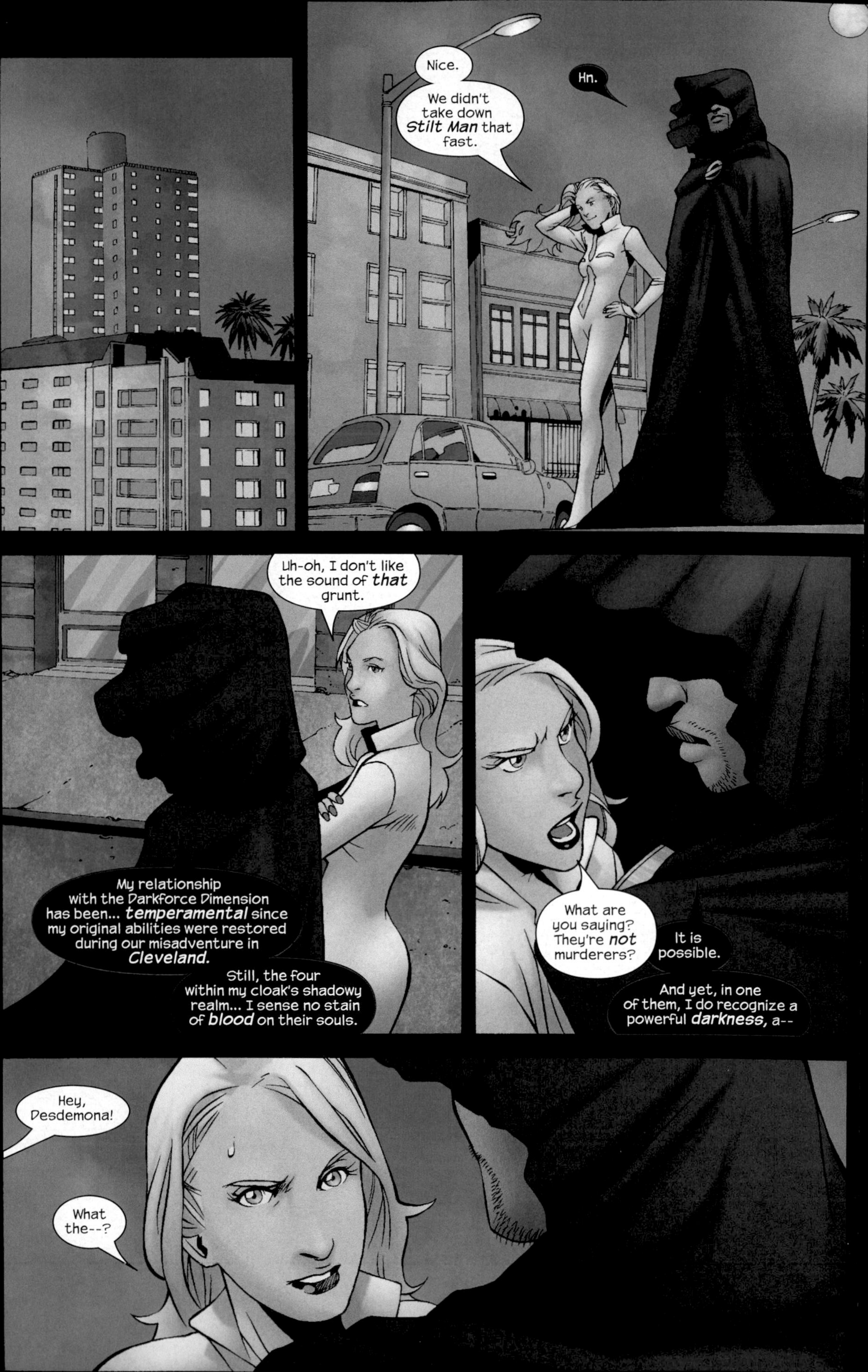
Nice.
We didn't take down *Stilt Man* that fast.
Hn.
Uh-oh, I don't like the sound of *that* grunt.
My relationship with the Darkforce Dimension has been... *temperamental* since my original abilities were restored during our misadventure in *Cleveland.*
Still, the four within my cloak's shadowy realm... I sense no stain of *blood* on their souls.
What are you saying? They're *not* murderers?
It is possible.
And yet, in one of them, I do recognize a powerful *darkness,* a--
Hey, Desdemona!
What the--?

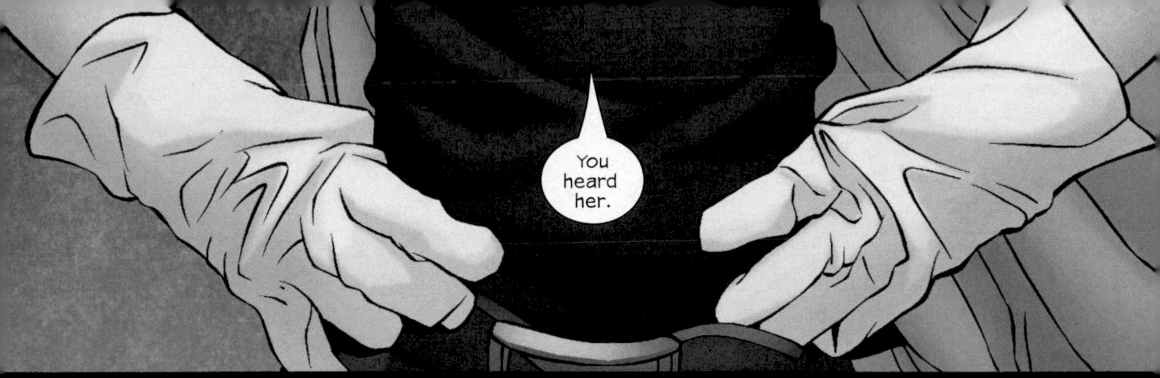
You heard her.

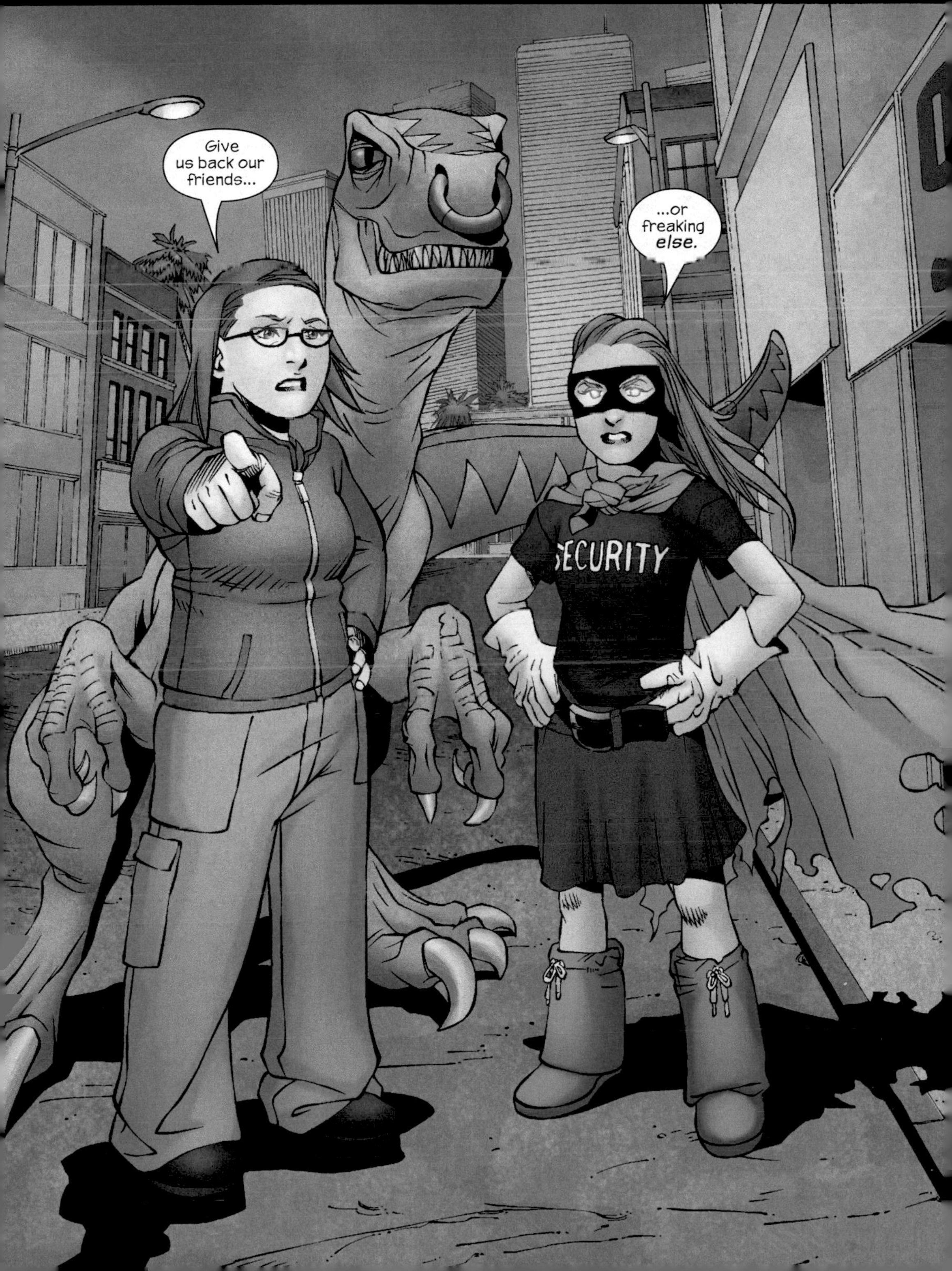
Give us back our friends...
...or freaking *else.*
SECURITY

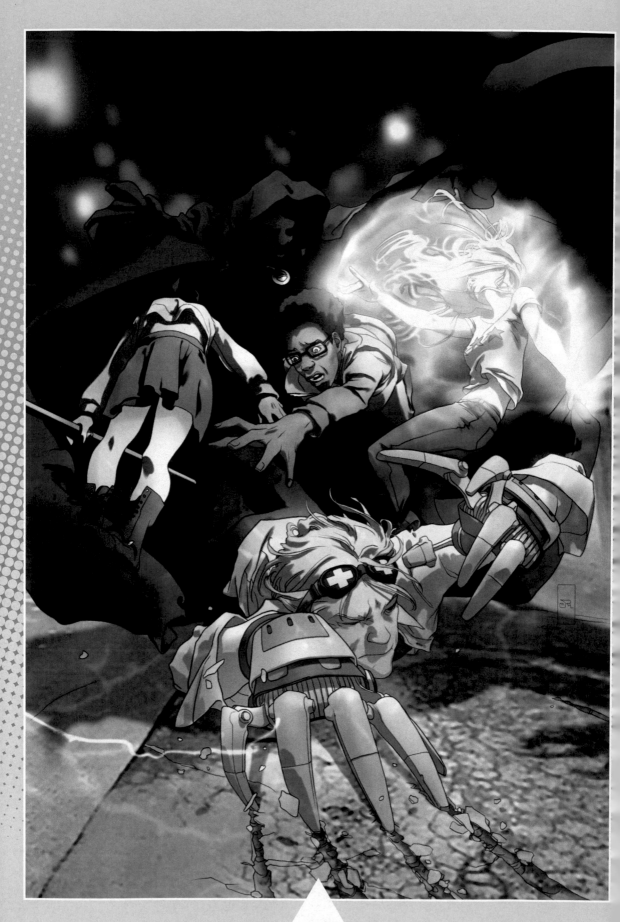

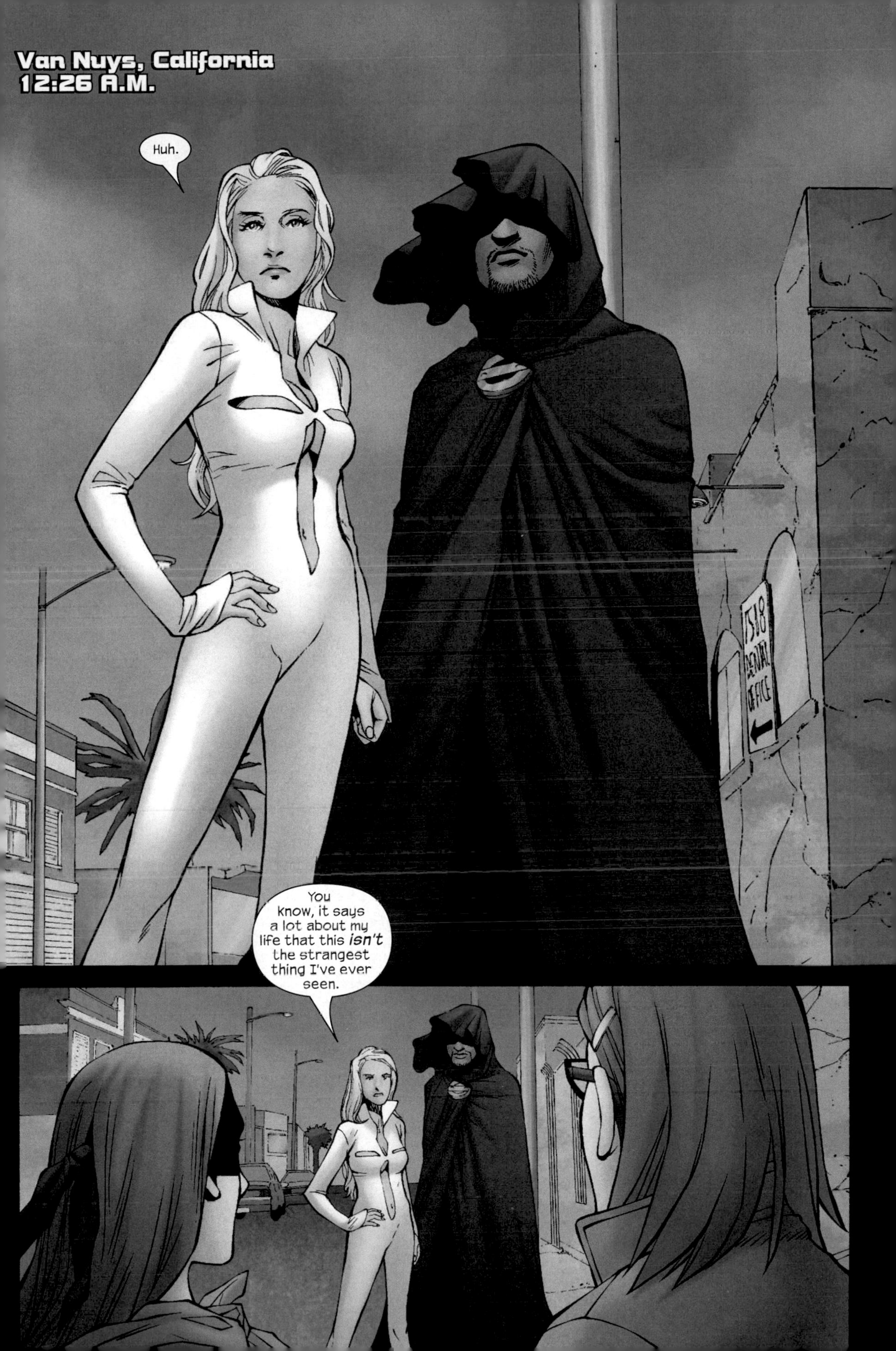
Van Nuys, California
12:26 A.M.
Huh.
You know, it says a lot about my life that this *isn't* the strangest thing I've ever seen.

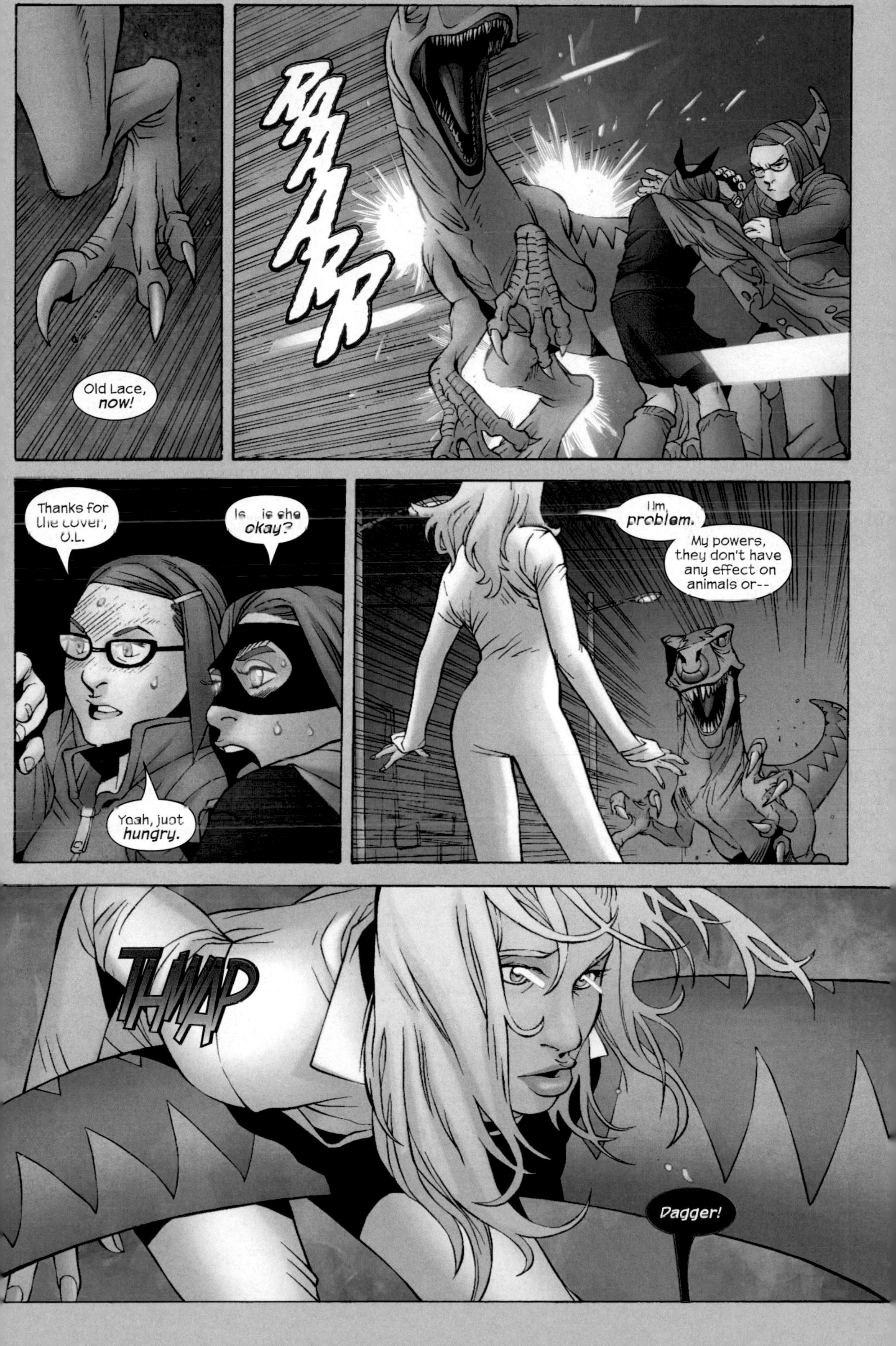
Old Lace, now!
RAAARR
Thanks for the cover, O.L.
Is... is she okay?
Yeah, just hungry.
Um, problem.
My powers, they don't have any effect on animals or--
THWAP
Dagger!

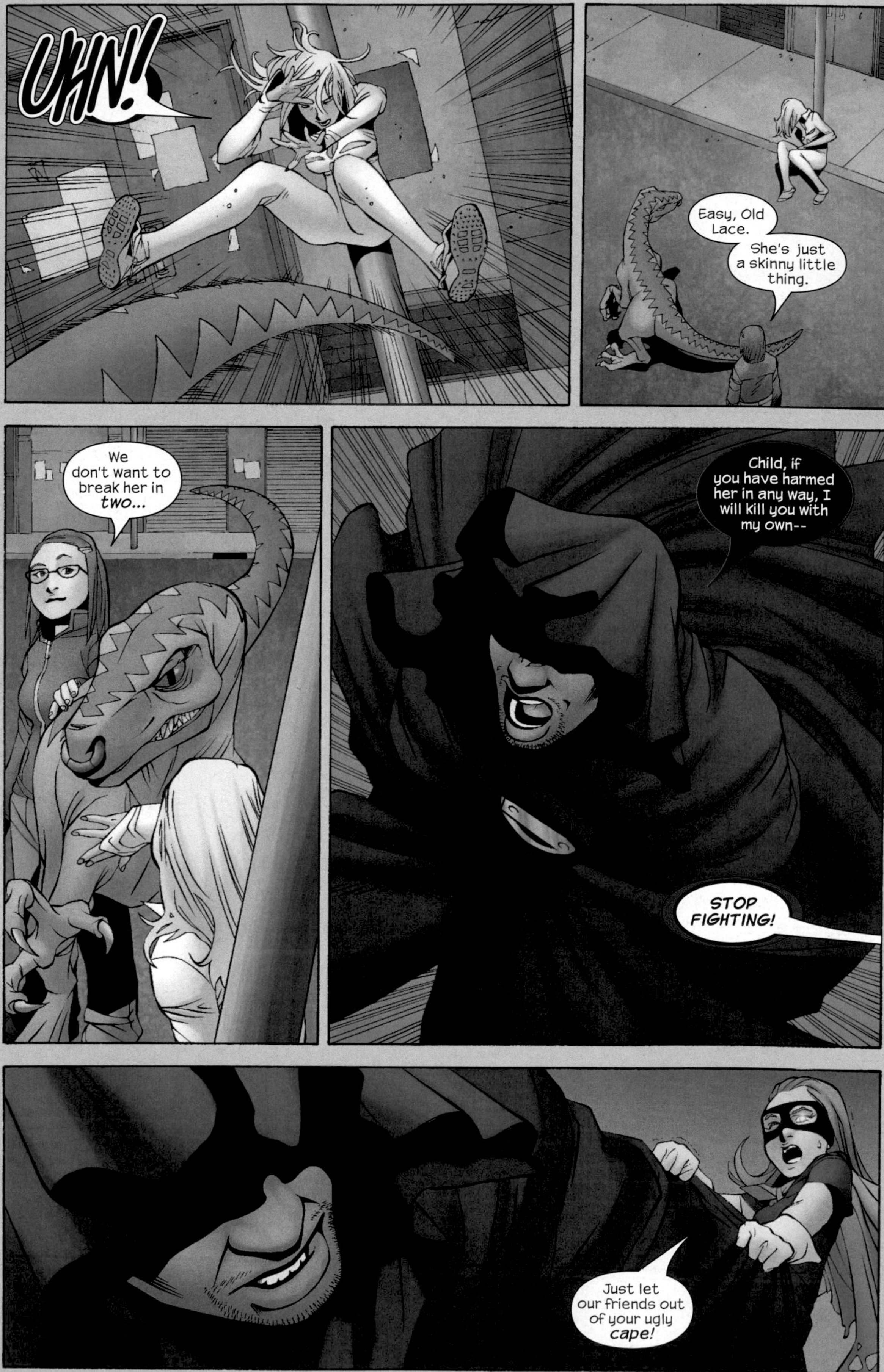
UHN!
Easy, Old Lace.
She's just a skinny little thing.
We don't want to break her in two...
Child, if you have harmed her in any way, I will kill you with my own--
STOP FIGHTING!
Just let our friends out of your ugly cape!

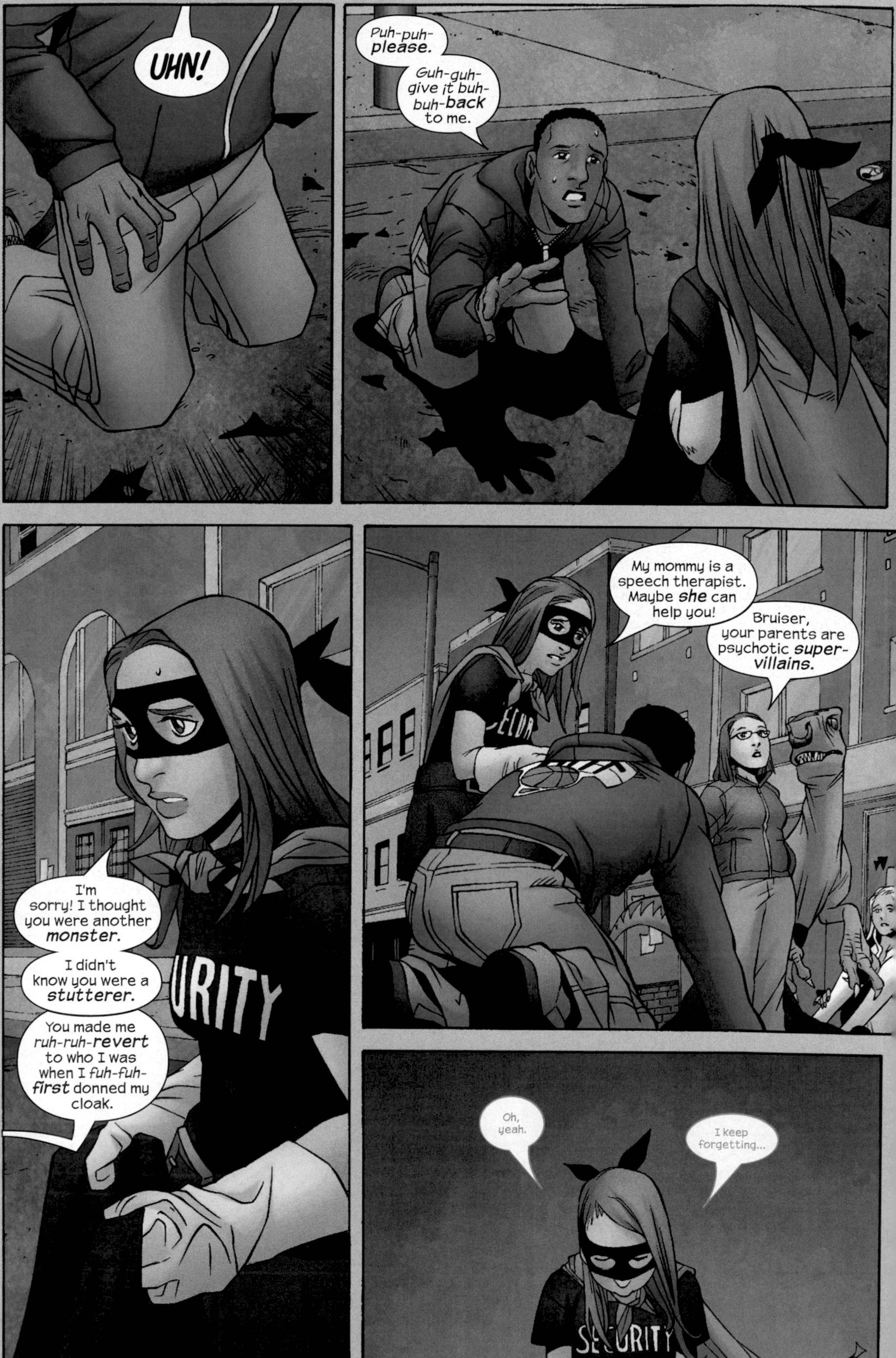
UHN!
Puh-puh-please.
Guh-guh-give it buh-buh-back to me.
I'm sorry! I thought you were another monster.
I didn't know you were a stutterer.
You made me ruh-ruh-revert to who I was when I fuh-fuh-first donned my cloak.
My mommy is a speech therapist. Maybe she can help you!
Bruiser, your parents are psychotic super-villains.
Oh, yeah.
I keep forgetting...

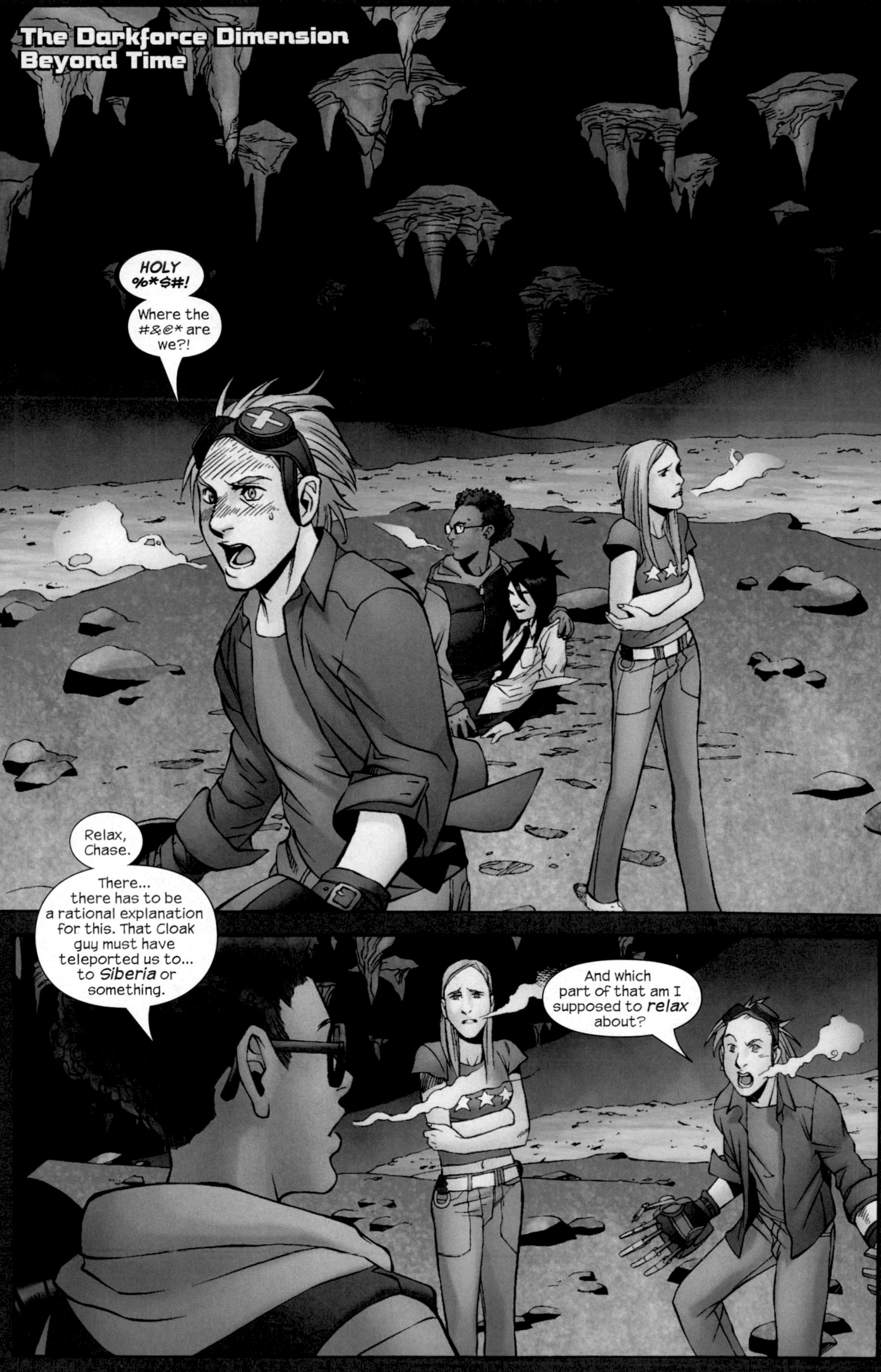

The Darkforce Dimension Beyond Time
HOLY %*$#!
Where the #&@* are we?!
Relax, Chase.
There... there has to be a rational explanation for this. That Cloak guy must have teleported us to... to Siberia or something.
And which part of that am I supposed to relax about?

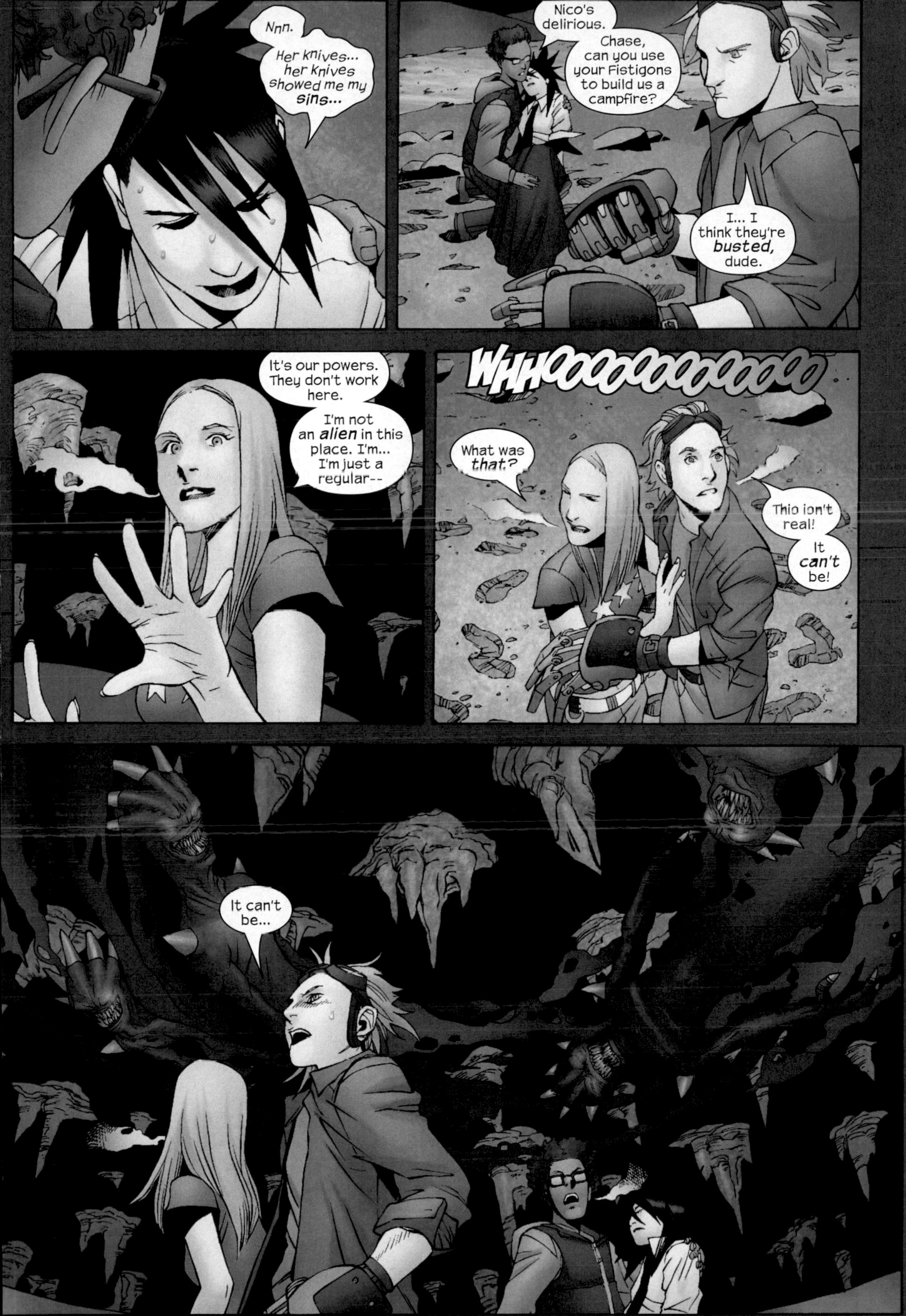
Nnn.
Her knives... her knives showed me my sins...
Nico's delirious.
Chase, can you use your Fistigons to build us a campfire?
I... I think they're busted, dude.
It's our powers. They don't work here.
I'm not an alien in this place. I'm... I'm just a regular--
WHHOOOOOOOOOOOOOO
What was that?
Thio ion't real!
It can't be!
It can't be...

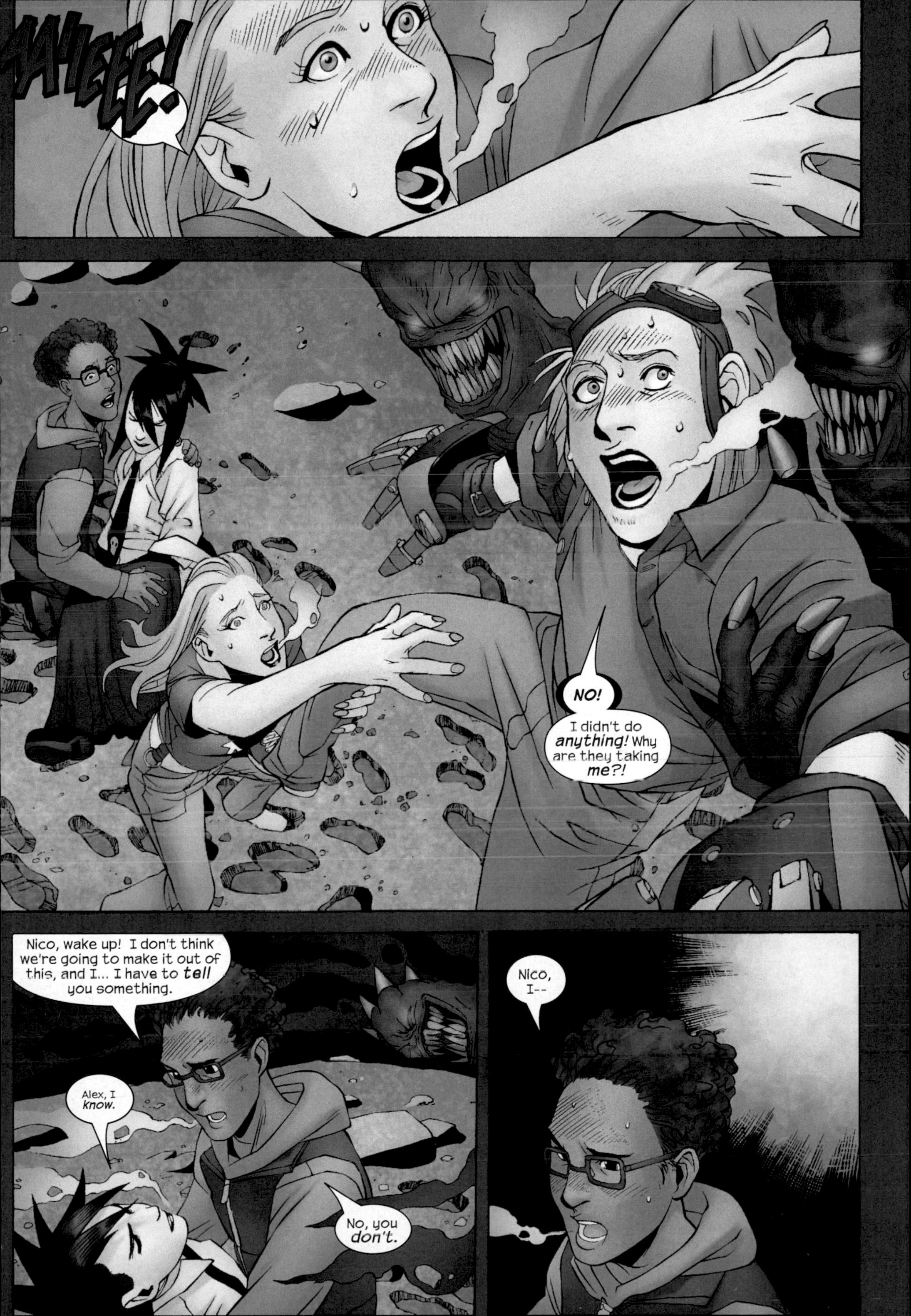
AAHEEE!
NO!
I didn't do *anything!* Why are they taking *me?!*
Nico, wake up! I don't think we're going to make it out of this, and I... I have to *tell* you something.
Alex, I *know.*
No, you *don't.*
Nico, I--

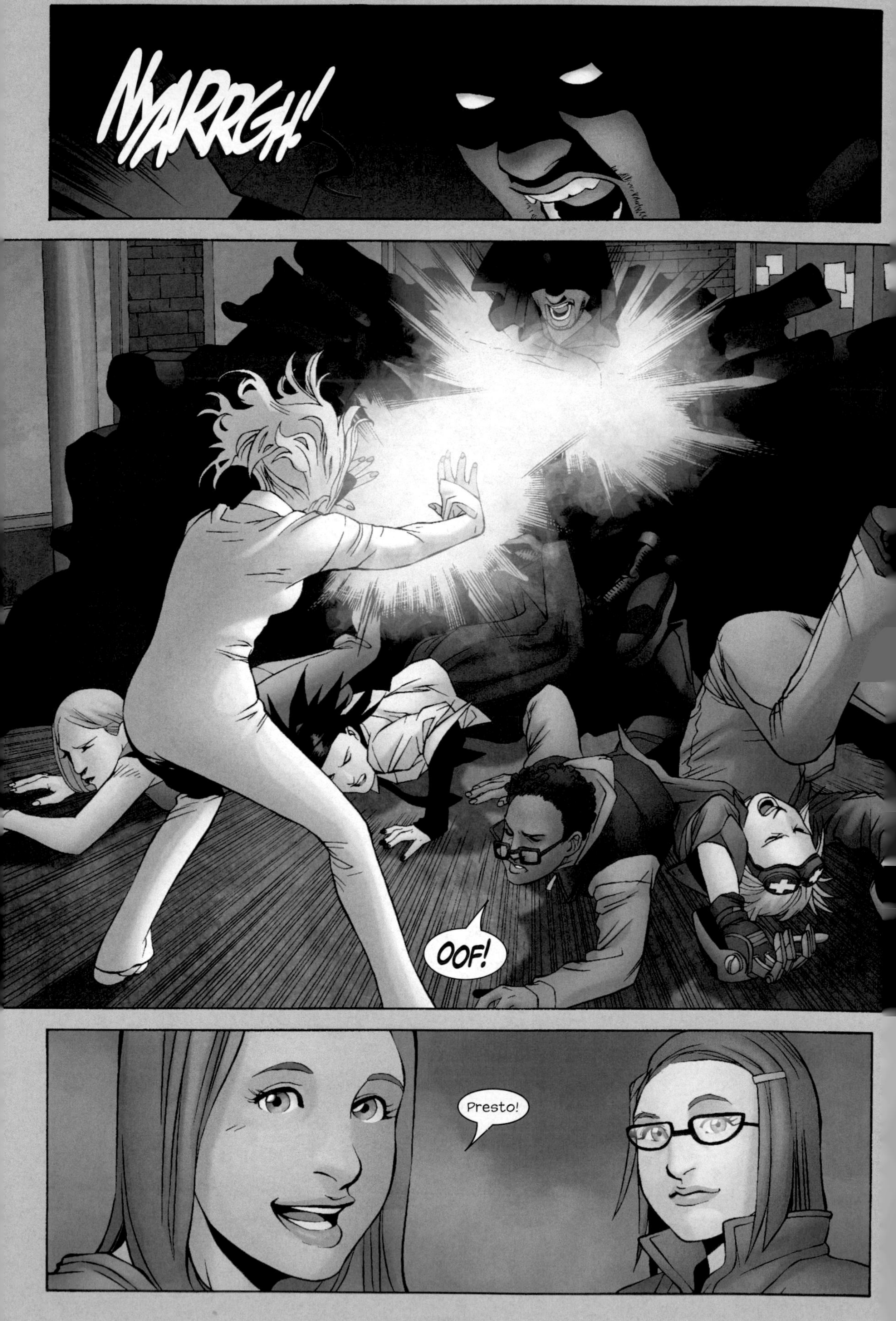
NYARRGH!
OOF!
Presto!

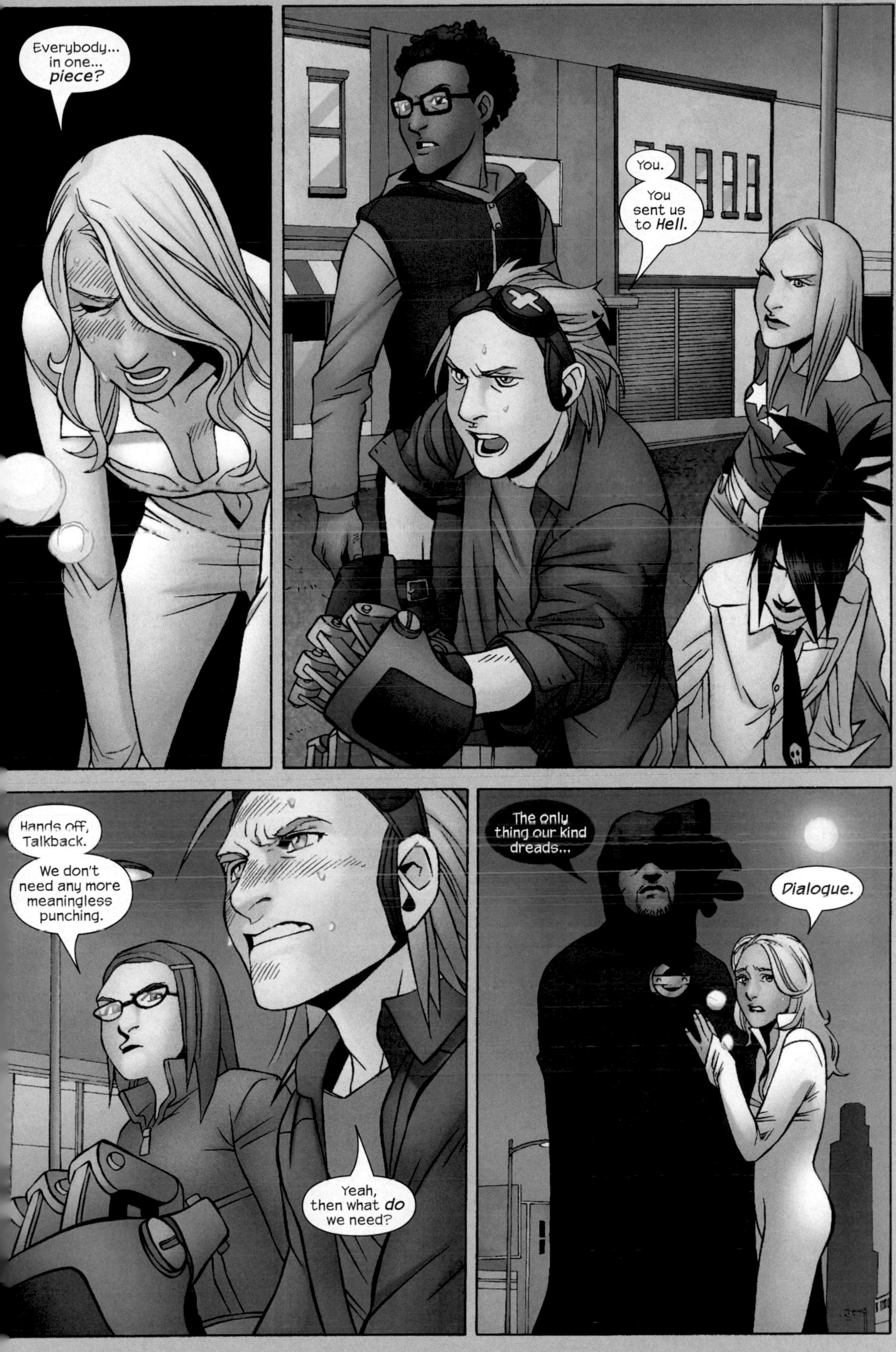
Everybody... in one... *piece*?
You.
You sent us to *Hell*.
Hands off, Talkback.
We don't need any more meaningless punching.
Yeah, then what *do* we need?
The only thing our kind dreads...
Dialogue.

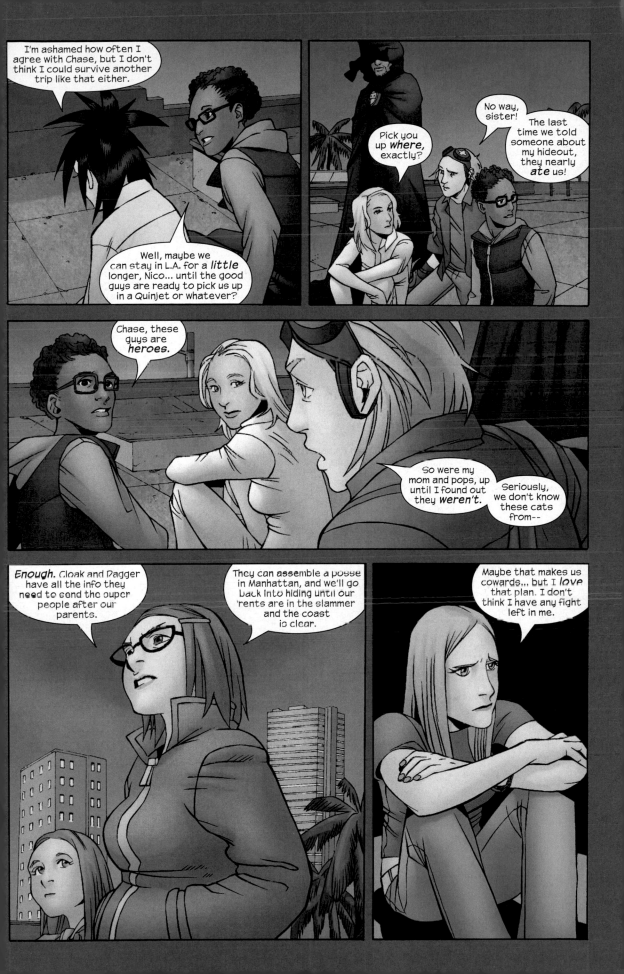

I'm ashamed how often I agree with Chase, but I don't think I could survive another trip like that either.

Well, maybe we can stay in L.A. for a *little* longer, Nico... until the good guys are ready to pick us up in a Quinjet or whatever?

Pick you up *where*, exactly?

No way, sister! The last time we told someone about my hideout, they nearly *ate* us!

Chase, these guys are *heroes*.

So were my mom and pops, up until I found out they *weren't*.

Seriously, we don't know these cats from--

Enough. Cloak and Dagger have all the info they need to send the super people after our parents.

They can assemble a posse in Manhattan, and we'll go back into hiding until our 'rents are in the slammer and the coast is clear.

Maybe that makes us cowards... but I *love* that plan. I don't think I have any fight left in me.

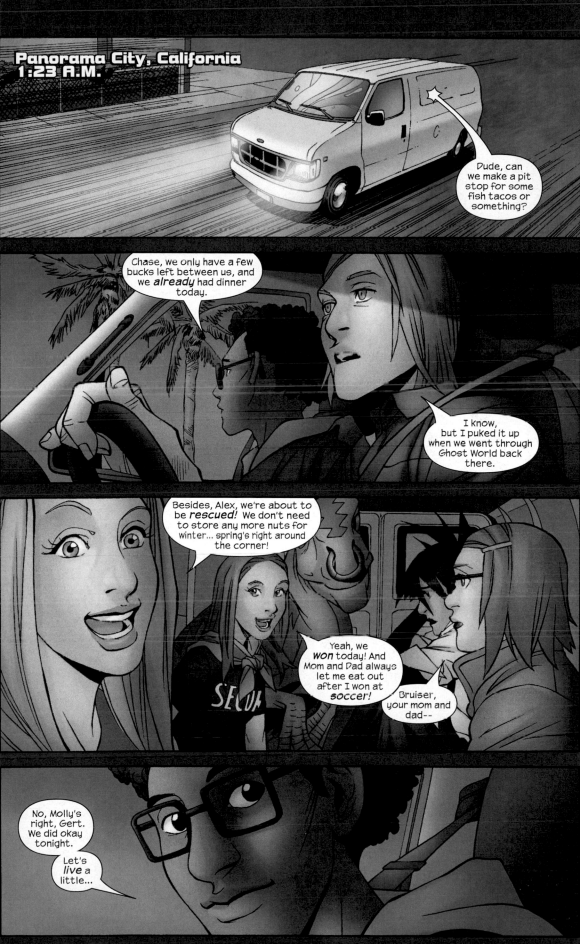

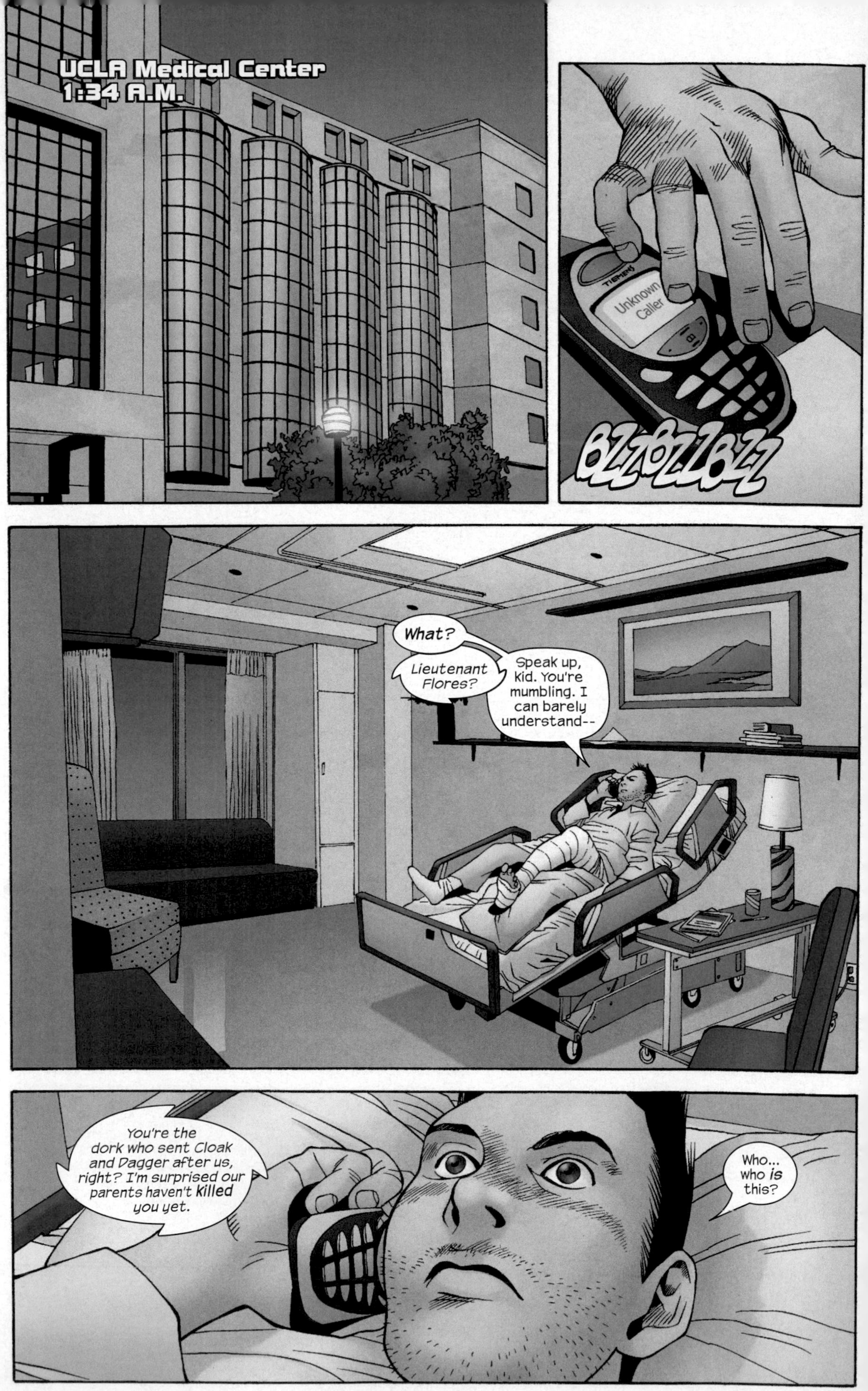

UCLA Medical Center
1:34 A.M.
Unknown Caller
BZZBZZBZZ
What?
Lieutenant Flores?
Speak up, kid. You're mumbling. I can barely understand--
You're the dork who sent Cloak and Dagger after us, right? I'm surprised our parents haven't killed you yet.
Who... who is this?

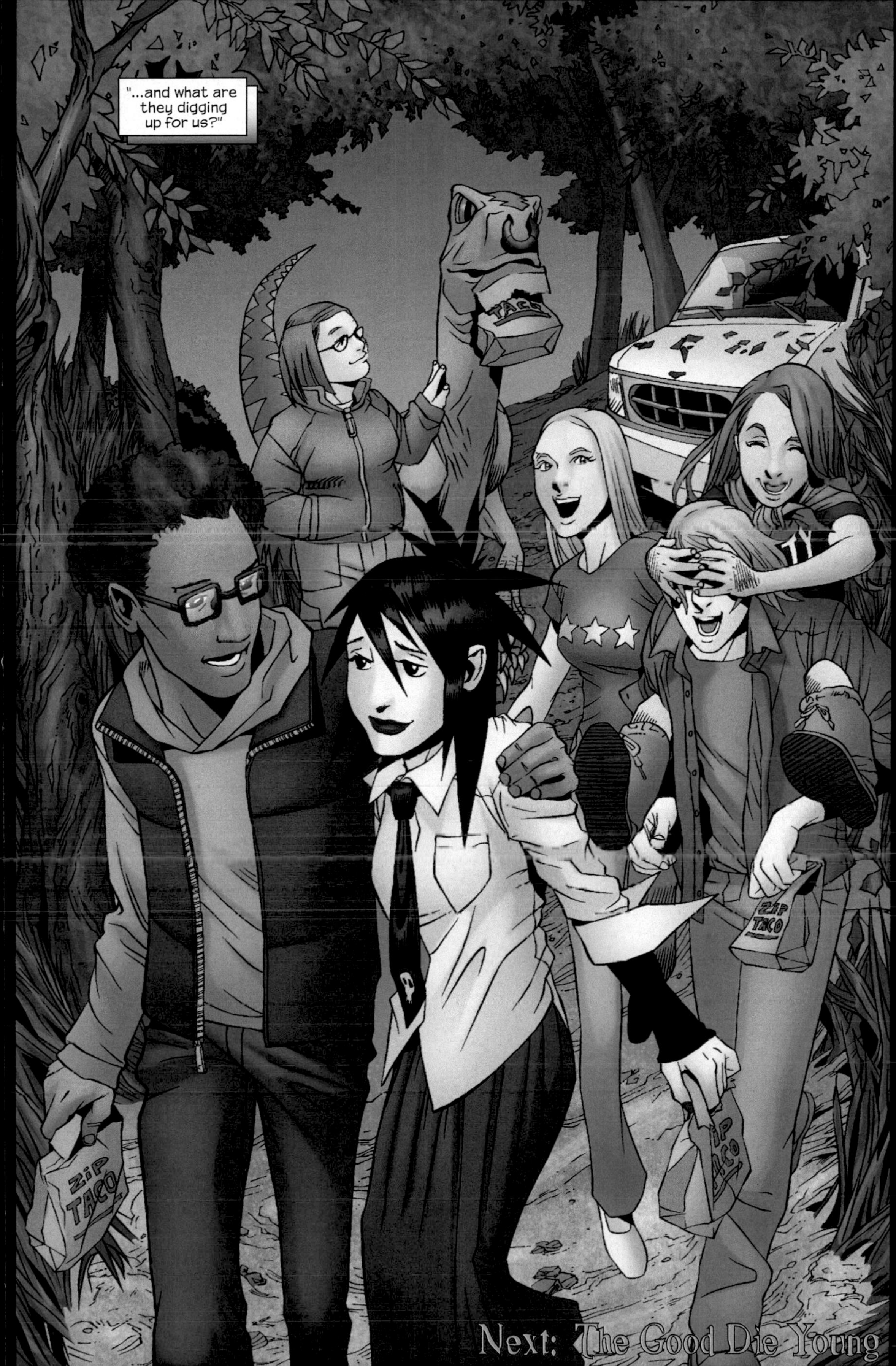
"...and what are they digging up for us?"
TACO
ZIP TACO
ZIP TACO
ZIP TACO
Next: The Good Die Young

PROMOTIONAL SKETCHES BY ADRIAN ALPHONA

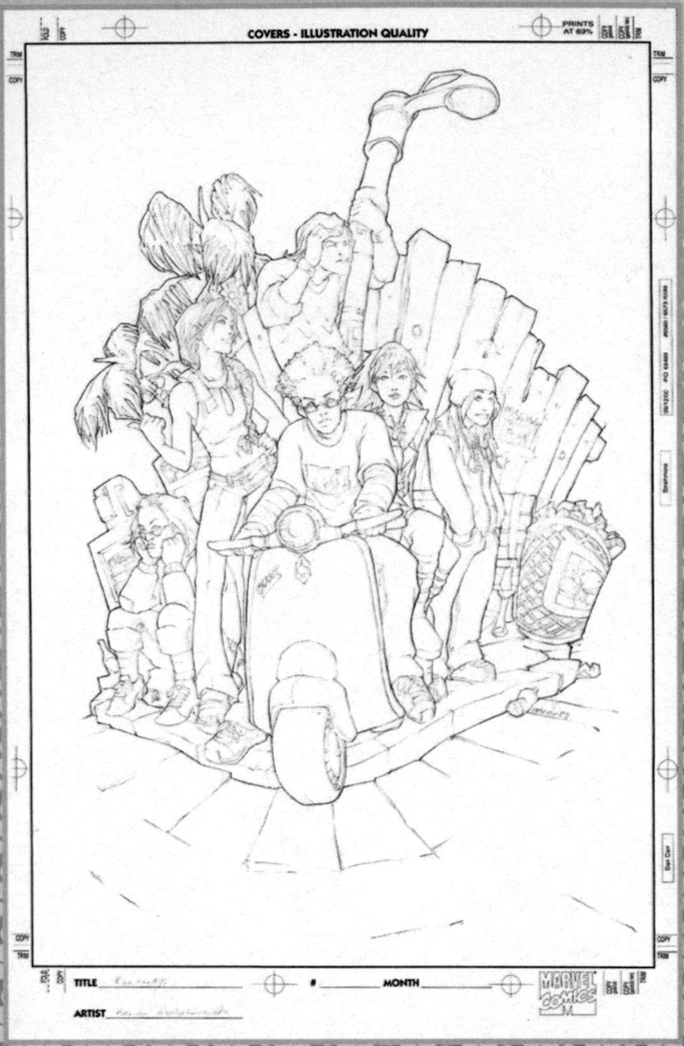
COVERS - ILLUSTRATION QUALITY
PRINTS AT 69%
TITLE
#
MONTH
ARTIST
MARVEL COMICS

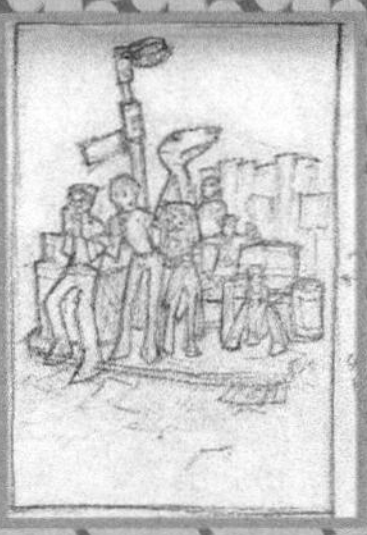

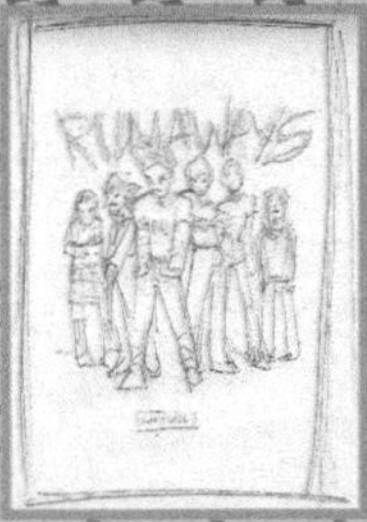
RUNAWAYS

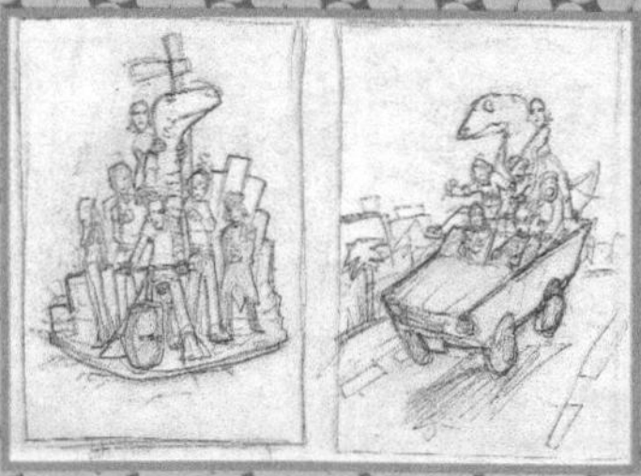

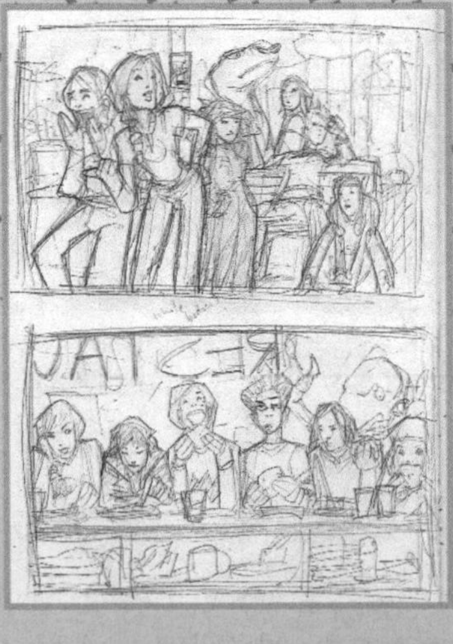

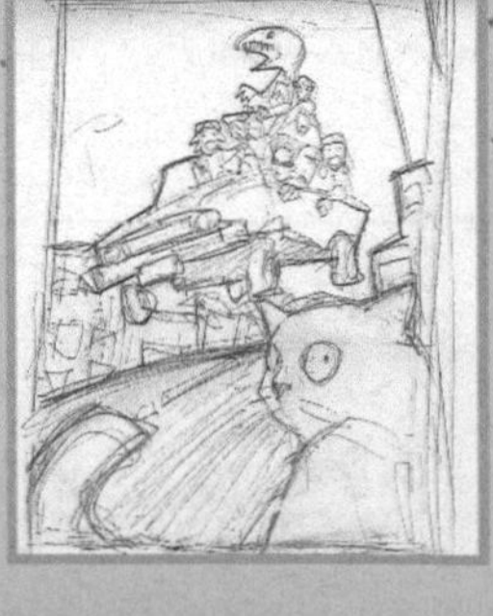

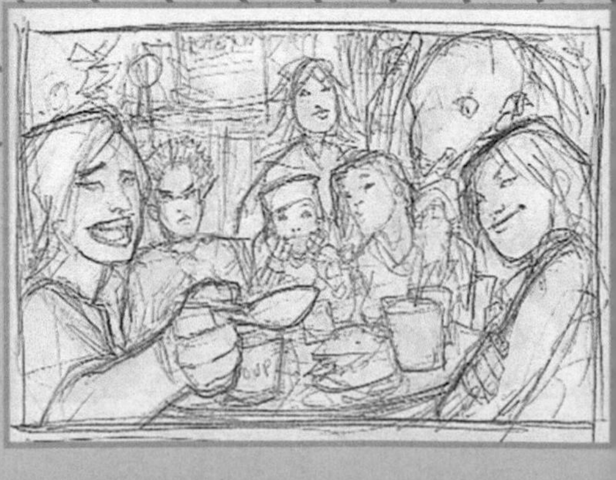

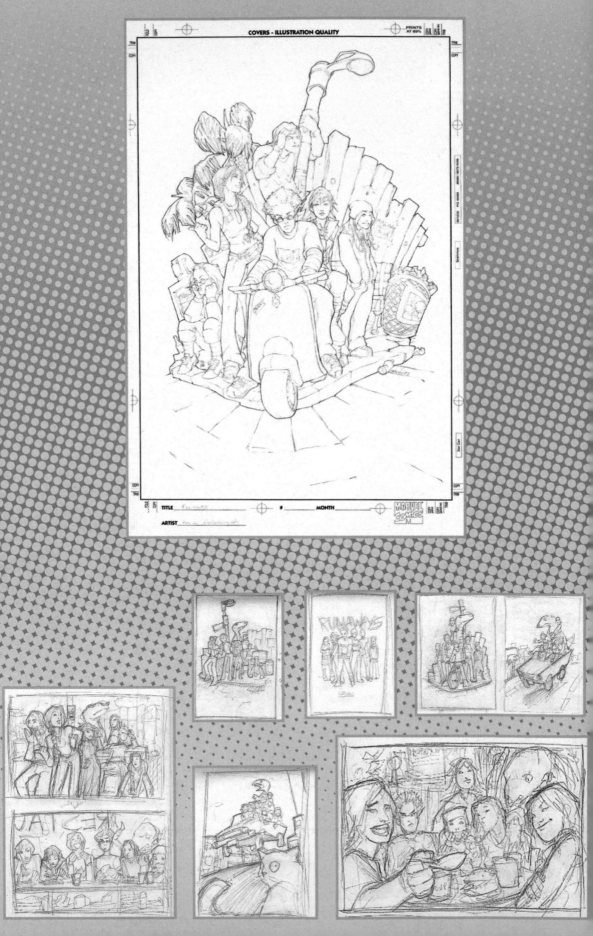

PROMOTIONAL ART BY
ADRIAN ALPHONA

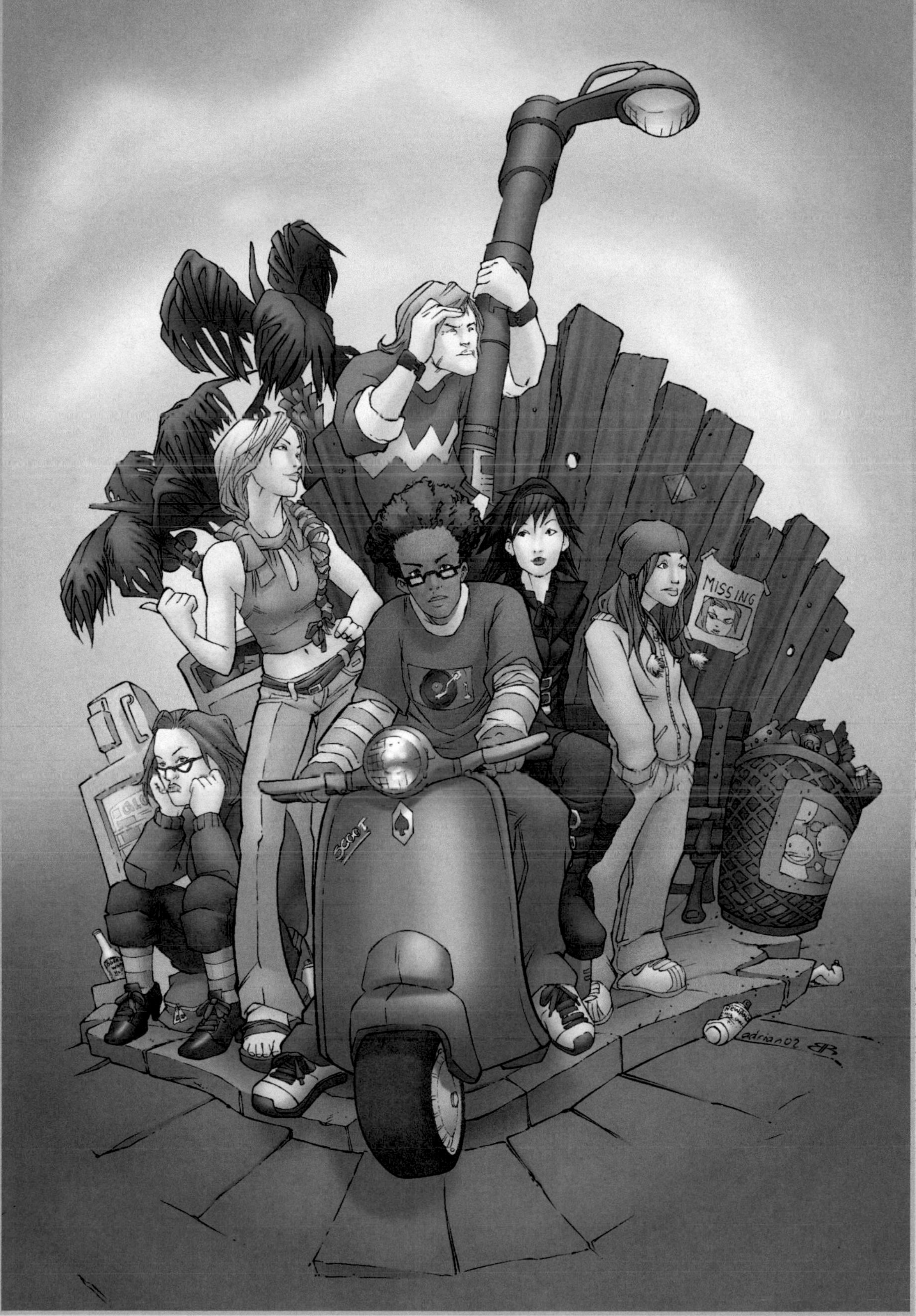
MISSING
SCOOT
adrian02

VOLUME 1 HARDCOVER
COVER ART BY ADRIAN ALPHONA

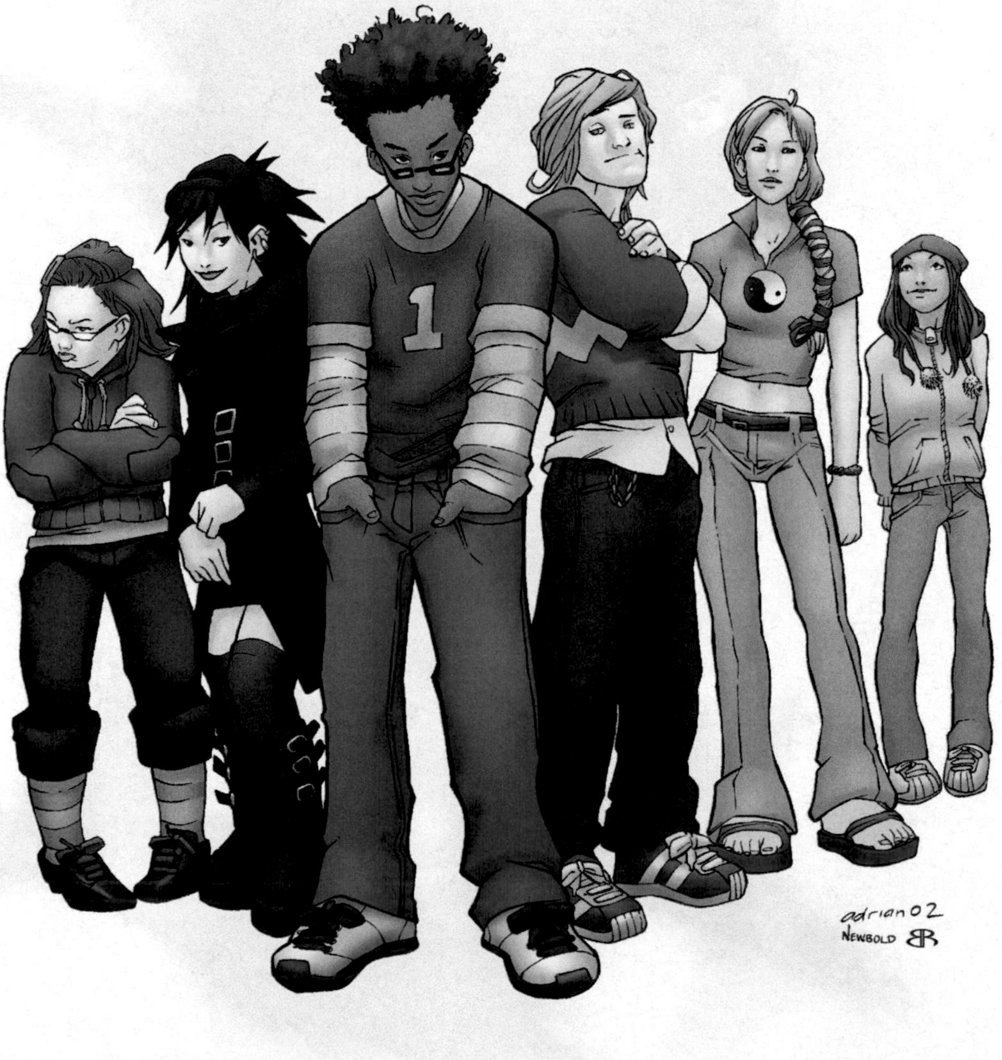
1
adrian 02
NEWBOLD

ADRIAN ALPHONA SKETCHBOOK

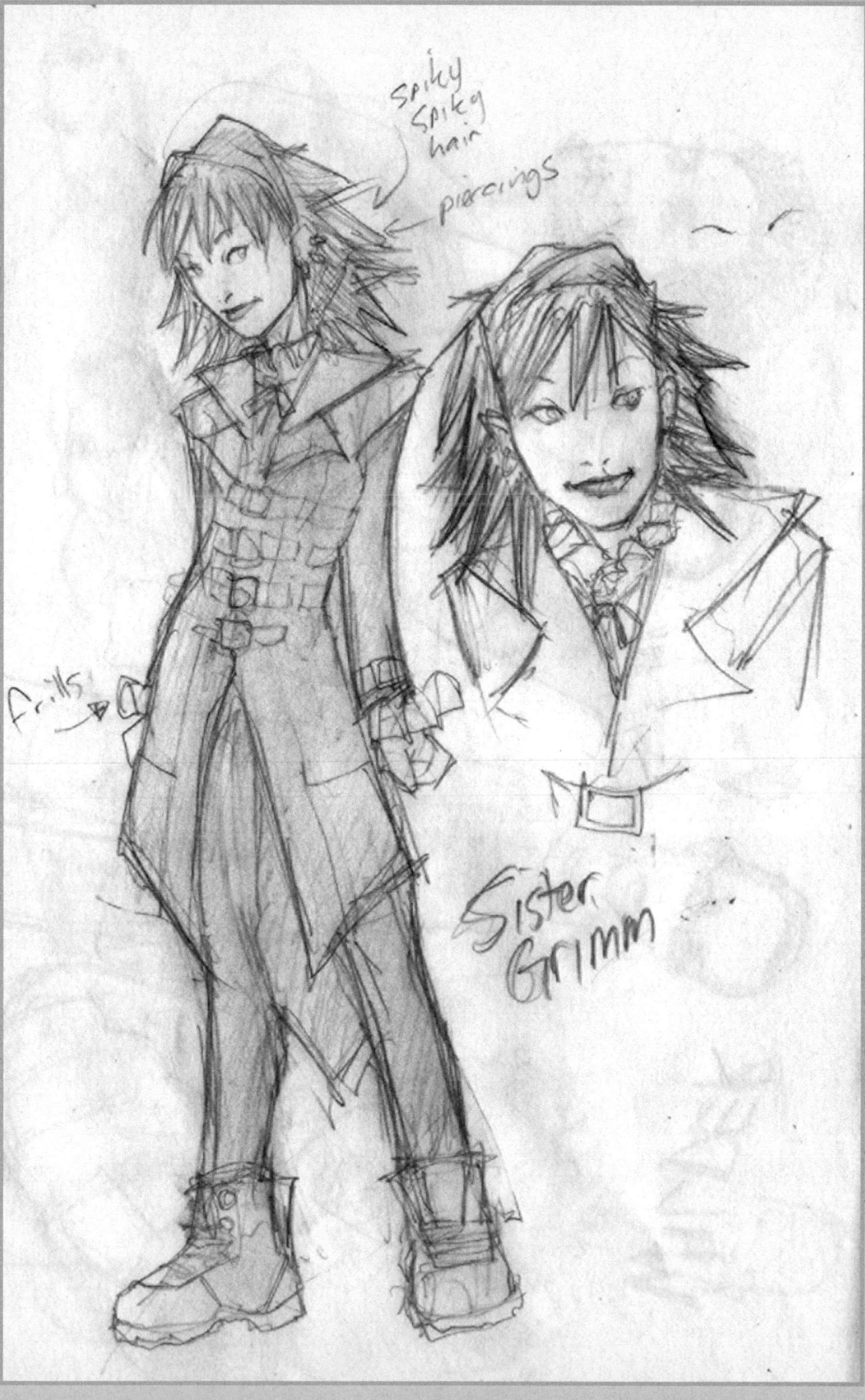
spiky spiky hair
piercings
frills
Sister Grimm

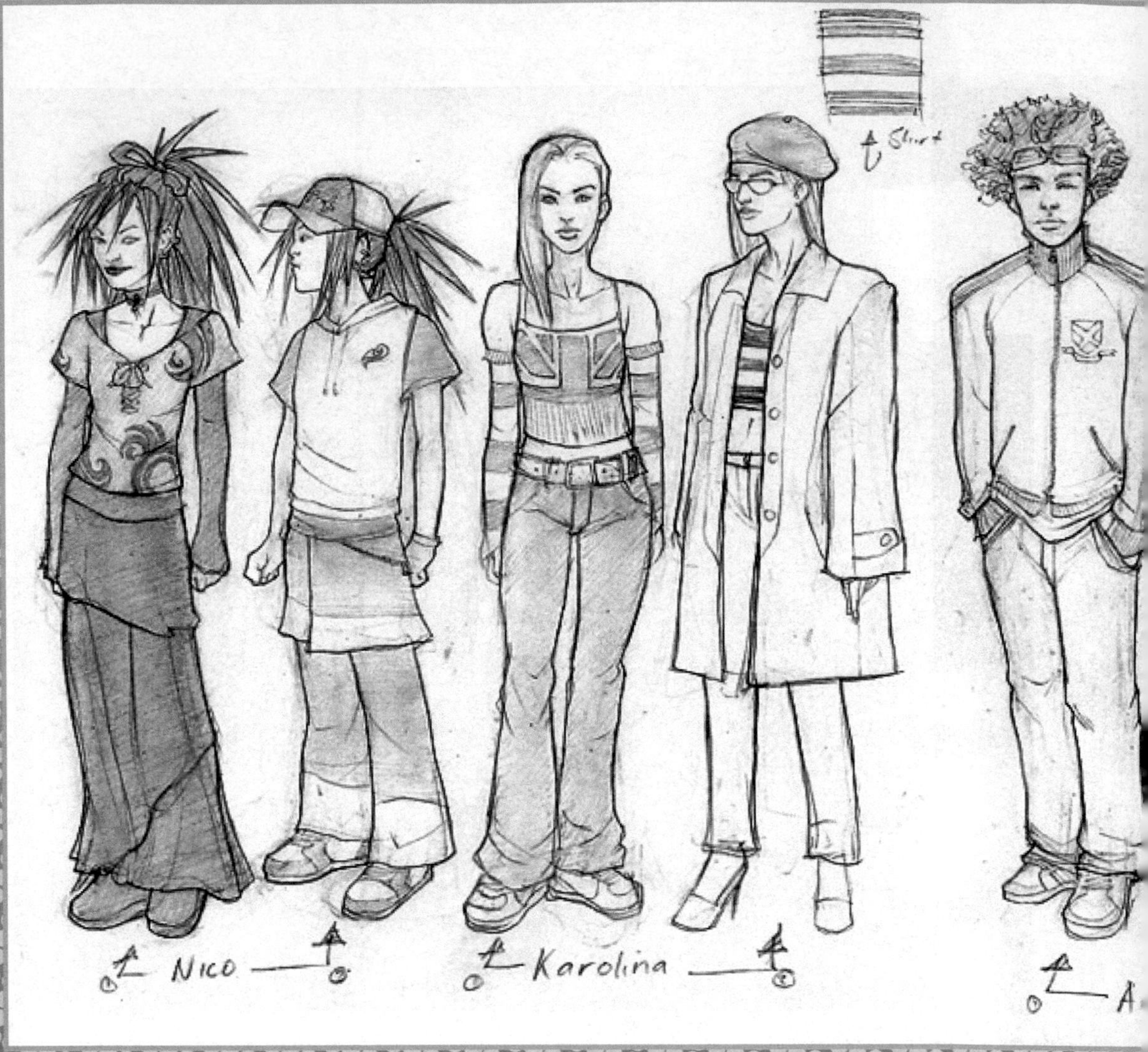
Shirt
Nico
Karolina
A

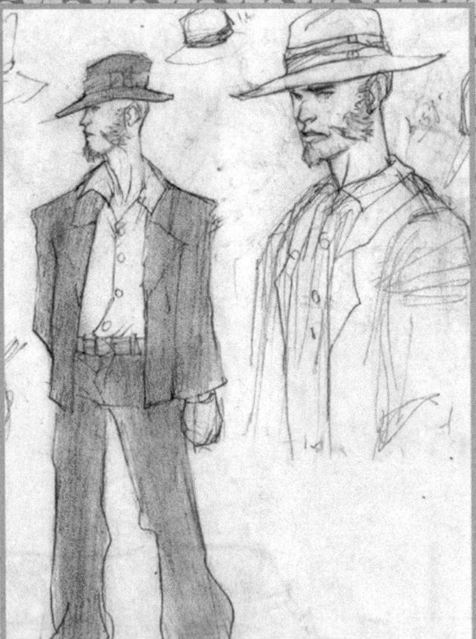

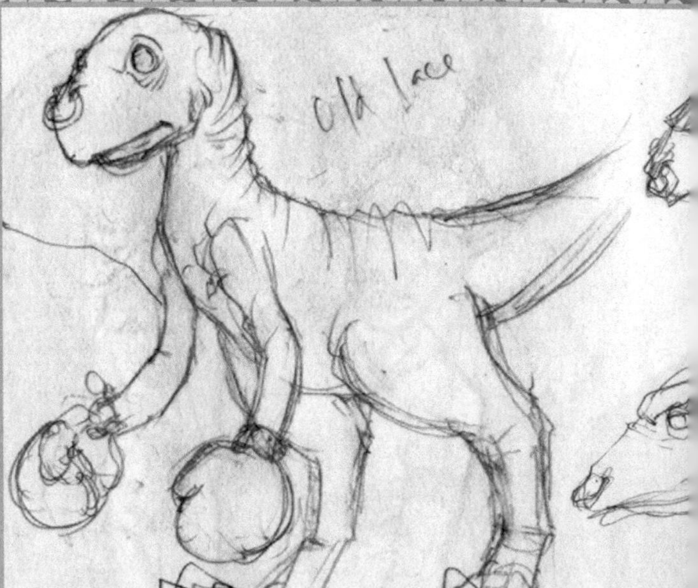
Old Lace

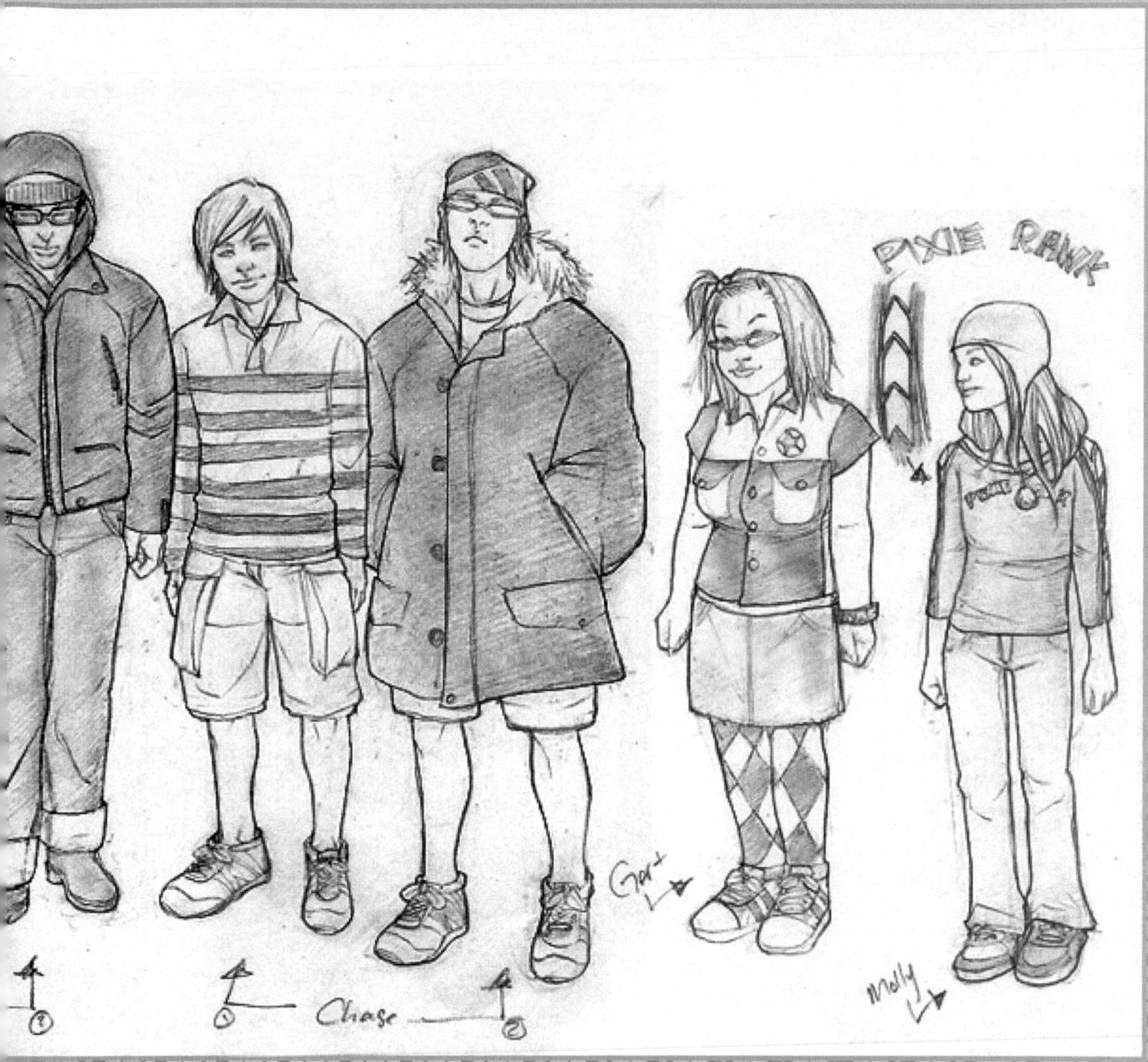
PIXIE RAWK
Chase
Gert
Molly

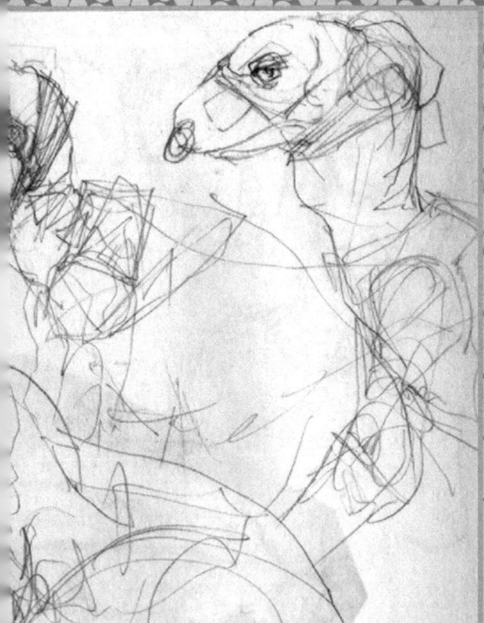

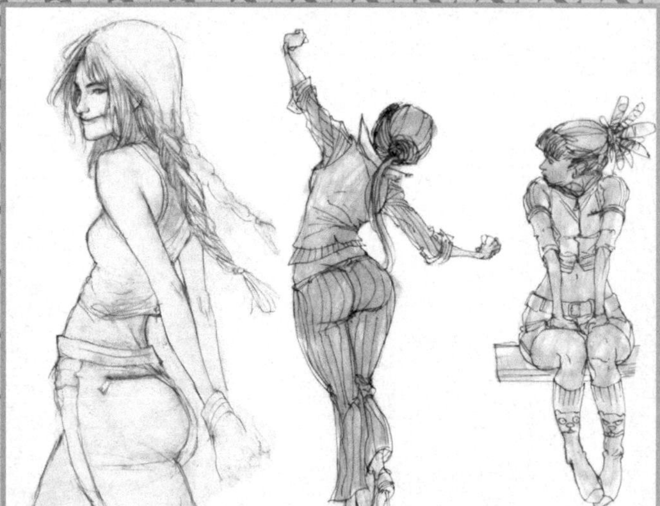

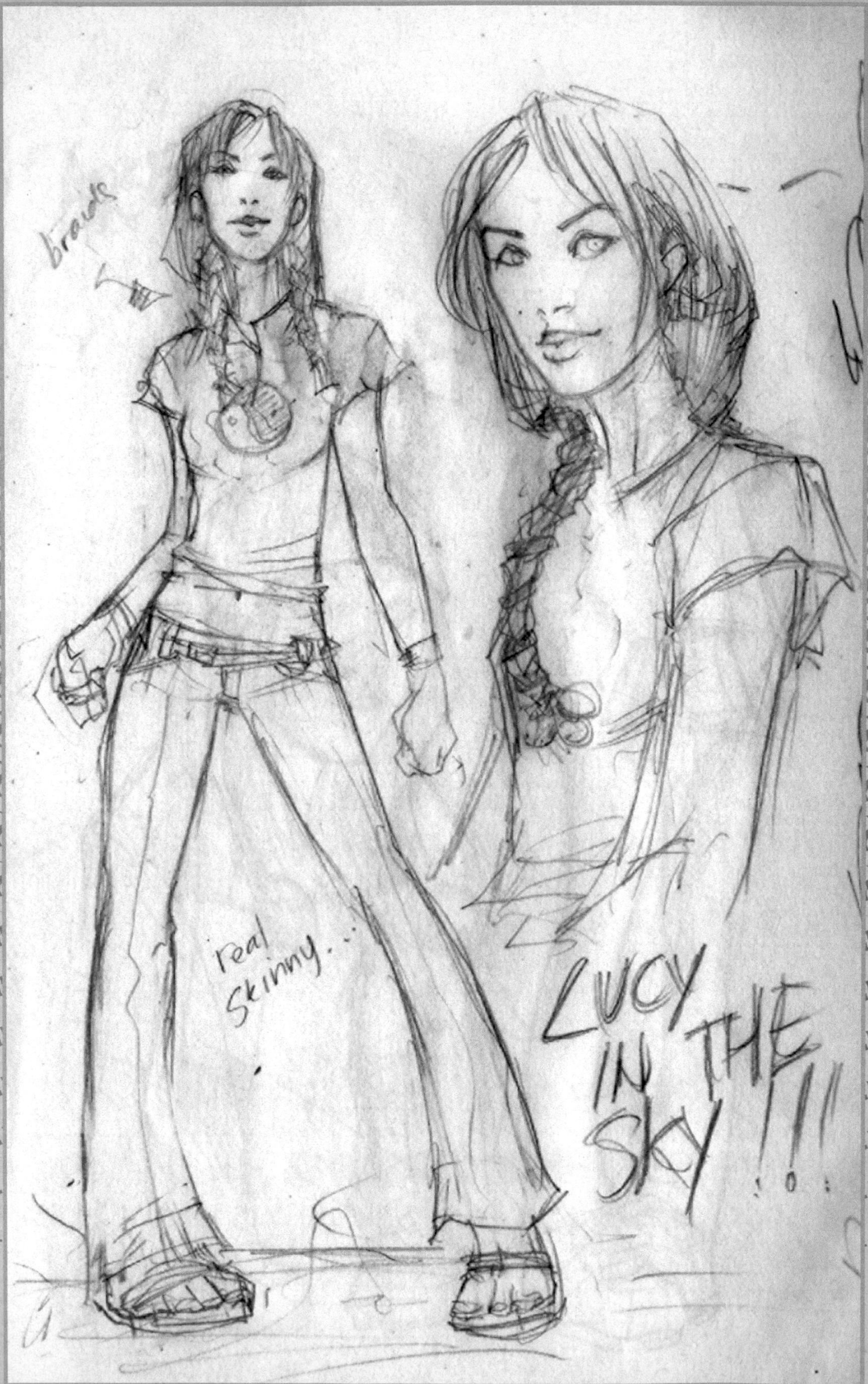
braids
real skinny...
LUCY IN THE SKY!!